PRAISE FOR *MY YEARS WITH TOWNES VAN ZANDT*

"We will learn about Townes Van Zandt, but we will be inside the story of his partner and friend, Harold Eggers. He shares his own stories of love and loss, family and friends, Viet Nam and, of course, his life with Townes. The book is an open heart for all to share."

—Kathleen Hudson, PhD, director of the Texas Heritage
Music Foundation (1987–2017), author of *Telling Stories,
Writing Songs: An Album of Texas Songwriters*

"Having had the great fortune of sharing some of this story with Harold and sharing the stage with and living with Townes over the years, I can honestly stand here and say that this book is the most authentic and insightful look into the life of Townes Van Zandt that I have ever read. Harold knew Townes like very few ever could, and to know Townes was to know a true poet, a brilliant mind, and a fine and gentle heart. Harold Eggers's book captures the essence of Townes and opens a window into the life of a unique and solitary soul, offering an honest and true version of one of the most amazing songwriters of our time."

—Michael Catalano, singer-songwriter, founder of the Nashville Film Festival

"A unique insight into one of the great songwriters of the twentieth century, and an entertaining page-turner, to boot. Harold Eggers lived, worked, and toured with Townes pretty much his whole professional life, and in [*My Years with Townes Van Zandt*], he finally tells 'the truth, no matter what.' Also includes some useful appendix material you won't find anywhere else."

—Nick Barbaro, publisher and co-founder of
The Austin Chronicle and co-founder of SXSW

"Over the years, my friend Harold has told me some of his escapades of his wild ride with Townes, a ride that sometimes eclipses the danger of his time in Vietnam. He has now vividly documented his time with Townes. His experience was most decidedly different from Col. Parker's time with Elvis. Harold's story has more heart, because that's who he was and is. And the whole story of Townes and Harold comes to life in *My Years with Townes Van Zandt*. This book is where the real music stories live."

—Rush Evans, music journalist, Austin DJ

"Eggers's memories give us a heartbreakingly intimate glimpse into the music and mystical madness of poet-songwriter Townes Van Zandt. Above all, this book is about friendship. It's about compassion and acceptance and the love forged in pain when we give ourselves to others."

—Sybil Rosen, award-winning writer

"Townes Van Zandt was one of the greatest songwriters of his time, a singer who knew that what Hank Williams and Robert Frost did were one and the same. Townes was also, as his best friend Guy Clark once said, 'a rambling kind of guy,' and one of his closest companions on that journey was the man who wrote this book, his tour manager, producer, and friend Harold Eggers."

—Sylvie Simmons, renowned writer, *Mojo*

"No portrait of Townes Van Zandt is more personal and compelling than Harold Eggers's narrative of life on the road with Townes. Having experienced all the highs and lows on a daily basis for twenty years, Eggers takes us beyond the cliché of the tortured genius. We learn that Townes's battle with his demons actually became part of his creative process. It gave him the insights that filled the poetry of his music and that he brought to his intimate performances. Eggers spins a narrative that flows like a novel—rich in details of settings, personalities, and remembered conversations—as we join his journey to understanding the complex genius of one of America's great songwriters."

—John Wheat, music historian at the Briscoe Center for American History, University of Texas at Austin

"The most important thing to be said about this book is that Harold Eggers was there, boots on the ground. Every student or fan of Townes Van Zandt can't consider their study or admiration of the man and his music without knowing all the stories. And Harold Eggers has plenty of them."

—Andy Wilkinson, music archivist, Texas Tech University

"Townes would often say of someone who met his highest standard of admiration, 'He's the real deal.' *My Years with Townes Van Zandt*, by Harold Eggers Jr., is most assuredly the real deal."

—William Hedgepeth, journalist and author

MY YEARS

— WITH —

TOWNES VAN ZANDT

MUSIC, GENIUS, AND RAGE

HAROLD F. EGGERS JR.
with L. E. McCullough

Backbeat Books

AN IMPRINT OF HAL LEONARD LLC

Published in 2018 by Backbeat Books
An Imprint of Hal Leonard LLC
7777 West Bluemound Road
Milwaukee, WI 53213

Trade Book Division Editorial Offices
33 Plymouth St., Montclair, NJ 07042

Printed in the United States of America

Book design by M Kellner

All photos are from the personal collection of Harold J. Eggers.

Library of Congress Cataloging-in-Publication Data
Names: Eggers, Harold F. author. | McCullough, L. E.
Title: My years with Townes Van Zandt : music, genius, and rage / Harold F. Eggers Jr. with L.E. McCullough.
Description: Montclair, NJ : Backbeat Books, 2018. | Includes bibliographical references and index.
Identifiers: LCCN 2018027326 | ISBN 9781617137082 (alk. paper)
Subjects: LCSH: Van Zandt, Townes. | Country musicians--United States--Biography. | Lyricists--United States--Biography. | Eggers, Harold F.
Classification: LCC ML420.V248 E37 2018 | DDC 782.421642092 [B] --dc23
LC record available at https://lccn.loc.gov/2018027326ISBN 978-1-61713-708-2

"One has to pay dearly for immortality; one has to die several times
while one is still alive."

—Friedrich Nietzsche, *Ecce Homo: How One Becomes What One Is*

"A part of a man's praise may be told in his presence;
the whole in his absence."

—*Babylonian Talmud*

CONTENTS

INTRODUCTION
"THE TRUTH, NO MATTER WHAT"
by Harold F. Eggers Jr.

THIS IS ONE of the scariest books you'll ever read. It's a personal memoir about spending nearly a third of my adult life with Townes Van Zandt.

It's scary, because it's all true.

I was in the close gravitational orbit of Townes Van Zandt, a gifted and tragic singer-songwriter, over a span of twenty years—a two-decade roller coaster ride during which my primary goal was to help him survive his gauntlet of emotional and artistic obsessions as he made his way to the stage.

I was his road manager, business partner, and co–record producer. Mostly, I was his friend.

I loved him for his exquisite, sensitive songmaking; I was infuriated by what he did to himself and his career.

He was a genius; he was insane.

He was the most beautiful human soul I have ever encountered; his brutal honesty with words could cut like a razor.

He was born into a wealthy Texas oil family and spent most of his adult life living in self-induced misery and despair.

He was lionized by critics as one of the "towering figures" of American music; he was dismissed from his final recording session two days before his death.

A study in contrasts, to be sure. As he was fond of saying to interviewers, all he had ever wanted to do was "write the perfect song that would save someone's life."

Unfortunately, he couldn't save his own.

Life on the road with Townes was a 24-7 immersion in a lifestyle most observers would designate as clinically insane.

It involved years of coping with his drinking sprees, mental hospital commitments, and conversations with paranormal entities he classified as demons, angels, and various types of ghosts. Years of witnessing a musical genius in action, creating incessantly and trying to touch the world with song even as his own life ebbed into the wind.

Onstage he was riveting—a primal artist akin to the early country-blues singers whose performances emerged from deep within their psyche. Every night he sang differently. There was always a different mood onstage, always a different set of problems offstage that made for a totally unique live performance. Townes could not stop himself from re-creating his music or his life every minute he lived. The serenity of his music seemed to depend upon his life being in utter chaos.

It has been two decades since Townes Van Zandt died. It's time to tell his story the way he wanted it told.

No happy-face sugarcoating, no noble canonizing.

That wouldn't be the truth. That wouldn't be Townes.

Before he died, we talked often of putting together this book about his music and life. Townes was insistent that the good *and* the bad both be told:

"Don't forget, H, in the book of my life, the most important thing is to tell the truth, no matter what. I want everyone to feel my pain, as I have shared it with you. Do not whitewash anything. Let all the ghosts and demons have their say. That's what I've done my whole life."

This book lets the ghosts and demons have their say. And then some. It is alternately humorous and grim, uplifting and sordid, showing in vivid detail the many conflicting sides of this complex artist.

Yet this book is not an indictment or even a criticism. It's just the truth of one man's life told by a close friend watching it unfold.

It's a memoir of time spent in the company of one of the most unique creators of American music in our time.

You had to be there. I was.

And now you will be, too.

FOREWORD
by L. E. McCullough

"His influence as a songwriter towers over American country and roots music . . . his entire body of work serves as a gold standard."

—WALL STREET JOURNAL

A STRIKING, intuitive musical genius whose hard-living, rowdy lifestyle belied his sensitive inner nature, Townes Van Zandt created songs that were heartbreaking in their beauty and are proving timeless in their appeal.

Born into a prominent Fort Worth, Texas, family in 1944, Townes was groomed to be a corporate lawyer. But, like thousands of his fellow baby boomers, he tuned in to the siren call of sixties pop music and dropped out of college to become an itinerant singer-songwriter on the folk circuit.

In a little over three decades, Townes would write more than 130 songs, record twenty-two albums, and tour constantly around the globe—all the while influencing thousands of American folk, country, and pop artists with a songwriting style unmatched for virtuosic wordplay and emotional honesty.

To date, Townes's songs have been commercially recorded by close to five hundred performers worldwide, including Willie Nelson, Merle Haggard, Bob Dylan, Emmylou Harris, Don Williams, Doc and Merle Watson, Bobby Bare, Lyle Lovett, Steve Young, Kathy Mattea, Freddy Fender, Mudhoney, Bonnie Bramlett, Ricky Skaggs, Cowboy Junkies, Doug Sahm, Richard Buckner, Jimmy LaFave, Guy Clark, Lucinda

Williams, Nanci Griffith, Steve Earle, Jimmie Dale Gilmore, and Hoyt
Axton.

Clearly, he had a lot to say during his life, and he's still saying it.

My Years with Townes Van Zandt: Music, Genius, and Rage is a memoir whose central character is a remarkable singer-songwriter, a prophet
wandering the world in the guise of an outcast. It explores the source of
Townes's prodigious talent and seminal influence while chronicling his
relentless path toward self-destruction.

It is a memoir narrated to me by Harold F. Eggers Jr., whose own personal life journey of loss and redemption is inextricably entwined with
that of his friend and musical partner, Townes Van Zandt.

If there is any single person most familiar with the deepest recesses
of Townes Van Zandt's conflicted genius as it played out over his career,
it is Harold Eggers—or simply "H," as he was affectionately called by
Townes from their first meeting on.

It is Harold's vivid, firsthand accounts of the singer's tumultuous
onstage and offstage life that make up the heart of *My Years with Townes
Van Zandt: Music, Genius, and Rage*, and reveal the inner core of an enig-
matic troubadour whose music was a source of inspiration and healing
for millions, but was for himself a torment that struggled for dominance
among a myriad of personal demons.

Unlike many musical artists who peak early and spend the rest of
their lives on a downward spiral toward mediocrity, Townes Van Zandt
never stopped creating at a top level. Despite his advanced physical deterioration and periodic treatments for mental breakdowns, some of his
best work came at the very end of his life. On the day he died (New
Year's Day 1997—his idol Hank Williams Sr. had died 44 years before
on the same day), Townes Van Zandt was in the midst of a recording
project featuring material destined to surpass anything he had yet put
on disc.

New York Times critic Robert Palmer compared Van Zandt to the
legendary Hank Williams, saying, "Both men live in their music, as if
singing and writing and being human were the same thing and all as
natural as breathing. Their songwriting craft and vocal musicianship are

exceptional, but what you hear is beyond all that; it seems to be the direct, untrammeled expression of a man's soul."

Rolling Stone's Anthony DeCurtis called Van Zandt one of the "towering figures" of American music, "a songwriter who, at his best, rivals Hank Williams and Bob Dylan. If you're serious about American music, eventually you're going to have to enter this darkness."

More than a year before Townes died, he agreed to work with Harold on a book about his music, life, and career. As they traveled from gig to gig, Townes shared a profusion of details about his early life and experiences in the music industry, details ranging from the mundane to the harrowing. Townes was adamant the full story be told.

That's the story you'll read in these pages.

Two decades after his death, the songs of Townes Van Zandt continue to inspire a passionate fanaticism among music listeners throughout the world.

Type in the name "Townes Van Zandt" on Google, and you'll get 460,000 or so web page hits. That's a Market with a capital M, and it's up from 400,000 hits a month ago, 324,000 hits a month before that, and 288,000 a month before that.

A huge number of those hits are fan sites, tribute articles, current radio playlists, and active references within performer discographies that demonstrate the ongoing impact and interest Townes has on contemporary music of multiple genres. The rest are commercial sites promoting the sale of the more than forty Townes Van Zandt albums and CDs available, with more on the way.

Posthumously, Townes's music continues to elicit recognition and reverence.

- In 2002, *Poet: A Tribute to Townes Van Zandt* earned a pair of Grammy Award nominations, for Best Contemporary Folk Album and Best Male Country Vocal Performance, for Willie Nelson's rendition of Townes's "Marie."
- A 2004 film documentary, *Be Here to Love Me: A Film About Townes Van Zandt*, appeared at Sundance Film

Festival and film festivals throughout Europe and North America, garnering awards and acclaim. *Heartworn Highways*, the groundbreaking 1976 film featuring Townes, was rereleased on DVD in 2003.

- In October 2016, Townes was inducted into the Nashville Songwriters Hall of Fame, an event covered in *Billboard*, *Rolling Stone*, the *Washington Post*, and other major music media. In March 2017, the South by Southwest music festival initiated the annual Townes Van Zandt Award, honoring career achievements of Texas singer-songwriters.

- In 2004, his "Be Here to Love Me" was included on the Grammy-winning album *Feels Like Home* by multiplatinum pop vocalist Norah Jones; in 2017, his "Buckskin Stallion Blues" was featured twice in the Oscar-winning film *Three Billboards Outside Ebbing, Missouri*.

- And for musical history tourists, the Kimpton *Hotel Van Zandt*—described by its website as "a true Texas charmer that speaks to your inner rebel with distinguished, laid-back style"—opened in 2015 in downtown Austin, in honor of Townes and his third great-grandfather, Isaac Van Zandt, a founder of the Texas Republic in the 1830s.

Such achievements and events have all helped keep Townes's music very much "in the present," creating a perfect moment for an authentic memoir to appear.

Yet even among his most devoted followers, Townes Van Zandt remains a mythic, mysterious figure.

Who was he, really, offstage?

How did he create his remarkable music?

What sort of Faustian bargain did he make that nourished his indomitable creative spirit but left his outer human shell wounded and vulnerable?

My Years with Townes Van Zandt: Music, Genius, and Rage has the answers to those questions . . . and many more.

PROLOGUE
1978: "EVERYBODY HERE'S CRAZY EXCEPT ME!"

The ringing phone echoed through my small apartment on Belmont Boulevard in Nashville, interrupting my first cup of coffee on a chilly morning in early December. Picking up, I heard a woman's voice screaming and sobbing.

"Harold, it's an emergency! You need to get out here right away! He's flipped out!"

She paused, her breath coming in ragged gasps. "Harold, please hurry—it's really serious this time."

The screams, sobs, and gasps belonged to Cindy, the eighteen-year-old second wife of Townes Van Zandt, the critically acclaimed singer-songwriter with whom I had been destined to work as road manager by a perverse, prankish, music-loving committee of Fates.

"I'll be right there. Just keep him calm."

"He's chained to a damn tree. It's as calm as I can get him for now."

I sighed and hung up, grabbing my coat and keys and rushing to the car for the picturesque ride to the Van Zandt homestead in rural Franklin, about thirty miles distant. No doubt about it: the next few hours were going to deduct a year or two from my life span.

I drove past Music Row and turned onto 21st Avenue, threading my way quickly through lingering rush-hour traffic and keeping a sharp eye out for cops, a skill I had honed during my time touring with Townes.

I followed 21st Avenue out of Nashville as it turned into Hillsboro Road and moved deeper into the rolling countryside. Born and bred in suburban Long Island, I couldn't help but feel a mixed sensation of uneasiness and liberation whenever I ventured into a non-urban area . . . especially the three thousand acres of isolated backwoods where Townes had fabricated a survivalist retreat and occasional drinking club for Nashville's renegade singer-songwriters.

Chained to a damn tree. I couldn't resist a chuckle at the thought of Cindy, frizzy mane of bright red hair streaming over her thin shoulders, wrestling the big logging chain around Townes. Soft-spoken with delicate, elfin features, Cindy was, nevertheless, the daughter of a long-distance trucker and possessed of fierce determination with regard to her man. Within a few months of living with Townes, she had become adept at the art of physical restraints.

I turned off the main highway onto a two-lane blacktop, wheeling past a medium-size critter carcass mashed into the asphalt. Following the road's winding course through the hills along the Harpeth River, I reflected on having made it through my first full year as Townes's road manager.

And wondered if I'd make it through another.

To a great degree, the partnership of solo performer and road manager resembles a short-term shotgun marriage born of economic necessity and scheduling convenience. It is an intimate relationship that crosses all personal boundaries, as the partners work, travel, eat, sleep, converse, and carouse in the closest proximity every hour of the day for months at a time.

An efficient road manager must be prepared for every conceivable situation and challenge that could possibly arise during the course of the tour. In my case, the chief challenge was to get Townes from one gig to the next without either of us dying in the process.

I had gotten the job through my older brother Kevin Eggers, founder and president of Tomato Records. In 1976, Tomato had reissued Van Zandt's first six albums, recorded from 1968 to 1972 for Poppy Records (Kevin's earlier label), including 1972's *The Late Great Townes Van Zandt*, which had received enough distribution and radio airplay to make national tours feasible and even—were it not for the excesses of Townes's touring regimen—potentially lucrative.

Unlike those of his more notorious musical peers, Townes Van Zandt's pop-star idiosyncrasies did not involve group sex, expensive limos, or trashed hotel rooms. Instead, his preferred method of unwinding after a gig was to have us drive to the local skid row, where we would seek out winos sleeping on the sidewalk or huddling around trash fires.

Townes would distribute $10 and $20 bills, joking, "If I'm ever here again, at least I'll be able to score a drink."

While I was moved by Townes's genuine compassion toward the poor, homeless, and mentally ill, I was less enthusiastic about the surprise occasions when Townes would invite a particularly down-and-out street person to spend the night in our hotel room.

I learned to sleep with my hands in my pockets, holding on to our travel money and praying I'd awaken alive and in one, un-strangled, un-stabbed piece.

Even more disconcerting was Townes's propensity for sealing newly made friendships by taking out a pocketknife, digging a deep chunk of skin from his wrist, and offering to be "blood brothers."

This ritual, I discovered, could just as easily occur within the same hour that Townes became enraged at an antagonistic stranger and issue the chilling statement "I'll slit your throat and drink your blood."

It was a dark, unpredictable side I had not anticipated. Townes had been a frequent visitor to our family home during the late 1960s when I was a teen. He had even served as a co-godfather for Kevin's daughter Mary in 1972.

For me, getting the call at age twenty-seven to be road manager for my brother's top label act was a personal honor and profound responsibility. It was like acquiring a hipper, more exotic godfather of my own generation while having the chance to be involved with Kevin, whose success as a rising music executive I hoped to emulate.

Naturally, I jumped at the chance and laughingly remarked to friends that traveling the U.S. with Townes couldn't be any more dangerous than my in-country tour of duty in Vietnam. *Boy, was I wrong about that*, I mused as I approached the Van Zandt homestead.

The whiff of fresh cow dung hung in the air as I brought the car to a stop at a cattle guard, after passing through the sedate confines of an exclusive new housing district recently carved from the rump acreage of an old tobacco farm. Beyond the guard, the road sank into a rutted dirt path, barely wide enough for one vehicle. A mile across the fields and through a creek, past a long-abandoned farmhouse, the path ended at Townes's "cabin"—a decrepit shanty inhabited in past decades by sharecroppers.

I sat at the wheel for several moments, engine idling, envisioning the scene that lay ahead. *Maybe I should turn back and get the hell out of here. Work for some rational person, at least somebody half-less nuts. It's not like this folkie stuff is going to make anybody rich . . .*

I gunned the motor and forged ahead. *What the hell . . .* a brother was a brother, blood or otherwise.

I topped a rise and saw three vehicles parked thirty or so yards up ahead. Cindy was crouched behind one of them—a Chevy four-door sedan that belonged to John Lomax III, Townes's business manager. He was now crouching behind his car alongside Cindy.

John was the grandson of John Avery Lomax and nephew of Alan Lomax, renowned Texas folklorists and collectors of American folk song who had reshaped and revitalized the country's popular music by bringing songsters like Leadbelly, Willie McTell, Woody Guthrie, and countless other blues and country performers to widespread public notice during the 1930s and '40s. Cindy had called John after rousing me, hoping that strength in numbers would prove a settling influence on her husband's mania.

I parked my car and got out. I looked past Cindy and John and spied two figures lying at the base of the oak tree—Townes and the family dog, Geraldine.

Townes's eyes were closed, and he held a shotgun in his right hand and a half-gallon jug of vodka in his left. Geraldine, a bright-eyed, two-year-old German shepherd–husky mix, sat by his side, panting patiently and glancing intently at the crescendoing medley of morning critter noises peeping from the surrounding forest.

I could hear Townes muttering. "The Plan . . . ever'body jhhoin The Plan . . ."

I went over to Cindy and John. "He's driving me crazy," Cindy whined. "Look inside the cabin—he tore up the whole damn place."

According to Cindy, the human half of the oak tree duo had been drinking steadily for three days without any sleep. This was not in itself unusual when Townes was at home off the road, but that morning, she reported, he had wordlessly chopped off his shoulder-length hair with a chipped butcher knife and daubed his face with red, green, and yellow finger paints in an effort to achieve the classic Plains Indian battle design.

After shouting for a half hour at a stereo speaker he thought resembled a promoter who had once cheated him, he'd pulled out his .357 Magnum and shot a few holes in the rear cabin wall, thinking he might get lucky and nail one of the "black ghosts" he believed inhabited the back part of the residence. Pausing to reload, he had told Cindy to chain him to the tree so he could meditate and work on The Plan.

Were it not for the modern trappings of overhead phone wires and automobiles in the driveway, the moaning, paint-streaked man with a chain cinched around his waist could have been mistaken for a nineteenth-century Sioux warrior in the last throes of a mighty vision quest.

The Sioux had used fasting and prayer to seek a personal guiding spirit that would strengthen the warrior through his life journey. The quest sometimes involved significant suffering and deprivation, but lasted no more than four days.

Townes Van Zandt's vision quest was into its second decade with no discernible evidence of guiding spirits other than alcohol and rage. Some people might have been freaked out. I'd come to view it as artistic evolution.

This was, after all, the same Townes Van Zandt who just three years earlier had charmed his way through the movie *Heartworn Highways*, a groundbreaking documentary about a bold new wave of Nashville singer-songwriters, in which Townes accounted for two of the film's most captivating moments, eliciting both laughter and tears.

With a bottle of whiskey in the crook of his left elbow and a shotgun in his right hand he had introduced himself, Geraldine, and Cindy to the camera, proceeding to regale the gullible film crew with a wild story about raising giant rabbits in his back yard. And then suddenly, he'd slid feet first into a hole, completely disappearing into the ground, yelling that the giant rabbits were pulling him down.

A few scenes later, Townes sang "Waiting 'Round to Die" for Uncle Seymour Washington, an elderly black man and neighbor. Tears rolled openly down Uncle Seymour's face, with the line "Seemed easier than just waiting around to die" evoking a shuddering burst of lamentation from the old man. Seamlessly shifting between hillbilly clown and cathartic healer, the Texas-born troubadour Townes had already established his stage persona as an eccentric but powerful musical shaman who could render a packed room spellbound with a simple guitar chord and the merest whisper.

He had also begun creating a body of lyrical work that would outlast his own tortured life and premature death in just twenty years, at age fifty-two. Two of his songs, "Pancho and Lefty" and "If I Needed You," would in five years be huge crossover hits for several top country music stars and ensure his place in the American musical canon as a gifted, innovative songsmith.

But now, as the pale winter sun dappled the valley, the notion of a promising future as a major recording artist seemed as implausible as the surrounding forest suddenly parting to reveal an ocean liner loaded with vacationing Sioux vision questers.

"The Plan . . . ever'body jhhoin The Plan . . ."

The mantra was evolving, taking shape as a melody, perhaps eventually a song. When it verged into a howl, Geraldine lent backup harmony with a series of sharp barks and yelps.

I turned to Cindy. "Do you have the key to the chain?"

She sighed and handed me the key. "Make sure you get the shotgun from him first."

Townes shouted for me to come to him. I began a slow saunter toward the tree. His lanky, six-foot-one frame was stretched out along the ground, his back against the tree, the crown of his head pressed into the bark. The fine-boned cheeks on his thin face were flushed red against the pale skin not covered by his dark, bushy brows, disheveled mop of black hair, and week-old growth of gray-flecked beard. Curiously, his brown eyes—when they fluttered open—betrayed no hint of turmoil or angst; they gazed seemingly unperturbed at the sights and sounds of a private universe.

I stopped a few feet away, as he issued a slurred but undeniably cheery greeting. "H-how's it goinnn'?"

"Pretty good," I replied. "How about you?"

"Not bad. Got Cindy and Lomax totally freaked out, huh?"

I nodded my assent. "That's for sure. Can you hand me the gun?"

He lifted it and pointed it at my chest. "No," he replied loudly enough for Cindy and John to hear.

I walked a few steps closer, stopping two feet away. I had no reason to believe he would intentionally shoot me. But accidents do happen. I'd seen several in Vietnam.

"Can you hand me the gun?"

He looked into my eyes, smiled, and raised the shotgun to point at my head. "No!" he shouted. I had a feeling Cindy and John were getting ready to make a run for it, but I just kept looking at Townes and thinking: *This would be a heckuva way to go out, but it would generate plenty of press, for sure.*

After a couple of minutes, Townes lowered the shotgun and let me take it.

"Thanks," I said. "So, what do you want to do?"

Townes struggled to his knees, and motioned me to unlock him. "Okay, here's The Plan." His voice had suddenly lost the slur, though the trembling had morphed into a rapid-fire, staccato delivery that meant his thoughts were outpacing his speech and the sobering process was starting its slow ascent. "They've got a program at the state mental hospital where you check in and dry out for fifteen days, then they let you go. Sounds like my kind of place, don't it?"

I had been through the express dry-out drill before and saw no reason to disagree. His next performance wasn't for another month, which meant I could get him clean and ready to travel with time to spare. With

Townes under clinical supervision, I could spend the next few days preparing for the trip instead of being on 24-hour intervention call.

I conferred with John and Cindy about procedure. "We'll take him to Vanderbilt Hospital first," John suggested. "You need a doctor's referral to get into the state facility." Townes stumbled a few feet away, unloaded the shotgun, and tossed the shells to the ground. Geraldine stared at him with intense interest, then began to paw at one of the shells.

John gulped. "Jesus, he keeps that thing loaded?"

"Only when he's drunk," Cindy shrugged.

The ride into downtown Nashville felt surprisingly short, and Townes's renewed lucidity made it mildly entertaining. He was a natural-born storyteller. I was a natural-born listener.

Lying across the back seat, his head tilted and resting on his palm, he recounted the first time he'd played with folk singer Don Sanders in the early 1960s at a Houston hole-in-the-wall called Sand Mountain, on a night when the only audience member—besides the proprietress, an elderly widow named Mrs. Carrick—was a surly, middle-aged man.

"There was this song I used to do at the time called 'The KKK Blues,' and I sang it that night. It was a talking blues about a guy dropping out of the second grade to join the Ku Klux Klan, and after I sang it, the customer said, 'Son, you got too much education.' Then he walked out, and the old lady, Mrs. Carrick, I looked to her for some encouragement. She smiled real sweet and said, 'Well, that was real good, darlin'. But we just don't do things like that around here.' My first, last, and only engagement at Sand Mountain."

Townes's comic timing was dead-on, as he mimicked the characters' accents, facial expressions, and body language. *It's like he's onstage right now introducing a song,* I realized, wondering if this whole craziness with the paint and chain and now the hospital was simply another elaborate Townes Van Zandt prank.

In the emergency room, we waited outside the curtained cubicle where Townes was being examined by an earnest young resident. "There's nothing wrong with you," the doctor told Townes. "You just need to stop drinking." Townes stuck his head outside the curtain and winked at me as if to say, "Listen to this."

"Doc, I make my living as a guitar player, but there's just one problem." Townes looked down at his hands, then back at the doctor with a completely straight face. "I want to cut off my hands. But if I cut off one, how would I cut off the other one?" The doctor blinked but said nothing, leaving the cubicle and making a phone call at the intake desk.

A few minutes later we heard a loud car siren screeching outside the ER door. Two Nashville P.D. officers raced toward us down the hall, one with club in hand, the other brandishing handcuffs. They cuffed Townes, who talked to them calmly while simultaneously pissing them off.

Five minutes of my vigorous pleading and stolid assurances persuaded the doctor to dismiss the police and let us drive Townes to the mental hospital. A queasy feeling in my gut suggested The Plan was going to take some unspecified detours. "You'd think I was askin' to get into Fort Knox," groused Townes. "I just wanna go to the nuthouse."

Back in the car, on the way to the mental hospital, Townes demanded we stop for a half pint of vodka. I spotted a liquor store, got the bottle, and Townes sat in the back seat guzzling until we turned in at the Middle Tennessee Mental Health Institute.

Before passing through the entry gates, Townes blurted, "Whoa! I gotta get another jug, cuz once I'm inside, it's cold turkey, jerky."

I turned the car around, drove back to the liquor store. By the time we returned to the institute, Townes had finished his second half pint. And decided he needed one last topper. Back to the liquor store, score another half pint, return to the institute.

This time he was ready to go inside. It was almost dark.

John and I half-carried, half-staggered him up to the entrance of the austere, gray-stone building. The main glass doors whooshed open automatically, then locked behind us with a sharp, loud click. At the counter, the nurse asked, "Who is checking in?" Townes pointed at us, and we pointed at him.

The nurse had obviously been through this routine before. "You can check in together on the buddy program," she said, with no visible trace of humor.

Three stocky male attendants in white appeared and surrounded us. With a sheepish grin, Townes finally stepped forward. He waved and chuckled as the attendants led him down the hall. "Keep a jug on ice," he said as he disappeared around the corner. "I'll be thirsty when I get out!"

The next day I visited the institute. To my dismay, I discovered Townes had been placed in the Dangerous Patient Ward, behind three locked doors with very long corridors in between. Men and women under extreme medication wandered aimlessly, mumbling, or sat still, staring straight ahead, expressionless as zombies amid a cacophonic soundscape of television noise, chair and table scraping, flurries of shouts and yips.

Townes was sitting by himself in a light-blue patient smock and paper slippers, scared and shaking. He'd been shaved and bathed and had his hair evened out, but his face was white as a sheet, his eyes dilated with drugs and panic. "They made a mistake and put me in the wrong ward. They don't even *have* a dry-out program here," he said. "I'm not crazy like these folks, but if I stay here, I will be. You gotta get me out of here, H. Everybody here's crazy except me!"

I was sure I'd be able to straighten out this mess, one way or another. That was what a road manager did—straighten out messes, all sizes, all shapes, all levels of crazy.

As long as he doesn't die in here, we'll pull this off. He's too good to flame out this soon. He's got too much life and music left in him.

I gripped Townes's arm. "Buddy, I'll get you out of here."

"I know you will, H." For the first time during the visit, Townes smiled. It was his Zen smile, his holy-man smile, his all-wise, total enlightenment, glimmer-of-God smile that summoned images of insight and bliss, of order and reason, of a funky wondrous destiny beyond words just waiting around the bend, a secret smile that hinted, "Don't worry . . . it's all in The Plan."

It took three days of phone calls with institute administrators for me to learn that Townes's remarks about cutting off his hands had served as justification for the severe commitment. He would have to undergo an additional week of extensive evaluation to determine if he would be released.

If. A very small word that, in this instance, packed an enormous amount of dread. Was it possible he could be confined to this place for a year? Two? Forever?

On the day of his court hearing, Townes sat between Cindy and me at a long table. Across from us were arrayed a judge, stenographer, social worker, and five institute doctors. Nobody was smiling. In fact, the judge was completely inscrutable, his hands folded so that they almost entirely covered his face.

Earlier, in the hall, Townes had whispered to me, "If they decide I gotta stay, I will dive through a window. You have the car ready, and we'll break out of this loony bin."

"Sure, no problem," I replied, chuckling. *At least he still has a sense of humor. I mean, seriously, why wouldn't they let him go? He's not really crazy.*

Turned out that was a minority view. The doctors unanimously concluded that Townes should stay for six months to a year, then receive another hearing at which time a final determination would be made—which could result in an indefinite commitment.

Under the table Townes tapped my leg, glancing toward the window. I gave him the flat-hand-on-the-knee "wait" signal. He sat frozen, sweating, eyes as wide as I'd ever seen them, as Cindy stood and spoke, saying she loved him and that she would be there for him always.

The judge turned to me, his hands still blocking his face, so that only his dark, somber eyes and furrowed forehead were visible. "You're his friend. What do you have to say?"

I said a lot. A whole bunch of a lot, trying to touch on every possible reason Townes should be granted release. Mostly, I focused on Townes's work as an acclaimed songwriter and performer and how his intent in approaching the institute had been to enjoy a simple, short sabbatical, if you will, to get himself in shape to write and perform better.

He was as completely rational and responsible as any of us here today, I avowed . . . even as a part of my brain was calculating how quickly I could dash to the car and facilitate an illegal breakout.

The judge trained his gaze on Townes. "What do you think?"

Townes swallowed hard, raised his head, and looked straight at the judge. The room was completely silent. In a soft but steady voice, he said, "My mom told me, 'When you need to take a drink, don't.'"

The judge hesitated for several seconds. "That was good advice," he said, finally moving his hands from his face to reveal a bulbous, beet-red, W.C. Fields nose. With a smile, he issued his decree: "Let him go."

As we walked out the front door, it started to snow, picking up as we drove back to the cabin. Each mile put the institute further in the past, and Townes relaxed and told jokes, ribbing Cindy gently, talking about love and happiness, vowing to write new songs and get back on the road again. When we got to the cabin, the snow had transformed the rustic landscape into a winter wonderland.

Townes strolled to the tree where he'd been chained that day of the vision quest. "Sure is good to be home," he said. "Won't try that fifteen-day so-called program again. Think I might stick with Mr. Tree next time."

We all hugged one another, and Townes shook my hand, holding it tightly. With tears in his eyes, he said, "Thanks. H. You have a merry Christmas and say hello to the family."

It was only then that I realized it was two days before Christmas— the holiday had snuck up on me totally unawares. Townes's release was a great Christmas gift. An even better one would be driving straight through to my parents' home on Long Island.

Navigating the snow-filled wheel ruts leading back to the main road, I looked in the rearview mirror and saw Townes with one arm around Cindy, his other petting Geraldine. Townes Van Zandt had shot craps again with the vagaries of life and come out a winner once more.

For the next twenty years, he would roll the dice night after night, day in and day out, shuttling between ecstasy and despair as he sang his life in concert halls and roadhouse joints across the U.S. and Canada, throughout Europe, and Down Under in Australia.

He would keep beating the odds and keep creating passionate, riveting music that touched the souls of total strangers, firing their imaginations with his fevered muse, each line of a new lyric buying him time, or so he believed, until the fateful hour he would return to Our Mother the Mountain, from whence all creation came.

What follows is the story of that music and the sublimely terrifying fusion of genius and rage that birthed it.

1

I First Meet the Late, Great Townes Van Zandt

THE FIRST TIME I met Townes Van Zandt was in 1967, when my brother Kevin unexpectedly dropped by the family home in Stony Brook, New York, for a visit. Kevin's visit may have been sparked by chance, but ended up shaping my life in ways I couldn't have imagined then, and can still barely fathom.

I was seventeen years old, a student at Port Jefferson High School, and an ordinary late-'60s Long Island teenager with five siblings (Nonie, Peggy, Kathy, Kevin, and Dennis), a homemaker mother, and a father employed by the New York Telephone Company, where he would eventually be elected union president for Suffolk County Communications Workers of America. Solid American middle class all the way around.

Seven years my senior, Kevin had been in the entertainment industry since the early part of the decade, when he moved to Los Angeles and became friends with two other recent L.A. arrivals—Elvis Presley and his close friend Lamar Fike—and began a rapid career rise from mailroom clerk at New York's General Artists Corporation to executive assistant for legendary booking agent Sid Bernstein.

That's the Sid Bernstein who, along with Kevin, presented the Beatles' historic 1964 Carnegie Hall concert and initial U.S. tour and then proceeded to introduce a slew of British Invasion bands—like the Rolling Stones, the Who, the Moody Blues, and the Kinks—to American audiences. Kevin ended up coproducing those early tours, along with shows by Tony Bennett, James Brown, Ray Charles, and other 1960s icons. During my teen years, he often brought numerous entertainers of note to our parents' house, not just to impress the family, but also to let his clients take time off from the showbiz grind and spend some time with regular folks—which my parents, Honora and Harold Sr., certainly were.

I'm not sure if Mom and Dad truly appreciated the full cultural significance of various pop music stars of the day having cake and coffee in our kitchen, but they were always gracious, nonetheless. These visits would set me to wondering if I could emulate Kevin's success in show business.

On this particular day in 1967, Kevin brought a distinctive visitor with an even more distinctive name. Townes Van Zandt was a tall, soft-spoken twenty-three-year-old Texan whose debut album of original songs, *For the Sake of the Song*, Kevin had just recorded for his Poppy Records label and would release the following year.

I had been bitten in earnest by the music bug three years before. For my fourteenth birthday, Kevin had taken me backstage to meet the Rolling Stones when they played Carnegie Hall. He opened the door to their dressing room, led them in congratulating me on my birthday, and then left me there for fifteen minutes as they tossed out pictures of themselves to fans on the street below. As I watched them interact with one another in hip Brit-Mod slang, I thought about how cool it must be to be famous at such a young age. They laughed and joked with one another, pointing out the pretty girls, and waving to the fans, enjoying every moment.

I walked out of that dressing room profoundly different from when I entered. From that day on, I wanted to be in this world of crazy pop music, anywhere, any way.

This Townes Van Zandt fellow was immediately intriguing. I hadn't seen anyone like him hanging out in Stony Brook, that was for sure. My first impression was that he seemed almost ghostlike, especially with his intense, straight-on gaze. In the ensuing conversation, he was quiet and reserved, very respectful, saying "sir" to my father and "ma'am" to my mother. Townes blended in very quickly, cracking jokes to my dad and telling my mom how great the meal was.

From this very first encounter, the family embraced him, and he embraced them. As Kevin continued to record albums with Townes, the singer-songwriter would drop by frequently, attending many family functions and eventually coming to refer to my mother and father as "Mom" and "Dad." In fact, Townes and blues guitarist Albert King served as co-godfathers to Kevin's daughter. I believe that of all the artists Kevin recorded, Townes was the artist he believed in the most.

During one visit, Mom told Townes about her own show business career as a dancer with New York City's legendary Radio City Music Hall Rockettes in the 1930s. After marrying Dad in 1939, she had operated her own dancing school in Brooklyn. When my mom finished telling this story to Townes, she got up and danced around the room.

As for me, despite growing up in a comfortable middle-class home, I was itching to break out of the suburban mold. When my draft notice came in high school, I immediately enlisted in the Air Force. I had acquired the notion that if you volunteered and chose your service (picking your poison, as the saying goes), your chances of seeing front-line combat were greatly minimized, if not eliminated altogether.

That notion would turn out to be radically incorrect, as I'll detail shortly.

Like so many talented young recording artists of the late '60s and early '70s, Townes Van Zandt had seemingly arrived onto the music scene wholly baked and already iconic. However, he had paid serious musical and personal dues, starting from his early twenties, when he dropped out of the University of Houston's prelaw program and took to performing in local music spots.

Pursue a career as a lawyer or become a folk singer? There was no contest, Townes would later tell me. "Mr. Guitar won out, hands down."

Townes had gotten married in 1965 at age twenty-one to a college schoolmate, Fran Petters. Making an effort to live a straight and normal adult life, he had tried to enlist in the Air Force, but was turned down when they learned of the extensive shock treatment therapy he'd undergone in a mental institution just a year or so before.

That rejection was the accidental spark that set a bunch of random kindling ablaze and eventually became a lifetime of artistic fire.

In the small apartment where he and Fran lived, Townes made a closet into a writing room. He began playing at Houston coffeehouses and nightclubs, where he met musicians like renowned bluesman Sam "Lightnin'" Hopkins, who would serve as a musical and philosophical mentor.

Throughout 1966 and 1967, Townes found his performing persona and matured into a polished stage entertainer. He picked up gigs across Texas and at clubs and festivals in the Northeast, opening for progressive rocker Todd Rundgren in Philadelphia, co-billing with bluegrass maestro Doc Watson in Oklahoma City, serving as the house act at New York's Bottom Line, and playing his own nights at Gerde's Folk City, the revered Greenwich Village folk music club where a teenage Emmylou Harris would occasionally open for him.

Jerry Jeff Walker, another up-and-coming singer-songwriter working the Houston music milieu at the time, suggested Townes start writing his own songs. "It's easier to remember what you wrote than what somebody else wrote," Walker advised. It also made a performer stand out as somebody a record label might want to take an interest in.

Townes's break came in 1967, when Houston singer-songwriter Mickey Newbury heard one of his demo tapes and gave it to Nashville record producer Jack Clement. Clement was contacted by Lamar Fike— Elvis Presley's confidant and a Nashville publishing executive—who knew my brother Kevin had just started a label (Poppy Records, with distribution by MGM) and was looking for a unique performer to inaugurate the imprint.

Clement played Kevin a demo recording he'd made of Townes's "Tecumseh Valley." Kevin knew he was hearing an incredibly distinctive and original American songwriting voice. On the spot, he asked Clement to produce a Townes Van Zandt record for the initial Poppy Records release.

Townes's *For the Sake of the Song* was recorded at MGM Studios in New York and released in December 1968, the first of six Townes albums issued by Kevin on Poppy Records through 1972. The albums were first-class productions. Arrangements and orchestration duties were handled by industry professionals like Ronald Frangipane, Bergen White, and Don Randi and employed a range of top-flight studio musicians like Charlie McCoy, David Briggs, Kenny Buttrey, James Burton, Larry Carlton, Chuck Cochran, Harvey Newmark, and David Cohen, among others. The album packaging was graphically sophisticated as well, with intriguing cover art contributions by the likes of illustrator Milton Glaser and photographers Allen Vogel and Steve Salmieri.

For the first time in his performing career, Townes's music was sold in major record stores and played on radio across the country. The Poppy/MGM affiliation linked him to a touring network that put him in front of audiences across North America and, more important, brought him to the attention of his songwriting peers. In November 1969, Townes headlined a Poppy Records showcase at Carnegie Hall and was instantly catapulted into the Big Apple rock-and-pop music circus of the time.

However, *For the Sake of the Song* sold poorly despite receiving positive reviews by critics. None of Townes's albums or singles released during this period sold well relative to record industry standards.

Yet those who did hear the records—or experienced Townes in concert—became die-hard fans who avidly followed his musical activities for years.

Traveling with Townes later on, I spoke to countless people who told me that his music had changed their lives in many positive ways.

His songs, they would say, hit them "right where they lived" emotionally, with lyrics that were concise, evocative, memorable. Listeners felt they were getting an intense, condensed dose of Vital Life Truth that alternately inspired, consoled, and guided them as they made their way in their own world.

It's the kind of truth everyone needs to confront at certain challenging times in their lives. For me, those times were about to start in earnest.

2

Moving Forward,
One Backward Step at a Time

MANY TIMES during the next two decades, Townes asked me to tell stories about my time in the military. After a while, I realized it was for more than just to pass the hours on long drives. It represented a part of him that was strangely unfulfilled—a yearning, deep-rooted element of his psychological makeup that continually drifted toward the shadowy world of violence and despair.

When Townes was refused by the Air Force and labeled as mentally unstable, he could have simply receded into a life of quiet melancholy, as a quote-unquote normal person who moved on after their life's dreams had been denied. It's a typical response for countless people each day all over the world.

Instead, he set about diverting his emotional distress into creating music that plumbed the depths of his personal pain and uplifted the spirits of complete strangers. But when he wasn't performing or creating, that pain remained a constant factor in his everyday consciousness. Whatever catharsis he may have felt through music was fleeting.

Slowly, over many years of rambling conversations and uproarious incidents, I began to see how important that single incident at the Air Force recruitment office had been in shaping his future. If he couldn't be in the military, Townes would make his civilian life as a touring musician into a kind of perpetual war zone that reflected the unceasing turmoil in his mind and heart.

And maybe, I'm thinking now, that was why I stayed with him all those years. I still needed an occasional war zone in my life, too. I guess you could say with some truth that I was Townes's vicarious battlefield warrior. And that Townes was my postwar Vietnam.

I graduated from high school in 1968. It was an exhilarating time to be a young American. Hippies, psychedelics, street protests, bell-bottoms and tie-dye—the buttoned-down world of our adolescence was changing day by day, never more so than in music.

My senior-year soundtrack included songs like "Sittin' on the Dock of the Bay," "People Got to Be Free," "Chain of Fools," "Hello, I Love You," "Green Tambourine," "Jumpin' Jack Flash," "Born to Be Wild."

And "Sky Pilot" by Eric Burdon and the Animals.

Like every American male turning eighteen, I was legally required to register for the military draft. The year before, in 1967, the U.S. had sent 100,000 fresh soldiers—many of them draftees—to fight a war in Vietnam. A little over eleven thousand would never return home.

My oldest brother, Dennis, was in the Air Force Reserve, and he highly recommended I join that branch of service. There was less likelihood of me being sent to Vietnam, he believed. He also was of the opinion that, of all the military branches, the Air Force treated its enlistees the best.

I joined the Air Force while still a senior. After basic training at Amarillo Air Force Base in Texas, I was posted to Castle Air Force Base in Merced, California. The proficiency I retained from high school typing classes secured me a typist position in an office shared by three airmen like me, a pleasant master sergeant who was my immediate boss, and a bad-tempered second lieutenant with a two-bottle-a-day cough medicine addiction he barely bothered to disguise.

I grew my hair longer than was allowed by regulations and was consistently reprimanded by the second lieutenant, brought up on charges, and then reprieved by our colonel, who would order the two of us to get along. To me, the colonel would say, "Harold, try to keep your hair cut to regulation so he leaves you alone. And stop giving him a hard time every chance you can; we know he has personal problems." In the military, even small acts of nonconformity generate conflict.

As an East Coast transplant, I totally dug the Golden State lifestyle. I spent weekends off taking bus trips to San Francisco, Santa Monica, Los Angeles, Yosemite Park, all through California. It was great to be in a state where you could go to beaches filled with pretty girls in bikinis one day, and then snow ski the next day in the mountains.

After a couple of years, I had adapted comfortably to the military regimen. However, the news from the war overseas wasn't getting better. President Richard Nixon had not ended the conflict as he'd promised; in fact, he'd widened the war to Cambodia and Laos, bringing harm to millions more. I decided I wanted to understand war firsthand and do my part to protect America. I volunteered for Vietnam duty and arrived at Bien Hoa Air Force Base in Đồng Nai Province in 1971, where I was assigned to the helicopter air-traffic control office and oversaw thirty helicopters.

That night, the local Viet Cong fired mortars on the base, and a small enemy ground force attacked us. Welcome to Vietnam, soldier.

Bien Hoa AFB was in the process of being transferred over to the South Vietnamese Air Force, so there weren't that many Americans there. It was garrisoned by a contingent of South Vietnamese army forces and a small Korean Special Forces unit. Bien Hoa had actually been overrun by the VC in 1968 during the Tet offensive, so security was intense. The base was classified as "restricted access"; we were not allowed off base because the enemy was situated just beyond the 20-foot barbed wire perimeter.

Within my first week we received a ground assault by the Viet Cong, and these assaults continued during my entire time at the base. As the incoming mortars exploded, a siren went off, meaning we were under attack. I would dash up onto a tower post and watch as tracers and rockets lit up the sky, mortar rounds whistling as they sailed over us and landed with a thump inside the base . . . two or three seconds of silence, then *KA-BOOM*, the explosion flare blinding you for an instant.

I had an infrared rifle scope, so I could see the enemy at night. It improved the chances of hitting them, but it was like shooting at shadows. The skirmishing would go on and off until sunrise, and then repeat the next day or two days later.

Even when I wasn't at my regular job working for helicopter air-traffic

control, I had to stay loaded up with a rifle, extra ammunition, and gre-
nades. I looked like a stereotypical Mexican bandito, crisscrossed ammo
belts over my chest.

My nerves got pretty well shot within this initial period and only got
worse as time passed. You don't adjust to this type of madness—you just
get numb to it and assume that, sooner or later, you will be shot or blown
up by an incoming mortar. Existence in a war zone is anticipating the
worst at any moment.

By my third week, I was more or less acclimated to the extreme jun-
gle humidity and the alternating states of sleep deprivation and paranoia. Each morning, the area outside the perimeter was sprayed with
Agent Orange to kill foliage that would conceal the Viet Cong as they
approached the base. The wind wafted the chemical clouds back over the
whole base. We thought nothing about it, other than that you could see
hardly anything and the smell burned your throat; we learned to avoid
being outside when the spray came.

I made friends with the Vietnamese mama-sans who cleaned our
clothes, squatting down in the showers and washing the base laundry by
hand. I noticed they all had black teeth. I asked a GI about it, and he said
it was the result of chewing betel nut, a hallucinogen.

At first I was uncomfortable taking a shower while the mama-sans
washed, especially with them pointing and laughing at me. But the next
time I was in the shower, I laughed along with them; they got quiet for
a minute, and then proceeded to laugh, and I laughed along with them
again. I didn't understand a word of Vietnamese, but they nodded at
me to let me know I was okay with them. From then on, I made more
and more Vietnamese friends just by being nice and letting them know
I would make fun of myself in front of them to gain their trust and
respect. Once I got to know them more, they let me know they liked me,
too, especially since I was small like them. I always treated them with
respect and never referred to them with the common ethnic slurs used
by other American soldiers.

I started smoking marijuana to put my mind in another place. The
weed helped distract me from the rising twinges of self-loathing nibbling

at my conscience whenever I thought about shooting at other human beings.

Of course, it couldn't eliminate the insanity of war itself. We learned the Viet Cong were terrorizing the local villagers, at one point beheading a village elder and posting his head on a stick. They brutalized the villagers into attacking the base—women and old men used as cannon fodder. I realized that some of the Vietnamese friends I kidded around with during the day were in my rifle sights at night. I had probably killed one or two.

I was promoted to sergeant and reassigned to the air-traffic control office in Saigon. I'm not sure whether I felt safer in the bustling metropolis or at the isolated air base. There was the time I was sitting at the bar of a favorite nightclub, an intimate rooftop lounge on top of a three-story building in the red-light district. It was a favorite spot for ladies of the evening, and over time I had become casual friends with several of them.

One night, four of these women and I were sitting together, just relaxing, when a Vietnamese man suddenly approached and grabbed one of them roughly by the arm, pulling her out of her chair and yelling at her. He reared back his hand and slapped her face, hard, knocking her against the table. He raised his hand for a second blow—but it never landed. The other girls jumped up and stabbed him several times in his back and sides; with a choking grunt, he fell to the floor, dead.

No one else in the club appeared to take much notice, and, without a word, the women dragged his body to the balcony and threw it off the roof. They came back to the bar and sat down next to me. I am certain my visage showed some level of anxiety. They perceived this and told me not to worry. "We won't hurt you—you are our friend. But if you hurt one of us, you see what happens."

What I saw was that anyone can be murderous, if you push them too far past a certain line. My time in Vietnam was teaching me how to be a more astute observer of where those lines might be.

I also absorbed the importance of keeping to a schedule. Saigon had a nightly curfew enforced by the home guard militia, which meant that no one—*no one*—could be on the public streets during those hours.

Helicopters would fly over the city, sweeping the streets and alleys with lights to see anything and everything moving on the ground. Anybody the patrols found on the streets after curfew was assumed to be VC or a spy and was shot. On the spot.

Racing against curfew became a sport; you'd wait till as late as possible, then catch a cyclo—a motorized version of a pedicab—and see if you could get home to the air base in time. If it didn't look like you could, you'd stop in the nearest cheap hotel and rent a room to stay till sunrise. I'm not sure how effective the curfew was at preventing espionage, but it gave hotels and cyclo drivers lots of extra business for many years.

For me, it reinforced a growing attraction to danger I would find irresistible for years.

In Saigon, I met a Vietnamese girl named Lien, which means "lotus flower" in that language. She didn't speak much English, but we were in love and got an apartment together. A kind, gentle, soft-spoken soul, Lien had married very young and had lost her husband and children to the war, but was still full of love and hope.

Our apartment had a small garden and was on the top floor of a four-story building in an area with numerous battle-damaged structures. No one in the building spoke English except me, but all the other tenants accepted me because I was with my Vietnamese girlfriend.

As I got to know the Vietnamese, I could never wrap my mind around this basic paradox: they were the poorest and most devastated people I had ever met, yet they were the happiest people I've ever encountered to this day.

This insight would always come back to me as I traveled with Townes, who was simultaneously the happiest and saddest individual I've known, truly war-torn in his own way. I can't help but wonder if he was somehow inhabited by a returning spirit of one of my Vietnamese friends who had died but couldn't remain on the Other Side.

Christmas Eve, 1971. The armies had called a twenty-four-hour truce, at least in South Vietnam. American planes continued bombing enemy targets in Laos and Cambodia all through Christmas Day, but in Saigon, as the clock ticked toward midnight marking December 25, you stopped hearing jeeps, you stopped hearing helicopters. The street din that *never* completely stopped for even a minute, merely faded to a whisper in the hours before dawn . . . suddenly, it wasn't there.

And then the singing started.

Lien and I leaned out over our apartment terrace. In the courtyard below, next to a partially blown-out church, hundreds of people had gathered for Midnight Mass and were singing "Silent Night" in Vietnamese. Every person held a candle. From where we stood, the flickering lights were like a bright orange wave surging up and down through the dark.

I knew there were Viet Cong mixed in down there. The enemy I had a responsibility to kill, who had tried to kill me. But tonight they were all singing for peace. Praying for peace. And tomorrow, after the truce, willing to kill and die for peace.

Tất cả đều bình tĩnh, tất cả đều tươi sáng . . . All is calm, all is bright.

I broke down and cried. Then and sometimes now, remembering the sound of those voices in that tropical midnight hour. Despite all the madness and killing these people had suffered—and would suffer for years to come—this night they sang about hope, faith, and love.

As my departure date from Vietnam drew near, I asked the military authorities if it would be possible to bring Lien home with me to America. Permission was denied; even my offer of marriage was not granted. On the day we parted, Lien and I hugged and cried; she would not let go of me and kept saying, "Please don't leave me!" over and over. I made sure I got a window seat on the plane. Instead of waving her hand back and forth as Americans do in bidding farewell, she extended one arm, waving her hand in small motions up and down—this actually meant "come here" among the Vietnamese.

Though we had exchanged our parents' mailing addresses, and I called and mailed numerous letters to her over the next few months, I was never able to reach her again.

I arrived in the U.S. with an honorable discharge and an incipient case of what would come to be classified as post-traumatic stress disorder.

PTSD wouldn't be formally admitted to the *Diagnostic and Statistical Manual of Mental Disorders* until 1980, but it was a mental condition soldiers and civilians touched by violence had experienced for centuries under different labels: nostalgia. Melancholia. Soldier's heart. Gross stress reaction. For me and my war, the label was shell shock.

It's a condition that manifests many different ways, not always because of a particular crisis or incident. To this day I'm haunted by memories of standing on the runway at Bien Hoa and seeing an arriving plane filled with fresh U.S. military personnel, likely as naive as I was . . . while at the other end of the strip, a crew loaded coffins of dead soldiers onto a plane bound for America.

My mental state wasn't aided by the general alienation I felt readjusting to nonmilitary life. Returning from Vietnam following my discharge, I had arrived at the airport to find my mom, dad, and sisters Peggy and Kathy waiting to greet me. I was in full uniform and, departing from the plane onto the tarmac, drew the unwanted attention of several members of the crowd. Suddenly, I heard the words "Baby killer!" and some muffled shouts, growing in number. It took me a few moments to realize the clamor was directed at me. I spotted my family, and then felt something wet on my shoulder. *Spit? Someone had just spit on me?*

My mind went into immediate defense mode. I dropped my duffel bag, freeing both hands, and strode straight up to one of the shouters, my face convulsed and eyes furious. The shouts stopped as suddenly as they'd started. Two or three backed away, fear in their expressions; others averted their gaze and were silent. After a few seconds, I turned away, found my family, and embraced them, glad to be home again but realizing it was not the same place I'd left four years before.

In Vietnam, you felt as if you were always on the brink of getting shot, which is natural for any soldier in any war zone. Back home in the U.S., that hyper-alertness could morph into an addiction pattern where you sought danger in normal daily life.

For me, that was driving a cab in New York City on the night shift. One, two, three in the morning, I'd go to the airport or Broadway and pick up Puerto Rican girls and drive them to Harlem. They'd give me weed and say, "What are you doing taking us to Harlem? You're one crazy white man gonna get himself killed!"

They didn't realize I *needed* the crazy. The attraction to dangerous people and situations is a characteristic common of those with PTSD. In fact, I found myself drawn to bad parts of the city, looking for trouble. After what I'd seen in Vietnam, I was like, "What the hell? You get shot, you get shot. You die, you die. It'll be a heckuva rush, no doubt about it."

I moved in with my brother Kevin and his family in their Brooklyn Heights brownstone, just the other side of the Brooklyn Bridge. I lived on the top floor in a couple of rooms where Townes would often stay when he was in the city. Kevin had changed his label from Poppy Records to Tomato Records and was at peak activity with a staff of forty or so people, including our brother Dennis, who had coproduced the label's Dick Gregory *At Kent State* album.

Kevin saw the readjustment stress I was going through. He offered me a job as road manager for a French group called Magma, who played what can best be described as avant-garde rock fusion. The drummer was situated in front of the rest of the band, and their song lyrics were composed in a special language they had created. Their music was totally out there, but they had fans among their pop music peers, including members of the Beatles and Rolling Stones.

Magma was to perform at the Newport Jazz Festival, which that year was held at various clubs throughout New York City. I met them at the airport and learned that neither the band members nor their wives, girlfriends, or road manager spoke a word of English. Which perfectly suited my nonexistent French. Somehow the necessary communication among us all was achieved, and the tour went off without a hitch.

It was my first taste of being a road manager. Like driving a cab in New York City or surviving a mortar attack in Vietnam, it had its own unique set of up-tempo adrenaline moments.

I was hooked, even if I didn't yet know it.

From 1968 to 1972, Kevin put out six Townes Van Zandt albums on Poppy Records: *For the Sake of the Song* (1968), *Our Mother the Mountain* (1969), *Townes Van Zandt* (1969), *Delta Momma Blues* (1971), *High, Low*

and In Between (1972), and *The Late Great Townes Van Zandt* (1972).
With each new record and via Columbine Music, the ASCAP publishing company they co-owned, Kevin worked to introduce Townes and his music to the huge number of industry people he knew, in hopes their artists would record a Townes song.

During visits to New York, Townes met the Beatles, the Rolling Stones, and the Who, along with their producers and managers. But Kevin's pitch efforts went largely unrewarded, except for placing "If I Needed You" on Doc Watson's 1973 *Then and Now* album on Tomato Records. Doc's acceptance meant a lot to Townes, and he would mention it often through the years.

Even so, Townes's audiences were expanding beyond the boundaries of country-folk; the early 1970s saw him sharing stages with Frank Zappa and the Mothers of Invention, John McLaughlin's Mahavishnu Orchestra, bluesmen John Hammond and Freddie King, progressive rockers Mandrake Memorial, and well-known performers like the Allman Brothers, Arlo Guthrie, Seals & Crofts, the Flying Burrito Brothers, and Charlie Daniels. In July 1971, he appeared on David Frost's popular television show with a bevy of Hollywood actors, the Lettermen singing group, and famed Vietnam War journalist Kate Webb.

Yet his personal life remained in flux, particularly his romantic relationships with women. Divorced from his wife in Houston, Townes surrounded himself on the road with hard-living ladies as lovers and traveling companions, women who aided and abetted his addictions while eliciting a passel of tender, plaintive songs from his lyrical muse.

One particularly tragic incident seems to have left a strong impact on his songwriting and his state of mind.

In August 1971, Townes was in a California recording studio finishing up tracks for his *High, Low and In Between* album. A woman with whom he had fallen deeply in love was murdered while hitchhiking home from one of his recording sessions. Leslie Jo Richards would be immortalized in one of his songs, "Snow Don't Fall." It was a song he would never perform live, no matter how insistent the request.

I always felt this was a key turn in Townes's life, leading to a profound embitterment and a deepening of his already pessimistic outlook. A couple of weeks later, while in Houston, Townes overdosed on heroin. He was rushed to Ben Taub Hospital, revived, and narrowly saved from death.

My life story, meanwhile, took a series of rapid 180-degree reversals. I quit driving cab and became a union carpenter, married a nice Long Island girl named Joan Murphy, and started inching toward solid-citizen status. I still regularly smoked marijuana, of course, and could never quite unsee in my mind what I'd seen with my eyes in Vietnam.

But the construction business was good to us—until one day, it wasn't. Joan and I had a one-year-old daughter, Megan, our debts were piling up, and two of our cars were repossessed. We moved in with my parents in Stony Brook, and I went down to Houston, where my sister Nonie Beard lived with her family, chasing rumors that a big building boom was happening there.

It was a rare instance in my life when a streets-of-gold rumor panned out. I found a construction job right away, got us an apartment, and arranged for our household furniture to be moved down. A month later, the plan was, my wife and daughter would fly in and join me. Everything back on track.

But when Joan arrived in Houston, she informed me she had met a rich man and wanted us to divorce. She was in love with him, she said. And I was broke and unable to provide for her as she believed he would.

We didn't argue much. I figured we'd sort things out in a few months, and so I put her on a plane back East. But she immediately remarried, cut off all communication, and disappeared into thin air. I didn't see her or my daughter for sixteen years.

To say I was depressed and disoriented would be an understatement. To say I began self-medicating with massive substance abuse would, again, barely convey the intensity of my hitting emotional rock bottom . . . and then digging an even deeper hole.

My mom got wind of my downward spiral and told Kevin. She may have asked him what he could do for me; or maybe Kevin instinctively figured out that the best fix for my problems was to hook me up with someone who had even more.

He called Townes in Nashville, related my circumstances, and suggested that once the singer's upcoming *Flyin' Shoes* album was done, a road manager would be needed for the tour. Townes agreed and said for me to give him a call. I did.

The line picked up, and Townes's disarming twang crackled over the wires:

"Son, I hear you have a broken heart. Well, move up to Nashville and be my road manager. Your broken heart will be right at home here."

That's all I needed to hear. I left Houston that night with only the clothes on my back and a small bag of travel essentials. I had no idea what I was in for in the weeks, years to come.

Even if I had, I wouldn't have—probably couldn't have—changed a thing.

3

Welcome to Nashville: Would You Rather a Knife in the Chest or the Back?

Townes Van Zandt had found a songwriter's paradise in a small cabin nested in a remote valley in the scenic Harpeth River watershed thirty miles south of downtown Nashville.

It would serve as his artistic retreat, his romantic getaway, and the site of a tragedy that upended his career in one swift smashup.

The "cabin" was, for all intents and purposes, a three-room shanty. It had been built decades before to house the seasonal migrant laborers formerly employed on the three-thousand-acre tobacco farm that surrounded the residence. As an actual habitation, it was as primitive as you can get—hand-pumped water in the kitchen, wood-burning stove, no shower, large gaps in the weather-beaten wooden walls and floorboards, an outhouse that depended on the silvery moon as a light source.

The landscape was beautiful, though, with grand sunrises and sunsets. At dawn and dusk, clouds of misty fog hovered over the land. There were no extraneous human or automotive noises, only the sounds of field animals, bugs, birds, the weather . . . Mother Nature at her rural finest.

For the two months I stayed there in late 1977, until moving to an apartment in Nashville near Music Row, life seemed timeless, moving at a lazy, carefree crawl. After my recent domestic troubles, that was quite consoling.

At the time of my arrival, Townes shared the cabin with his girlfriend, Cindy Morgan, destined to become his second wife in a few months. And with Geraldine, a friendly German shepherd–husky mix of indeterminate age and marital status.

Cindy was the daughter of a truck driver, a tall, pretty, red-headed Texas girl, generally soft-spoken but capable of the occasional temper outburst. Young as she was, she was already thick-skinned when dealing with Townes and his foibles. They wouldn't be officially married until September 1978, but for now they were a tight couple.

The day I arrived, Townes greeted me warmly when I reached the cabin, and made me feel welcome right off. Picking up from our phone conversation, he assured me that a broken heart was a major part of life and always would be.

"Don't ever ask a woman the truth, unless you're ready to lose your mind," he chuckled.

As stated by Townes, my rules of engagement were simple. "The deal as road manager is two things, H: One, you don't work for me, you work *with* me. Two, all your expenses will be paid, including food, and you get paid at the end of each tour when we return to Nashville." He paused and smiled. "I guess that's three things, but from now on, you're in charge of the number stuff."

"Also," he continued, "I hear you smoke a lot of weed. I don't smoke weed much at all; I prefer hooch. People give me weed for free all the time, so I will give it to you, one less expense for you."

That kind of fringe benefit was typical of the occupation and the era. Given my mental state at the time, it was highly welcome.

"Oh, and by the way—"

There was one more hard-and-fast rule . . .

"I always carry my own guitar. You never have to carry it."

Of course, there would be the odd occasion when he claimed he was too weak, sick, or depressed to carry his guitar, and then I would carry it at his request . . . and as I loaded the case in the car or truck, he would burst out laughing and say, "Got you again, H!"

I never minded this "con," because it showed he was still capable of merriment, especially toward the end. In a strange way, the pranking showed he was thinking about our friendship and able to break loose— even if for just a few moments—from his deepening state of gloom.

Townes's insistence on always carrying his guitar never seemed to be so much about him being the consummate professional always in charge of his instrument, as much as it was about him always having control of at least One Sure Thing, even as everything else in his life spiraled out of control. "Mr. Guitar won't ever break my heart or leave me," he'd say.

Despite all of his acclaim as a deft songwriter and emotion-laden singer, you don't hear the critics talk that much about Townes's actual guitar-playing technique. This, I believe, is a serious undervaluation of the innate musicianship that was part and parcel of his ability to reach audiences and communicate the essence of a song.

Watching him perform over a two-decade span in a wide variety of circumstances, I saw him use the guitar to not just carry the lyrics, but also frame them, like a skilled painter using subtle shades of color to finesse each individual rendition of a portrait—a portrait that would change in some interesting way every time you looked at it. Townes's guitar-playing always added a dimension to the vocal that added up to more than the sum of each individual element.

I credit the heart of his style to his intense study of the guitar technique of Lightnin' Hopkins, the legendary Houston bluesman, whom Townes had met at an important juncture in his musical development. Of the many African-American blues guitarists with deep, country-blues-style roots discovered in the 1960s by pop audiences, Hopkins was one whose guitar style was most accessible to newcomers.

Townes told me there were times during his first year at college when he would stay in his dorm room for days on end and listen to records, exploring new musical styles and trying to adapt what he heard to his emerging guitar technique. The two artists he found himself listening to the most, he said, were Bob Dylan and Lightnin' Hopkins. Dylan's early recordings helped bring traditional American ballad writing and writers like Woody Guthrie and Ramblin' Jack Elliott to the notice of young singer-songwriters. Blues composers like Hopkins offered a tight lyrical framework that was pithy and pointed, often using humor to make ironic and provocative comments on social and political topics.

When Townes moved to Houston in 1965, he would meet Hopkins and become even more immersed in the man's music. Many times over the years, Townes would tell me how great an influence Hopkins's music had had on him and how much he still enjoyed listening to it. The very last weeks of his life, Townes was still listening to his treasured tapes of Hopkins, as well as another personal favorite, Hank Williams Sr.

For Townes, the guitar was more than a work tool; it assumed an almost living role of a performance partner. Townes used several guitars over his career, and they were always christened "Mr. Guitar." He believed a guitar had to do "time" in a pawn shop to accrue the necessary "soul." I saw instances when he would pawn his guitar for a short period so it could earn its musical stripes, so to speak.

Once when we were returning to Nashville from Europe, the neck of his guitar got damaged in flight. I told Townes I would arrange to get a new replacement guitar. He got very upset. "H, if your cousin broke his leg, would you throw him in the Dumpster and get another cousin?"

I said I likely wouldn't, and he replied, "You bet you wouldn't. And I'm not gonna throw my best friend, Mr. Guitar, in the Dumpster and replace him with a look-alike."

Immediately after my arrival in Tennessee, Townes introduced me to several of his friends and musical cohorts. It was a diverse collection of humans, all of them busily embarked on their own vivid and unique life journeys. Looking back, it's pretty remarkable that so many were able to express their journey in eloquent songs that reached so many other people around the world and still do.

Townes's morbid sense of humor had led him to title his sixth album for Poppy Records, released in 1972, *The Late Great Townes Van Zandt*. It was not a savvy marketing move: numerous fans, deejays, promoters, and other music industry folk failed to grasp the joke and truly believed he was dead and no longer on the scene. While recording an album for Poppy later that year tentatively titled *Seven Come Eleven*, his heroin use dramatically resurfaced; Kevin judged the music too dark to release and shelved the project, which would appear only in 1993 as *The Nashville Sessions*, on Tomato Records.

Over the next five years, Townes's depression deepened as his recording and performing career stalled and drifted in the shallows of the commercial music world. Even though the 1970s saw musicians continuously crossing (and inventing) genre boundaries, the industry seemed unable to decide whether to categorize his music as country, blues, or folk.

Pop influences had been nibbling at the edges of Nashville's musical core since the late 1960s, with Bob Dylan's *Blonde on Blonde, John Wesley Harding*, and *Nashville Skyline* albums, the emergence of "outlaw country" artists like Willie Nelson, Waylon Jennings, and Kris Kristofferson, and country-influenced rock in the early 1970s by groups like the Byrds, the Flying Burrito Brothers, Commander Cody and His Lost Planet Airmen, Poco, Pure Prairie League, and New Riders of the Purple Sage. Yet Nashville in 1977 was still primarily a town controlled by record executives who favored two types of music: country and western.

The heart of Music City was Music Row: the block of music publishing offices, record labels, recording studios, and booking agencies situated in the area surrounding 16th and 17th avenues. These were, and still are, the rhinestone-paved streets of country-music success and failure, where platinum dreams have been found and lost.

While hundreds of musicians were involved in the daily business of writing songs, publishing songs, recording songs, and selling songs, Nashville wasn't known for having a commensurate thriving live-music network—especially during the zenith of the disco era.

Some of the nightclubs that featured country and folk music were Windows on the Cumberland, J. Austin's, Springwater Club, Douglas Corner, Exit Inn, Old Time Pickin' Parlor, Station Inn, Mississippi Whiskers, Bluegrass Inn, and, in downtown Nashville, the famous Tootsie's Orchid Lounge in the alley behind the Ryman Auditorium, which hosted the Saturday night Grand Ole Opry. The Exit Inn was more geared for the major acts; the others featured local stars and unknowns trying to work their way up the Music City food chain.

Most of the Nashville clubs Townes took me to ranged from classic American honky-tonks to small listening rooms. Invariably built with dark, wood-paneled walls to suck up the low-level lighting, they served mainly beer and usually had a bar and pool table in the front room.

There would typically be a long, narrow back room with a small, one-foot riser stage against the end wall.

My initial impression of the patron population was that they were a mixed bag of characters possessed of mercurial personalities running the gamut from charmingly bizarre to downright dangerous—a rotating mélange of songwriters, music business executives, and various showbiz celebrities, along with run-of-the-mill thugs, footloose nomads, seedy hucksters, petty criminals, and the occasional clueless college student slumming 'cross the tracks.

These gentle souls soon constituted my entire social universe. A post-graduate course of study that taught me numerous life lessons beyond what I'd absorbed in Vietnam.

For example, there was a night Townes and I were in the Springwater Club on 27th Avenue North. Said to have been established in the 1890s, the Springwater fitted the popular description of a genuine dive bar. It was also rumored to be a favorite stop-by of local prisoners enjoying weekend furloughs.

Townes was sitting in with the band in the back room, and I was standing at the bar, drinking a coffee. My bar neighbors were two large, loud-voiced women. I'd stoked up earlier on some potent marijuana, and my olfactory senses were extremely sensitive, leading me to detect that one, or possibly both, of the women urgently needed a bath.

I felt a sharp jostle in my side. I stepped back, turned to my neighbor, and said, in what I thought was an amusing tone, "Hey, don't rub against me! I don't wanna get what you got!"

My next memory is that I was lying on the floor, waking up from being knocked out, groggily realizing she had just punched me full in the face. As I clambered to my feet, she sneered, "Got anything else to say, dumbass?"

"No, sorry about that," I replied, staggering toward the back room.

After Townes got offstage, he found me and saw my puffy, bruised face. "Heard you been playing with death, H. This is no place to be mouthing off to anyone. A lot of these folks don't care nothing about nothing."

And that was how the concept "Keep your mouth shut anywhere Townes plays" became part of my survival skill set for the next twenty years.

The owners of the Springwater Club also owned a club called Cantrell's that was two blocks off Music Row and typically a whole lot safer, its audience being primarily a mix of music-related people. Townes played there often, frequently with Guy Clark. Cantrell's was a building made of logs, inside and out; there was a bar when you first walked in, and to the right was a long, wide room with a raised stage at the other end and fairly good acoustics. In the back was another room with tables for an eating and listening audience.

The Exit Inn on Elliston Place was the main music club in town, where major traveling acts performed and a lot of Nashville's upper-crust singer-songwriters happened by. It was across from the Gold Rush, Townes's favorite Nashville watering hole, where he would meet up with music friends like Guy and Susanna Clark, Steve Young, and David Olney, and enjoy the company of the more dangerous characters who always seemed to be lurking around him.

Townes would perform now and again at J. Austin's on Hillsboro Pike heading out of town. It was a downstairs club, with a long, narrow, dark room as you came in the bar and, at the other end, a small stage. The shows were always filled with other musicians. I recorded Steve Earle and his band there, when he was a young artist pursuing his career.

In the early 1980s, J. Austin's closed, and the Bluebird Cafe club opened upstairs, quickly becoming renowned as the center of the new singer-songwriter movement popping up in Nashville that decade. The Bluebird was a very intimate room, with a small stage and excellent acoustics. Along with noteworthy up-and-comers (Garth Brooks would first come to notice there), there was no telling what music celebrities you might run into; one night I saw Waylon Jennings perform a solo set.

Townes would perform at the Bluebird in the 1980s and '90s, and the *Together at the Bluebird Café* album with Townes, Guy Clark, and Steve Earle was recorded there in 1995.

But the very first person I met in a club context with Townes was Guy Clark, when they played a gig at the Old Time Pickin' Parlor. Guy was, like Townes, a Texas native and a masterful singer-songwriter. They had met in Houston in the mid-1960s and migrated to Nashville at about the same time in the early 1970s. Guy and his wife, Susanna, loved and admired Townes beyond words. Townes was the best man at Guy and Susanna's wedding. The last couple of years Townes was alive, Susanna talked with Townes every morning for hours.

Guy greeted me with gusto that night at the Parlor and helped ease my initial acceptance into Townes's Nashville world. Guy and Susanna ceaselessly promoted Townes to other songwriters and other artists—in fact, to anyone who would listen. I often heard Guy tell people that the best-written song in the world was Townes's "No Place to Fall," and he would always include a Townes song on his recordings.

Even so, Guy and Townes enjoyed a friendly competition when performing on the same bill. They would flip a coin to see who opened the show. Often, they would play together on two or three songs, and the duets weren't always planned. At a Guy-Townes gig, you had to be prepared for one of them to pop up onstage in the middle of the other's set, to sit in. This always got the audience going, and it was always apparent how much each enjoyed playing with the other.

Guy fully understood how difficult Townes could be. When either one was in shaky shape, each would take up for the other, onstage or any place else. They both believed in and inspired one another. Guy once said of Townes, "He says more with silence than others do with words."

Guy and Townes had a strong champion in Mickey Newbury, the Houston-born singer-songwriter who had come to Nashville in the early 1960s and written major hits for Elvis Presley, Don Gibson, Eddy Arnold, Tom Jones, Andy Williams, and Kenny Rogers and the First Edition.

Over the years, Mickey submitted many of Townes's songs to the Nashville publishing community. But despite Mickey's well-established reputation, they were a hard sell, and he was extremely frustrated at his inability to place Townes's songs. Once he spoke personally to Wesley Rose, president of Acuff-Rose Music, the premier publisher in the country music world. Never one to beat about the bush, Rose told Mickey he just didn't see the appeal.

Mickey and Townes co-wrote a few songs, notably "Mister Can't You See" and "The Queen." Mickey told me Townes was the only songwriter who influenced him. Once, when Mickey won a major songwriting award, he called Townes and said, "Townes, your songwriting and music have influenced me more than anyone. Without your influence I would have never won this award."

Occasionally, Townes and Mickey would share the same bill. At the 1993 Willie Nelson Farm Aid in Ames, Iowa, I watched them talk in the dressing room, best of friends with admiration and respect for one another. As Townes and I left the dressing room, he said to me, very saddened, "Mickey doesn't look good. I don't think he's going to last long." I wonder if Mickey thought the same thing of Townes, whom he would outlive by five years.

The last time I saw Townes and Mickey together was in 1995, when we took time off a tour and stopped by Mickey's home in Oregon. Mickey went to his electric piano, started playing, and he and Townes began to make up a song out of the blue. I ran to the car, brought back my recording machine, and asked if they would do the song again. They laughed. "No way," Mickey said. "It was one of those songs that just flew into the room and out." I can only imagine the magic that would have resulted if the two of them had ever seriously recorded together in a studio setting.

Kris Kristofferson once said he'd learned more about songwriting from Mickey Newbury than anyone else he'd ever met. Townes held Kristofferson in similar esteem. "Kris made it work," he once told me— meaning, I think, that Kristofferson had his madman moments but didn't mess with the businesspeople. He was a public rebel, but smart enough to know when to be quiet. Townes didn't have the sense to be quiet, ever. And if he saw any injustice from any of the businesspeople, he'd let them know, too.

By and large, though, I never saw Townes make an effort to hang out with Nashville music celebrities or industry power brokers. They all knew who he was, but Townes never sought them out, and they never came calling for him in a social vein.

And when he did make an effort to "play by the rules" of Music Row, the inability to achieve instant success rankled. In the late 1980s, I arranged for Townes to meet with Erv Woolsey, who had gotten the careers of George Strait, Lee Ann Womack, and Clay Walker spectacularly off the ground. My thought was that several Townes songs would be perfect for any number of future George Strait recordings, and maybe the chart-topping lightning that had struck a few years before with "Pancho and Lefty" and "If I Needed You" would turn up again.

Armed with a folder of his best new songs, Townes dutifully showed up at Erv's office—on time, clean, and sober. Erv, however, was not there. Townes waited an hour before leaving, disappointed and angered. Later in the day, Erv called me and apologized profusely, saying a personal emergency had come up and asking if his meeting with Townes could be rescheduled as soon as possible. I called Townes and explained the snafu and Erv's sincere request to reschedule; Townes refused and said he'd never take such a meeting again.

In my first few weeks in Nashville with Townes, whether he'd finished a gig or just visited a club that night, we would always end the evening at a diner a few blocks from Music Row. Late at night, the place was a favorite of Nashville police, so when we entered in various stages of inebriation, our "blue paranoia" immediately intensified. The cops usually didn't bother anyone, unless someone made a scene—with the waitresses, other customers, or their own companions. The last thing you wanted to do in that environment was piss off a Nashville cop.

The waitresses were friendly, but could be terse. Townes was always a gentlemen to waitresses. I would eat a large meal; Townes would sometimes get just toast and a coffee, always a coffee. Mostly, we listened to the banter of the cops, servers, and other refugees from the bars. At the time, I wondered if this ritual was part of Townes's songwriting research.

As those first days in my new home went by, I learned additional things about my new acquaintance.

He Always Had a Plan. One day Townes said, "H, it's time for me to dry out, or go in the mental hospital." Townes always had a plan about his next project, be it making a record, booking a tour, or going into rehab. When he made up his mind on a certain course of action, he did exactly what he wanted to do. No one ever dictated to Townes.

He Had a Few Emotional Triggers. When Townes saw a hat placed on a bed, he reacted in terror. It was a deep-rooted superstition. He also spoke on a daily basis to animals, whether they were nearby or off in the distance, like a bird in flight, a deer or cow in a pasture. He mentioned to me often that "the animals are the closest thing to God."

When he came across a dead animal, it devastated him; he would become immediately quiet, and then sometimes cry out loud or weep silently, tears running down his face. He never said why these instances bothered him so intensely, but I suspected the loss of a beloved childhood pet might have been the root cause.

Never Get Caught Napping. Physically, Townes always rode his horses hard. "Sleepin' ain't allowed around here," he would say, only half-jokingly. He typically slept three hours a night when I first started working with him, if that.

On my first tour with him, after a gig in Madison, Wisconsin, he and the band went back to the hotel room with fans in tow, and a couple hours or so of lively partying ensued. Townes, however, faded into a stuporous state and appeared to fall completely asleep from overconsumption of alcohol. Then, as soon as the last guest had left or passed out, Townes suddenly revived, standing up and shimmying like a horse shaking off flies. "H, you wanna get a cup of coffee?" he asked, and we headed out the door to the nearest late-night eatery.

Referring to the party, he continued, "Did you hear everything they all said?"

"Sure."

"Well, don't forget it, and never let them know you heard and remembered. People when they are drunk will say what they really think. They will try to insult you, take advantage of you, steal your girl or money, not realizing they are doing this, because they are so drunk. This is when truth cuts like a knife, H. Listen to everything that's said, and you will see who you can trust and who you can't."

I learned a lot about Townes that night. I learned that he was suspicious to some degree of most of the people he encountered in life. He constantly tested almost everyone the whole time I knew him, usually in a quiet and subtle manner. If you failed the exam—and most did—in his eyes you were long gone with yesterday's newspapers. It was a protective mechanism he employed throughout his life, very similar to what I had taught myself to do in Vietnam, where miscalculating whom I could trust was almost certain to get me killed.

However, there was a major difference in our fundamental approaches. Townes had prepared himself to expect the worst from people, and that was what he usually got, in one form or another. It took me awhile, but eventually I embraced the opposite tack. I learned to give people the initial benefit of the doubt, while staying fully aware that the darkness we all harbor inside could pop out at any time.

I don't think either of us could have survived the other's company for so many years if that cognitive yin-yang hadn't existed.

Don't Ask a Question If You Don't Want the Answer. Then there was Townes's brutal honesty. The first while that I spent in his company, watching his public interactions with other people, I thought, "Man, this guy is intense!"

If someone asked him a question he thought too probing or personal, his response was both blunt and sharp. And that was that, which I thought was sending the message "Back off, buddy, and don't ask me that again."

He often remarked to me, "H, would you rather I stab you in the chest or in your back? At least when you get it in the chest, it hurts, but you can pull the knife out and move on from there. If the knife is in your back, you can't pull it out. And you won't be moving on."

I gradually learned not to take Townes's occasional briskness as a personal affront. Yes, he could hurt you—but only if you had hurt him first. I never saw Townes intentionally, premeditatedly attempt to hurt someone. But if you hurt him, you'd better get ready for serious blowback. At the time and in the method of his choosing, of course.

Townes's bluntness was also a way to keep people at a distance, for what he thought was his own protection, so that they'd never know what he was really thinking and doing. He possessed a talent for quickly spotting people's foibles and worst demons, and would expertly dissect their put-ons and façades; he'd invite them to try their hand at manipulating him, by acting vulnerable in some fashion, and then he would lower the boom.

If a fellow openly boasted of his wealth or success, Townes would listen awhile and then say, "You know, the true riches each of us have in life are within ourselves, not determined by worldly possessions or accomplishments. Would you kindly stop talking to me and try to be a real man for once in your life?" That typically resulted in the boaster walking away from the conversation fairly quickly.

Townes could be very intimidating when he wanted to. Often, rather than verbally respond to someone talking or acting in a jerkish manner, Townes would step up to the person, put his face very close to theirs, and stare intensely into their eyes without saying a word; the person would inevitably retreat.

I often looked at these people as a fresh stock of puppets, strings hanging above them, Townes pulling them back and forth mentally and often physically.

Years later, when he lived alone in Mount Juliet, Tennessee, Townes put up a crude wooden sign next to his front door that read "Bayou Self." He would often interject into the middle of a conversation, "Do you know what is the loneliest place in the state of Louisiana?"

No one, of course, could guess the answer. With a satisfied smirk, Townes would reply, "Bayou Self," the pun alluding to the solitariness not only of his isolated homestead but also his core spirit. Over the years, I realized Townes didn't have many close friends. It was a purposeful choice, though he never directly spoke of it.

When in Doubt, Roll the Dice. I wouldn't classify Townes as an addicted gambler. He simply really enjoyed gambling and engaged in it whenever he could. He liked to play dollar poker and also matching numbers or competing numbers in order. He would win the majority of times he played this game.

Townes would gamble for any reason, just for the sake of gambling. Whether he won or lost wasn't important; what he craved was the thrill that comes with anticipation. I once saw him bet on what color shirt the next person to enter the room would be wearing. Another time he bet his gold tooth against a .45 caliber pistol and lost; a friend was commissioned to pull out the staked tooth . . . but pulled the wrong one.

Sometimes a lot of money would be on the line, and Townes was adept at verbally inciting his opponent to make a rash move or a bad bet. However, he would not take money from those who didn't have it.

Not All Instruments Are Created Equal. After I first arrived at the farm in Franklin, Townes acquired a much-used alto saxophone. The only song he knew how to play was the Rolling Stones' version of the Mississippi Fred McDowell song "You Gotta Move." He would play it over and over. And over.

He usually played the sax at dawn or dusk, as if he were doing it for the ghosts of the land. He would try to play other songs besides "You Gotta Move," but he never succeeded, sounding worse each time. One day in disgust, he tied a string to Mr. Sax, hung it to a tree, and shot it with a rifle several times. Stepping to the tree, he said to the instrument, "Now you're dead and won't drive me crazy anymore."

A short time after, someone gave Townes a very cheap violin. At the outset, it was obvious Mr. Fiddle's days on the planet were numbered. Townes never learned how to play even one song. The sounds he did play resembled the proverbial nails being scraped across a chalkboard. "Sounds horrible, doesn't it?" he would grimace. I thought it was odd that we were in an area that had plenty of good old-time fiddlers, any of whom would likely have shown Townes the rudiments.

But Townes preferred to learn the fiddle his own way. When he didn't, Mr. Fiddle met the same lethal, up-against-a-tree fate as Mr. Sax.

I can't say I found the wanton destruction of musical instruments appealing, no matter how inexpensive and shoddy they might have been. He could have passed them on to someone who could put them to better use.

But the instrument episodes represented a paradox: onstage, my new acquaintance presented as a gentle, caring soul whose poignant music moved listeners to tears; offstage, in rare circumstances, he could be more volatile and dangerous than anyone else I had ever met. Being around Townes was like being back in Vietnam, waiting for violence to erupt at any moment.

His Family History Was Illustrious. Townes was a descendant of several notable personages from Texas history. His paternal great-great-great-grandfather was Isaac Van Zandt, one of the founders of the Republic of Texas in 1836. Townes was a great-great-grandnephew of Khleber Miller Van Zandt, a banker and civic leader who built up Fort Worth, Texas, in the 1860s. On his mother's side, Townes's great-grandfather was a founder and dean of the University of Texas law school.

Townes's great-grandfather, Isaac Lycurgus Van Zandt, occupies an interesting spot in the family chronicles. At some point in the late 1800s, the story goes, Isaac ventured into Oklahoma's Indian Territory with a large amount of family money for an investment. He returned to Texas, however, without any money—but with an infant of unmistakable Native American heritage he then adopted into the family.

I could never fully verify the total accuracy of this bit of lore, but I think the moral of the tale was that Isaac Lycurgus had clearly gone beyond the family tradition. Townes said one of his own aunts would frequently compare him to this ancestral "black sheep," implying that they both shared a similar tendency to behave in a fashion beyond the pale of family norms.

One of the first conversations Townes and I ever had about political topics involved him raging against America's unjust treatment of Native Americans, which was just coming to be documented in the 1970s in books like *Custer Died for Your Sins: An Indian Manifesto* and *Bury My Heart at Wounded Knee.* I didn't see the relevance at first, but when I learned of the family's purported Native American connection, Townes's enthusiastic embrace of black-sheep status and minority causes fell into place.

Years later, during one of our European tours, I was thinking of this story. Just before Townes went onstage one night, I said, "I think your relative was one of the great heroes to this tribe in Oklahoma. He probably used his money to save them from starvation."

He stared at me for several moments before breaking into a big smile. "Thanks, H, you may be right," he said. "And that's one less monkey for me to carry around."

Then he proceeded to play one of his best shows in weeks.

Townes Was What He Ate. In terms of diet, Townes consumed little solid food; in later years, he ate less and less. A meal for him might consist of chips and salsa, and he would proudly announce, "That was my vegetables." On the road, if he ate in the morning, it would be one piece of toast, maybe a cup of coffee—but never eggs and home fries or pancakes, bacon, sausage, anything with a substantial calorie count. For the afternoon, he would eat maybe half a sandwich, if it was available; in the evening again, he'd finish the remaining half. In later years, he began to favor Stouffer's frozen dinners when he was off the road.

Were he alive today, Townes would scoff at the ascendant omnipresence of bottled water. He seldom drank any water from any source, but he could drink more vodka than anyone else I ever saw. He was a maintenance drinker; except for an occasional over-the-top binge, his habit was to sip liquor throughout the day to sustain a steady, mellow buzz. It was like keeping a correct oil level in an old car engine—to avoid total breakdown, you had to continually add lubricant to preserve a balance.

He always drank the cheapest vodka—Popov when possible, with an orange soda chaser. Guy Clark asked him once, "Townes, how can you stand to drink that rotgut vodka?" Townes replied with his typical off-putting demeanor, "Guy, after the third or fourth drink, it all tastes the same."

Townes didn't drink the cheapest booze because of the cost, though. I think the cheapest booze magnified the misery, a self-administered alcoholic penance.

I remember a doctor telling Townes that his dietary habits were causing a progressive, long-term catabolysis—his body was breaking down internal fat and muscle tissue in order to keep him alive. In effect, the body was consuming itself. While that explained why he remained slender well into middle age, he didn't get dangerously frail until the last two years of his life.

From my time in Vietnam, I was well aware of the symptoms a heroin user displayed. Though I noticed some of the signs in Townes when I first came to live with him, he didn't shoot heroin in my presence. And he rarely did any heroin at all when we toured in later years. He attributed that to a curious epiphany he'd had in the mid-1970s while driving through Van Zandt County, which lay southeast of Dallas and was named for his third great-grandfather, Isaac.

Townes's vehicle had attracted the attention of a local police officer, who pulled him over and discovered in the back seat a container full of a suspicious brown substance. Townes explained that it was nothing more than dirt from Van Zandt County, his ancestral home. He said he had scooped it up to remind him of his Texas heritage and bring him good luck as he roamed the country.

After some consideration, the officer bade him be on his way. Townes realized that, if he had been found with heroin, a backcountry East Texas judge would likely have sent him to jail for years. So he stopped his ongoing use of heroin from that day forward, switching to vodka as his preferred palliative; in his mind, it was the closest high to heroin.

But he would tell me of his "war stories" of past heroin overdoses, relating the details nonchalantly, as if we were talking about having a tooth pulled at the dentist. One time, he said, he overdosed and was taken to the hospital, where he was pronounced dead and tagged for the morgue. Suddenly, the drug wore off, and he revived. "I was just taking a nap," he claimed. "Those idiots would have buried me alive."

Another time, he said, he'd overdosed on heroin and somehow glued his front teeth together; at the hospital they had to break his front tooth, so they could put a tube down his throat and pump out his stomach. "Lucky for me," he recalled, "I didn't glue my eyes together. I would have hated to miss seeing all these goings-on being done to me, just to keep my useless self alive."

Townes would laugh about these near-death experiences. "Sometimes

I wish they would've just let me die, so I didn't have to live under this veil of tears anymore."

But in the Tennessee foothills, where he'd come to restart his career, he seemed to be thriving.

Townes enjoyed living on the bare bones of life: hunting game on the land, keeping chickens, growing a small garden for salad greens. He and Cindy built a lattice against the cabin and planted morning-glory vines. There was a porch swing for sitting and watching the sunrise and sunset, listening to the wind, and watching the ever-changing skies as weather systems rolled over the ridges. After years of enduring the fierce urban intensity of Houston and the college-town wackiness of Austin, I found refuge and rejuvenation in this little blue-misted valley.

We would drive into nearby Franklin and visit the small country store, the garbage dump, the feed store. Townes loved talking to the local country folks. He was quiet and friendly in his interactions, and they really liked him, as he did them. Townes also liked having his music friends from Nashville come out occasionally to visit, play guitars, tell stories, and put one another on.

A few hundred yards away from the cabin was a small farm home occupied by Michael Ewah and his girlfriend. When Michael drank just a little beer, he became big crazy, especially if Townes got him wound up. Most of the time, their escapades concluded harmlessly.

Michael was a real naturalist, and he and Townes often hunted together. Often they fished for large, biting turtles in a pond on the property. When they got one on the line, Townes would needle Michael into wading into the water to pull the turtle out. Townes was amazed that Michael would even do such a thing, and if Michael hesitated, Townes would dare him to do it, and that would send Michael thrashing into the pond. Michael would soak the turtles, and then make turtle soup.

Michael was keenly interested in Asian martial arts. Townes would stand on the porch and hurl Michael's ninja throwing stars into a large field with neck-high weeds. Michael would run off into the weeds and come back with the stars. Townes would repeat the process and toss them off again in all different directions, and again Michael would retrieve them. They would do this for hours on end, to my amazement.

It was a perfect setting for a songwriter whose emotional lyrics were drawn from his life experiences. Settled into a state of bucolic bliss with a beautiful girlfriend and a tour and new album on the horizon, Townes was free to indulge in his eccentricities and his addictions—even as he created new songs that conveyed a sharper-than-ever writing skill.

With the pressure turned down to near zero, he seemed ready to move into a completely new phase of personal and artistic development. Anything seemed possible.

As 1977 came to a close and a new year beckoned, the number one thing Townes wanted was to get his music back on record shelves.

After not having recorded in nearly six years, he was booked to begin work in January 1978 on the *Flyin' Shoes* album for my brother's new label, Tomato Records. Chips Moman was the producer, and the legendary hit-making American Studios on Music Row was the recording site. An all-star cast of top Nashville studio musicians was recruited, including Gary and Randy Scruggs, Muscle Shoals pianist Spooner Oldham, steel guitarist Jimmy Day from Willie Nelson's band, keyboardist Bobby Emmons, and Irish guitarist Philip Donnelly, who had worked with the Everly Brothers and Donovan.

Chips was determined to cut a single for Townes that would get huge radio airplay. Over the past few years, Chips had produced monster hits like "Luckenbach, Texas (Back to the Basics of Love) " for Waylon Jennings and Willie Nelson and "Suspicious Minds" and "In the Ghetto" for Elvis Presley. His work with Aretha Franklin, Dusty Springfield, Neil Diamond, Merrilee Rush, B.J. Thomas, Joe Tex, Bobby Womack, Wilson Pickett, Herbie Mann, Carla Thomas, the Box Tops, and numerous trend-setting R&B and country artists all but guaranteed that any record he produced would end up near the top of every radio DJ's must-play list.

I was in the studio each day, watching intently and getting a firsthand look at Townes's unrelenting creative force in action. It was the first time I'd been witness to how an album was built from the ground up, falling into place piece by piece with each take and edit.

Townes was consumed in the recording process and clearly enjoying every moment. "These songs are my babies, and now I can share them with the world," he would say with unabashed pride.

Flyin' Shoes was finished in the spring, and Townes had several shows lined up for the supporting tour. As road manager and rapidly maturing veteran of the Nashville honky-tonk scene, I felt I was ready.

I would soon learn there was a lot more to "ready" than I'd ever imagined.

4

We Hit the Road; Road Hits Back

TOWNES WAS A traveling troubadour in every sense of the term. Living on the road was as much a part of the Townes Van Zandt mystique as his writing and performing were.

He started out alone, a self-accompanied folk singer. In the last few years of his life, he reverted to solo status, alone again onstage with just his guitar and voice. In the years between, he organized bands of no more than two or three sidemen, and they rode together in one vehicle, playing one-night stands all over the country.

To showcase his new *Flyin' Shoes* album on Tomato Records, Townes decided to perform with backup.

For someone who had been a solo artist over the last several years, putting even a duo or trio outfit together took some doing. Naturally, he had to find musicians who were interested, available, and capable of blending in with his unique songwriting and performing style.

And capable of blending in with his travel regimen. Which could at times be psychologically and physically demanding far beyond the normal sideman pay grade.

Townes brought me along for the initial recruiting. Ever since I'd arrived in Nashville, he'd have me accompany him whenever he went out. I think he wanted me to learn his business approach and his lifestyle from the ground up, so I could handle them eventually.

We dropped by Danny "Ruester" Rowland's house. He was Guy Clark's lead acoustic guitarist, a great studio musician, and had played with other great artists, such as country songwriters Billy Edd Wheeler (co-writer of "Jackson," "Coward of the County," and "It's Midnight") and Alex Harvey, who penned "Delta Dawn" for Tanya Tucker and "Reuben James" for Kenny Rogers, among others.

Danny was visually an exuberant beatnik and philosophically a veiled rebel with a sly wit. He was already very familiar with Townes's complete song catalogue.

While Townes was content with the duo format, he shortly also acquired fiddler Owen Cody, who came to the band in an unusual manner.

Known among musical peers by his last name, Cody was fluent in numerous styles, from Cajun and Mexican to bluegrass and contemporary country. He had played extensively with Freddy Fender and, when Townes heard about him, was in the middle of touring with Texas songwriter Billy Joe Shaver.

Billy Joe Shaver is a bona fide country-music legend whose songs have been recorded by a galaxy of stars, including Kris Kristofferson, Waylon Jennings, Patty Loveless, Willie Nelson, Bob Dylan, and Elvis Presley. As of this writing, he is still actively gigging and recording at seventy-eight years old.

But on this day in 1977 at the Gold Rush bar in Nashville, Billy Joe was at the peak of his unrepentant honky-tonk ways. He, Townes, Cody, and I were sitting at a front window booth catching up on the local music scene, when Billy Joe mentioned that he planned to remarry his ex-wife.

Townes remarked, "That's great, Billy Joe."

Cody laughed and asked, "Why are you marrying that fat cow again?"

Before I could reach a conclusion as to whether that comment reflected a special form of in-group humor on Cody's part, Billy Joe's eyes bulged, his face turned bright red, and he grabbed Cody by the hair and punched him in the forehead. Billy Joe wore a large ring on his punching fist, and when it made contact with Cody's head, it created a gouge from which spurted much blood.

Apparently, that was Billy Joe's answer. Part one, anyway.

Part two came a second later, when Billy Joe picked up Cody by his hair and the back of his pants, dragged him out the front door to the sidewalk, and slammed him up against a parked car. As Townes and I watched from inside the bar, Billy Joe raised Cody up in the air and swung him down hard, banging his head against the metal wheel cap. Once. Twice. More.

Townes ran out, and I followed. "Stop, Billy Joe, you're killing him!" he shouted.

Billy Joe appeared not to hear and slammed Cody's head one more time into the wheel cap. Then he paused and turned to Townes. "Do you need a fiddle player?"

"I guess I do," Townes answered. "Otherwise, you're gonna kill him."

Billy Joe dropped Cody onto the sidewalk in a pile. "He's all yours," he stated, walking into the bar without another word or backward glance.

Townes and I stood over Cody to see if he was, in fact, still alive. "This is a hell of a way to put a band together," Townes said.

Cody was in the band from that point on. I don't know how his synapses are holding up today, but the incident seemed to have no effect on his musical skills at the time.

The trio first played at the Vanderbilt University coffeehouse Good Woman Café, and it was magic from the get-go. There had been no rehearsal, but everything pulled together onstage, and I recorded it on my Nakamichi tape deck. The quality of performance and recording were excellent enough that several tracks could be included on the *Rear View Mirror* album Townes and I put out in 1993.

Basically, every show was a live jam, and Townes was in great vocal form at this time. The repertoire he chose consisted of his early "classics" from the Poppy albums—"Pancho and Lefty," "If I Needed You," "Our Mother the Mountain," "To Live Is to Fly," "Flyin' Shoes," "No Place to Fall," and the like—and he delivered them with an engaging sincerity and humility, an unmistakable sense of realness that won the audience over immediately.

In attendance at these early gigs were writers from the local press, a lot of songwriters, a smattering of renowned entertainers, and a cadre of devoted fans. The fans would hang on every word he sang; at times I would see some singing right along with Townes.

When Townes performed, his ability to silence the loudest of rooms was striking. He would tell me it was nothing, that when he sang softer, the audience naturally got quiet. I knew better than that. Even in his early years, he was able to project a stage presence that intrigued and captivated. He never bragged of his talents, just let his lyrics and Mr. Guitar do all the talking . . . then he slipped off into the night.

Townes often said to me, "H, the only place I feel safe is onstage." I believe that during those singular moments in his three decades of performing, that was when he truly was the person he wanted and strove to be.

As I got more familiar with Townes's various routines, I saw that he was not one to take up the guitar and idly pick away the hours. After a gig, Mr. Guitar would not come out of his case again until Townes's next show. For as accomplished a guitarist as Townes was, it seemed odd that he never practiced playing his instrument even once or twice a week, just to keep his chops up.

Townes always said his practice was onstage—the first song of the set. In fact, aside from when he was with Guy Clark, he rarely played his guitar when he hung out with other musicians.

For the *Flyin' Shoes* tour, we traveled in a rented four-door, red-hued Chevy Caprice—the Crimson Chariot, as it was dubbed. It was a tight squeeze for four people and instruments, but proximity fostered camaraderie. Except when it didn't.

The tour went from Nashville up the East Coast to the Midwest, and then struck cross-country to the West Coast, playing a mix of colleges, urban coffeehouses, and nightclubs.

I drove, collected receipts for all expenses, and performed basic business manager functions that occasionally included serving as sound engineer when needed, all while trying to keep my sanity. I drank coffee and smoked marijuana to stay "level." Surprisingly early on in the tour, I came to accept that Townes's behavior extremes were going to constitute the "norm." As he often said right up to the day he died, "Just remember, H: If you're in a cage with a monkey, you're a monkey, too."

I had taken up residence in his invisible, mobile mental ward. And stayed there. At that point in my own fragmented life, it felt completely natural. And, I must admit now, exciting.

Most of our drives were on roads beyond the lights of cities and towns. While the others would sleep, I came to appreciate the ever-changing scenery, and, especially on a moonlit night or at the first stirrings of sunrise, a sense that we were chasing time—or trying to outrun it.

Townes slept only three or four hours a day, so he always rode shotgun and helped keep me awake, reciting words from songs he liked, songs like Willie Nelson's "On the Road Again," Guy Clark's "Dublin Blues," and Bob Dylan's "Just Like Tom Thumb's Blues." He possessed a childlike excitement about White Freightliner tractor-trailer trucks. As we drove up and down the highways, Townes would say, "Bet you I can spot a White Freightliner from the furthest distance you can see!" Sure enough, he did it every time. The fact that his "White Freightliner Blues" has been commercially recorded over a hundred times by artists around the world says something about his gift for tapping into the wanderlust we all feel at some point in our lives.

Townes would often tell me that living on the road was the closest he ever felt to true freedom—genuine respite from worldly cares and fears. "Nobody knows where you are, how to reach you," he would say. "You're invisible."

He loved the hum of the wheels on asphalt. Where we were headed never really mattered. What was in front of him was more real than what was behind. "Home is a rest stop off the highway for me," he would say. "The more time I spend at home not doing anything, the more trouble I get in."

However, Townes did *not* enjoy the hum of jet wings through clouds and avoided traveling by plane whenever possible. Often, he would refuse to get on a flight until he felt the flight number was "right." In later years, when we toured in Europe, he would always ask if we could go by boat.

Once, while flying back home from a long West Coast tour, I was sound asleep—until I felt Townes shaking my shoulder and mumbling, "H, wake up, we're going down!"

I was annoyed. "What are you waking me for? If we're about to die, why don't you just let me die in my sleep?"

This was no prank, however. Townes was all shook up. "I don't want to be alone in the final minutes of my life," he whispered.

I looked up and down the aisles and sensed no one else was feeling any alarm. "I think we're good, Townes. If there's a problem, they'll let us know." He became more agitated, though. I closed my eyes. But didn't get back to sleep.

In fact, I looked out the window and noticed we were flying abnormally close to the ground . . . and would continue at this low altitude for another forty-five minutes before landing in Nashville without incident.

As we drove back to his home, not a word passed between us. When we reached Mount Juliet, Townes sighed and said, "That was a close one. Next time I *will* sleep in case we do go down. Won't even have to know about it."

On this initial tour, Townes laid out his checklist governing venue arrival, a series of tasks I executed from the first gig I did with him until the last. "Make sure there is a back door and that it's open. Check what is the straightest line from the stage to it. Also check to see if the bathroom or office has a window, is unlocked and big enough for Mr. Guitar and us to climb through. And see what is below the window."

My perplexity must have been obvious, because he continued. "H, you don't realize how dangerous it is, what we do. Those joints are filled with people looking for a fight, women trying to make their men jealous, a lot of cheating going on. You've got people who have no value of life, and mixed among them are some real nice folks."

This was pretty much the spectrum of humanity I'd encountered during my military service, minus the added dimension of armed enemy combatants actively seeking to annihilate me. Still, his caution was welcomed.

"Each night we are in a different town and club, so don't ever let your guard down," he said. "If you see somebody with a gun or a knife, let me know right away, so we can get out of there before the action begins."

I thought this was funny coming from Townes, since he excelled at verbally challenging people and riling them up to the max. Many times, I asked Townes to calm things down before he caused a riot or got us hurt. Whenever I heard him say, "I hope this old road is a friend of mine," I thought the real danger of the road was him and the havoc his antics threatened to bring into being.

When I was trying to deal with the worst of situations Townes was inciting, he'd grin ear-to-ear and say, "Cheer up, H—it's only gonna get worse." Which, I would learn, always had a fifty-fifty chance of bearing out.

Yet Townes never seemed to be truly afraid of anything, aside from the possibility of getting permanently confined to a mental hospital. He thought of himself as Jesse James, and the band and I were his gang. We would roll into town, do the show, get the money, and ride out in a cloud of dust before anyone knew we were gone.

In reality, this was not a bad strategy, because when Townes stuck around after a show, he had a habit of causing trouble in the club. The kind of trouble you find yourself running *from*, with someone running *after* you.

Townes might suggest to a club owner a quick gambling proposition: double or nothing the amount he was owed for the night. The bored or unsavvy club owner might agree, and most of the time Townes would win, enraging the owner beyond words as they were forced to honor the terms of the wager.

Or Townes would jokingly flirt with the girlfriend or wife of (a) the club owner, (b) an employee, (c) a customer, or (d) all of the above—just to see "what might happen." What occasionally happened was a looming down-and-dirty fistfight or someone pulling a gun to deal with Townes's behavior.

This was when my PTSD came in handy, I suppose. It was as if I were suddenly back in Vietnam . . . I could feel shadows filling the room, and it wasn't because the lights were dimming.

When Townes was really mad at someone, he would growl, "I'll slit your throat and drink your blood!" He followed this pronouncement by spitting in his hand, his expression intent and furious, his face and body close to the other person's. Then, in disgust, he would angrily wipe his hand on his shirt very slowly—meaning in classic primate-conflict language a full-blown "Back off, or else."

Every time I saw him do this over the years, people did indeed back off and walk away without a word. At these times, Townes was very pissed off and dangerous; anyone confronting him sensed this and let things cool. These situations were rare, but extremely intense. One minute he'd be a calm, friendly, easygoing guy—then, suddenly, the fuse was lit, and an explosion seconds away.

As he got older, he seemed to become more aware of the impending danger his behavior was causing—the likelihood of us being killed, to be precise—and so he would reach the point of de-escalation more quickly. While Townes had a gift for insulting people, he never did it out of the chute. Inevitably, it started only if they had insulted him, or if he saw someone acting like a bully toward another person. Sometimes we solved whatever problem had impelled him to speak up, but the solution could spark up a whole new set of problems itself.

As we drew closer to the start of the tour, Cindy announced she wanted to travel with us. What young, music-loving girl of the '70s married to a celebrated troubadour wouldn't?

Townes opposed this. He viewed wives and girlfriends on a tour as neither economically nor logistically prudent. When you're doing a lot of performances in a short amount of time across a long stretch of territory, it's all about getting in and out of a venue as quickly and cheaply as possible. A band tour is not a vacation or sightseeing trip, or—unless you're John Lennon and Yoko Ono gigging for a high-profile political cause—anything resembling a whimsy-filled media circus.

It's just a daily grind of nondescript food, less-than-comfortable lodging, and erratic sleep schedules. When the tour's over, you usually feel like Willy Loman's weeping widow at the end of *Death of a Salesman*, exclaiming, "We're free!"—or, as they say in Texas, "Been rode hard and put up wet."

I believe Townes also wanted to be the ringmaster of any drama or disruption that might rise up on the road. As I learned over and over, he didn't need additional help—from Cindy or anyone else—generating drama.

Except for the occasional show, Townes was generally able to enforce his no-ladies rule on that and subsequent tours. Consequently, while we were traveling, Cindy would purposely get busted back in Nashville. She would hang out at the Springwater Club, become intoxicated, and then get pulled over driving home. She was invariably arrested. Townes would get the call from jail and would be furious—which was exactly the point of the exercise.

During our tours, Cindy would run around with a guy named Chris the Pinball Wizard. When we got back in town, Chris was always, coincidentally, the first one to show up, greeting Townes and buying him a drink. Both Townes and I knew he was fooling around with Cindy, but Townes never let him know it.

I asked Townes, "Why don't you beat him up?"

He would demur and respond, "Remember, H: Always keep your enemies in front of you."

I offered to throw the Wizard out a window, or off a roof. Not to kill him—just to hurt him and get him to stay away from Cindy.

Townes said no, he would deal with it in his own way.

I knew Townes had the ability to destroy a person with just a few words; I had seen him do it many times. He possessed a semi-psychic ability to pick up on someone's worst fear or insecurity, and then zero in on it with a seemingly offhand comment that cut to the quick.

Townes didn't need to carry a gun; his words were much more damaging. But about six months into working with him, having seen some of the hostile behavior we encountered (and at times instigated), I did offer to get one and keep it in a holster, ready to use if we were ever threatened with robbery or serious assault.

"No way, H!" he shouted. "You'd be shooting people left and right. And on the wrong night, that could include me!"

Years before I started working with Townes, my PTSD had been diagnosed. But it's not always visible. You shake on the inside. I don't know if I started crying on the inside in Vietnam. I think so. I think all of us are crying on the inside, in some way, at some point in this life.

But that was one of my strongest bonds with Townes. He loved telling people when I came in the room, "Be careful, Harold's a Vietnam vet—he might snap." It was part of his entertainment. Then again, there were times when I probably would have snapped, to be honest.

Townes regularly played tricks on me. When I was rushing to get us out of the motel and on the road so we could make the next gig on time, Townes would wait in the room until we were about to pull out. I would come get him, and sure enough, I couldn't find the car keys.

I'd go into a semi-frenzy looking for them everywhere, finally going back to the vehicle, thinking it was the most obvious place I would have left them. And when I inevitably returned to the room empty-handed— sure enough, the keys would be in plain sight on the bed, a chair, or a dresser.

Townes would always say it wasn't him. "It's a road ghost playing with you, H. You must have done something to make him mad."

Looking back, maybe it was. And maybe I did.

I noticed almost immediately after coming to live at the cabin in Franklin that Townes's private conversations with me showed a marked spiritual and humanitarian side of his personality. This side appeared not only in his songs but also manifested in his daily life.

Manifested in unusual ways, of course.

There was a period of time during the *Flyin' Shoes* tour when Townes collected Gideon Bibles from all the motels we stayed in. At one point, he had so many Bibles stashed in the trunk, there was scarcely room for the band's instruments.

He would often read and quote from them as we drove from gig to gig. Townes was a lifelong aficionado of classic Western and world literature, and he maintained that the Bible was the best literary work in the entire canon. He also held the belief that frequent Bible readings would keep the Devil out of the car and away from him and us during the tour. Given the general hassles a band encountered roaming the country in those days, that extra psychological edge wasn't such a bad thing to have.

But mostly, Townes liked to get a rise out of folks.

Cody would tell Townes that cherry-picking parts of the Bible while he was drunk was blasphemous. Townes would get riled up and silence Cody with coarse words and epic biblical threats.

It passed the time.

At the end of the tour, Townes decided he would give all the Bibles to a religious revival outfit we met in Nashville. With some embarrassment, he presented them to the preacher. "I know these Bibles are for desperate people," he said, "to help them through the night."

The preacher didn't reply, but I sensed, as I looked in Townes's eyes—and at the preacher, who saw the cloud of depression and despair suddenly sweep over Townes's face—that this man of God could tell the Bibles had, in a very roundabout way, helped salve another lost soul. *Salve*, not save—because I'm not sure anything could have delivered the kind of absolution and restoration Townes spent his life seeking.

Even after that episode, it seemed there was always a Bible in our gear throughout the years I traveled with Townes. I still have one of them; it is in three languages, acquired by Townes in a hotel somewhere in Europe. He gave it to me at the tour's end, saying, "H, you may need this Bible someday. Always keep it close. It's given me peace when I needed."

In his own way, Townes was very spiritual, yet it was a spirituality rooted in the earthly miasma of suffering and pain. He believed there was only one God and could not understand why all the religions— "tribes," as he referred to them—would claim their God as the only true one.

The homeless and the downtrodden were an integral part of Townes's life and songs. I've mentioned Townes's "black sheep" great-grandfather and how his impulsive personal generosity conflicted with the Van Zandt clan's more traditional philanthropy, as realized through universities and civic projects. Townes had clearly inherited his ancestor's singular ideas about charity.

After a gig, he would often have us go to the skid-row section of a town, seek out the homeless and destitute, and give them money to get a meal or something to drink. It was more than "paying it forward"; it seemed to me like "paying it backward"—some kind of psychic restitution he was making for whatever possible wrong he felt he had committed in his own past. Or maybe it was just the unforgivable transgression of simply being born.

Townes hated money and all it represented. When people would boast about their wealth or material possessions, Townes would silence them with a few disarming words, and they would usually walk off. However, as de facto business manager during our tours, I couldn't let him carry any real amount of money; if the mood struck, he would give it away or crumple a bunch of bills into a small ball and throw it on the ground. "Money ain't no friend of mine," he'd mutter. Following behind, I'd usually manage to retrieve the bills and direct them back toward our always marginal travel budget.

Sometimes after I'd collected the gig money from a club owner, when Townes and I were alone, he would say, "H, let me just feel that big wad of money for a few minutes, and then I'll give it back to you for safekeeping." A big smile would come over his face, as if he were astounded he'd actually gotten paid for what he did.

Townes was very conscious of racism and extremely angered by it. If he encountered it in public, he would invariably make his feelings known no matter what the probable outcome. In 1979, Townes and Guy Clark did a show at a club in Birmingham, Alabama. We got there early to settle in, and Townes hit it off with an African-American waitress, whom he invited to have dinner with us at a small eatery down the street.

We walked into the restaurant, and an employee immediately confronted us, stating that our African-American companion was not permitted inside. Townes erupted, "This is my wife. How dare you talk to her like that!"

Townes ushered us into the restaurant and forcefully sat down. Long story short, the police arrived and escorted us off the premises. Somehow, Townes talked his way out of being arrested, and he was able to do the show that night.

During my travels with Townes, I learned many interesting things. One is that there are still public places in certain parts of our United States today that do not welcome Native Americans as customers. We managed to encounter a few of these establishments over the years in the Midwest and West, and when Townes realized what was happening, he would go ballistic.

Townes was also responsible for introducing me to extraordinary moments of beauty and solace. Driving through northern California's redwood country, we stopped alongside the highway for a quick lavatory break. Townes wandered off into the woods with a cassette player and a Mozart tape.

Fifteen, twenty, thirty minutes went by . . . Townes hadn't returned, and the guys were getting restless, so I forged into the woods, an intrepid search party of one. Like a hunter trailing their quarry by sound instead of scent, I would catch wisps of Mozart and head in that direction, only to have the music fade away as it seemed I was getting closer.

The forest can become an eerie world unto itself in a very short space of time. Sunlight and shadows intermingle in weird ways, creating images that play tricks on the eyes and imagination. You hear things you've never heard before. It's not automatically a feeling of fright—more like a rising sense of disorientation that could be magical or menacing, depending on who you are.

I finally found him, sitting on a fallen log, the cassette playing softly. He was lost in the Mozart and the redwoods. For a few minutes we listened to the music together, not speaking. If you closed your eyes, the woods noises became part of the music, making a whole new soundscape for your ears.

It was the unexpected appearance of genuine tranquility, something I hadn't experienced much of over the past few years, and for that temporary gift I was grateful.

I told Townes I'd been a little worried he might have lost his way in the thick woods. Not to worry, he replied. If he hadn't come back, he would have sent his ghost back to fill in for him the rest of the tour.

Another time, in the darkness of the night, as we drove to the next gig, many miles away, Townes said very quietly, "H, can you hear the music in the wind?"

"No," I said.

He rolled down the window. "Then let me turn the volume up for you."

There was silence between us for the longest time, listening to the wind and air moving past us quickly, both of us floating off into a trance watching the road and miles disappear from sight, lost in the dark of night, as the winds sang with music, ghosts, and who knows what else swirling in the atmosphere.

Of course, our night drives were just as likely to see Townes without warning climb out the passenger window and bend his upper torso onto the hood while I was driving seventy-five miles an hour, his face pressed against the windshield with a leering grin, and stay there for a minute or more before crawling back into his seat.

Turning philosophical, he'd say, "So, tell me, H: Is being on the edge of death, like I just was, is that what it was like to be in war?"

I would say yes and have to tell him a few Vietnam stories; it was like putting a restive child to sleep. I realized he wanted to experience the same type of rush you'd get in a war zone. One way or another, he was going to get that type of extreme-danger high by rolling dice with the Reaper each day.

As the tour progressed, there was one thing I grasped for sure: Just when I thought I had this guy almost figured out, he'd do something outrageous that would send me back to square one. To genuinely understand Townes Van Zandt, I would have to admit that I could never understand him. There was simply too much happenstance and contradiction in his behavior "patterns."

After the first few shows, I discovered that Townes never used a set list when performing live. He selected the order of his songs on the fly. It wasn't that he carefully analyzed the previous performance in a formal way, or discussed things with the band and then made changes. Each show was going to be different—probably—and every set was going to be different from any other, so everyone needed to be prepared. In a way, the unpredictability kept the musicians engaged to a higher degree than if they'd just been doing the same set each night.

The song choice was determined by what mood he was in. The moods were never the same, of course, because his highs and lows never worked on a schedule. If you were a true-blue fan, this made each performance you caught extra special.

In terms of stage fright, I've come to believe every performer has a moment just before stepping onstage when they have learned to convince a part of their brain that, for the next hour and a half—or however long they are in front of the audience—they will be in total control.

I've known musicians who would routinely throw up before going onstage. It was more than mere stage fright; it seemed to be, literally, a means of purging from their consciousness anything not relevant to the performance.

Townes didn't get physically sick. But he had his own peculiar mannerisms while playing, such as singing with his eyes closed. I asked him if that was because he was nervous.

"No," he laughed. "I don't sing with my eyes closed. I'm squinting and looking at the audience. I learned from Hank Williams that you sing a happy song, a silly song, then sing a sad song. You get them real high and happy and then take them to the depths of sad, and it drives them right into the ground."

Watching the impact of his music on his listeners' emotions was an important part of his process. "They don't get it," he'd say. "I'm looking at them; they ain't lookin' at me. You know, everybody is there to take your energy. But I'm getting energy from them."

Sometimes after a solo show, Townes would come offstage and be really weak, fainting almost. Backstage, he would sit and cry. I'd ask what was going on, and he'd say, "H, I'm singing some of my worst nightmares, my worst heartaches. Every night I sing to these people, I'm baring my soul."

I saw very quickly that songwriting and touring consumed Townes's life spirit. "I try to empty out the words and music in my head daily," he told me, "so I can make room for the next song. At times my brain is racing so fast with words to a new song, my hands can't keep up with trying to write them down."

Songwriting as explained by Townes was less about applying technical skill and more about being an alert observer and a willing receptacle for whatever random inspiration might be passing through the ether at a particular moment. "You have to put your mind in a place," he told me, "where the light will shine into, giving you the words at times first, then the music another time. The light can come from anywhere—the window, walls, floor."

It was the medieval Sufi poet and mystic Rumi who wrote to a disciple: "Don't turn away. Keep your gaze on the bandaged place. That's where the light enters you." Whether he consciously knew it or not, Townes never turned away from the bandaged places of his psyche; rather, he used them for constant artistic introspection.

Songs like "Mr. Mudd and Mr. Gold," Townes said, came to him in an unpreventable rush—"the light shone on me, my pen in hand, racing through page after page to completion, not stopping to think what I'm writing, as if a force had taken over my mind and hand, writing lyrics down as fast as I could write, then feeling completely drained out, from God's hand to mine. I know my talents are a gift from God. These songs I've written are His, not mine. I am only the messenger."

Even so, as the author of over 130 original songs, Townes nourished his divinely granted talent with a finely honed sense of craft. He claimed he wrote the lyrics first and then figured out the accompaniment and tempo; "the poetry comes first, then the music," he would say. There was always a sparseness to his musical textures; the melodies were never overembellished, and the chord changes weren't overly complex. "It's not what you hear," he would caution. "It's what you don't."

When you finish the first draft of a song, he said, take out half the words. Then take out more, and more, and more, so what remains says the most with the least amount of words. For Townes, songwriting was a slow, tedious process; he compared it to the work of a diamond cutter, who must calculate each cut and its ongoing effect on the rough stone to produce the final gem.

He was certainly his own biggest critic. When Townes finished a new song, he would call Guy and Susanna Clark and sing it to them over the phone, no matter what time of day it was. Their comments and approval were very important to him.

At his shows, someone would usually ask him how he wrote his songs. He would characteristically respond with something humorous or evasive. Later he would tell me, "They're trying to get my mojo, H. In time they will realize each of us have our own mojo, and no matter how you try, you can't steal somebody else's."

Even just two words can be poetry, Townes told a crowd one time, after sitting through an emcee's embarrassingly effusive and lengthy introduction. "If you add one note on a guitar, you've got a song. It's not nearly as difficult as everybody thinks."

And sometimes it might just come down to the melody or the chord progression. He once said to me, "You know, H, Mr. Guitar has a mind and life of his own."

People have said Townes's writing was best in the early years, but I disagree. He wrote great songs right to the end of his life, because he was writing *from* his life as it lurched and tottered toward its final destiny.

Take a late-career song like "Marie," for example. I've spoken to people who said they'd first heard the song while driving and had to pull over and stop the car—*had* to stop—because the oppressive power of the imagery was so compelling, they could do nothing but listen and be lost in the story.

Townes continued to listen to a variety of music through the years and was always interested in artists we met along the way. Toward the end, though, I noticed he was listening almost exclusively to Lightnin' Hopkins and Hank Williams Sr. They'd been among his earliest influences, and he would play them over and over when we drove cross-country, and even when he was at home, as if he were putting himself in a comforting trance.

His songs were not written in a vacuum; he definitely incorporated input from his daily life. As he traveled from gig to gig, he collected images and ongoing thoughts from each place he saw and experienced, constantly absorbing scenery, people, noises, and things as he moved from place to place. On one very long, dreary night drive, a line suddenly popped into my head: "Shadows of love, shadows of pain, run through my heart like rivers of rain." I mentioned it to him, and he thought a bit and then responded, "That's a good, dark thought, H. Let's write a song together now." As the miles sped by, that's exactly what we did, batting images and rhymes back and forth, spooling that tiny, dark seed into a full song lyric that's yet to be paired with a melody.

Townes once said, "Every time a song is played, it goes into the air and universe and goes on forever. One of the great things with music is that you can't hold it in your hand. It always moves on."

Two songs may be the best candidates to stand as Townes's personal anthems: "Waiting 'Round to Die" and "For the Sake of the Song."

He maintained that the inspiration for "Waiting 'Round to Die" came from a conversation he'd had with an old man who regularly drank at Houston's Jester Lounge, where Townes often performed in his early days. It was the first serious song he ever wrote that wasn't derivative of blues or old-time country ballads.

"For the Sake of the Song" also derives from the acceptance of a lifetime of alienation and loneliness. "If you want to write a great song," Townes once said, "you have to forsake everything in your life—material possessions, money, family, and love—buy a guitar and hit the road, and don't ever look back at what you left behind."

Townes believed you couldn't sing the blues unless you lived them—infusing your daily routine with a significant amount of blues-drenched strife and despair. To attain a life lived literally "for the sake of the song," he gradually forsook everything normal and paid a heavy price for it.

If you want to know the essence of Townes Van Zandt, just listen to those two songs; that's the path he set himself up to travel. He was barely twenty-one years old when he wrote them, but it was as if he'd preordained the entire rest of his life in those few stanzas.

I never saw Townes act as if he were a big-time celebrity. He never bragged about what he wrote or who else had recorded his songs. If someone he had just met would ask him about himself, he'd mutter a bit, and I would have to step in and deliver a short summary "pitch": *Yes, he is a well-known songwriter; yes, he makes records; yes, many of his songs you have probably heard by other musicians,* and so on. His humility in public was genuine, I think; he was a fundamentally shy person who preferred going through life letting his songs speak for him.

Paradoxically, I lost count of the times over the years that Townes and I were alone and he broke down in a funk over his lack of major success in the music industry. "Why is Bob Dylan so popular and I'm not?" was the most frequent refrain. The two actually had great mutual respect for each other's work, but in Townes's eyes, Dylan symbolized the ultimate golden peak of career fulfillment as a songwriter. Townes was stuck in the gray, barren valley below.

Townes didn't want to be a rich rock star, but he did want to be acknowledged as a great artist by the public. That's a tricky tightrope for anyone to walk, especially an individual whose inherent mental health issues and treatment for said issues had left him in an emotionally fragile state for his whole adult life.

From the day his first Poppy Records album appeared in 1968, Townes became a fixture on the national folk circuit and remained popular at premier coffeehouses and nightclubs throughout his career. He also performed over the years for large audiences at events like Willie Nelson's Farm Aid, the Kerrville Folk Festival, and the prestigious Cambridge Folk Festival in England. Yet it didn't take long for me to notice that Townes preferred the smaller, intimate venues. In fact, there were a few big-venue shows where it was obvious this internal conflict resulted in him purposely "underperforming," to put it kindly.

It was a conflict he was not able to resolve even toward the end of his life. In 1996, Townes was booked at a large music hall in Berlin. Wolfgang Doebeling, who covered music for the German edition of *Rolling Stone*, had gone to enormous lengths to promote the show, writing numerous articles and arranging all kinds of additional media coverage touting this amazing American singer-songwriter. A standout show would have tremendously helped Townes raise his performance fee and increase his bookability with presenters on his return European tour.

The audience had come to see a great performance by a great country-folk artist. Townes, however, appeared to have in his head that he was playing a rock 'n' roll venue. He hadn't had much to drink before the show, but I could sense his mind drifting away, and he gave an odd performance—singing softly in his usual way, but playing guitar with windmill strums à la Pete Townshend of the Who, a style completely incompatible with his songs.

He finished his set and headed offstage, but went the wrong direction and walked right into a concrete wall. The audience saw this; I crossed the stage to Townes and told him the audience wanted an encore. He stared at me in panic. "How can I get to the other side of the stage without them seeing me?" he asked.

Finally, he returned to the microphone and once again played his acoustic guitar like a hard rocker, letting the strings ring and then strumming them fast and hard again. He did two songs very quickly and then left the stage without a word. Sitting down in the dressing room, he broke down and cried.

In about ten minutes I was summoned to the front office by the promoter, who was wildly pissed off and yelling in the phone to Berthold Seliger, Townes's European booking agent. The promoter handed the phone to me, and I explained to Berthold my theory about Townes thinking he needed to play like a rocker to fill the room. Berthold listened and then patiently explained to me that, because of the show Townes had just put on, his agency would not be able to book him in larger rooms on the next tour.

Suddenly, Wolfgang Doebeling was at my shoulder, summoning me back to the dressing room. Someone, he said, was asking Townes to help them commit suicide.

In the dressing room, I found Townes consoling a German fellow who was expressing the strong and immediate desire to kill himself. There and then. I must confess that at this point, my patience with another sudden onset of Euro-strangeness had run out; I told the fellow, who spoke English, "We are very sorry, but Townes has to leave right now." I physically guided the gentleman to just outside the dressing room, where a policeman was standing. I explained the situation. The policeman said he understood and would get him to a hospital.

Returning to the dressing room, I saw Wolfgang calming Townes down from this final odd turn of an odd evening. Gradually, Townes came back to the present. Wolfgang was a good friend and said, "You deserve a good meal, Townes. Let's get something to eat."

Afterward, Townes confided in me that he'd blown the show intentionally, because—at heart—he didn't really want to play anything but small venues. A curious contradiction, using a negative action to achieve a positive goal.

But that was how Townes reasoned. I could argue with him until I was out of breath, but in the end, he was going to do what he wanted to do. That first tour through the U.S. heartland had taught me that in multiple ways.

Madison, Wisconsin, in the 1970s was a thriving university town with thousands of music-loving young people and a highly active counterculture contingent that had organized the world's largest toga party, planted a thousand plastic pink flamingos on the lawn of the UW administration building, and painted the downtown curbs fluorescent so drunken students could find their way home from the bars. Townes had a good following there.

The trio did two shows at the campus theater with noted bluesman John Lee Hooker and his combo, which included Deacon Jones on Hammond B-3 organ and Wild Bill Randolph on bass. Hooker was also on Tomato Records, and he and Townes paired up for several gigs on the tour. They would alternate who was opening, depending on whether it was a blues or a folk club.

During the first show in Madison, something set the bluesman's mood awry, and he started improvising in the middle of a song with lyrics like "If I catch you messing with my wife, I'll get my boys to slit your throat."

It was a common motif in the blues lexicon, of course, but Hooker's delivery was so intense that about a third of the audience left. As intense as Townes might get, he could never silence and scare off an audience to that degree.

In mid-May, Townes and the trio played two nights at New York City's famed Lone Star Cafe, a hotbed for great music by Southern and especially Texas musicians. Blues guitar star Johnny Winter sat in for a song on the first night. As an albino, Johnny had extremely limited eyesight. Yet after tossing back a few drinks with Townes at the end of the gig, he hopped on a motor scooter and drove off into the Big Apple darkness, long white hair flying in the wind. Townes opined that, after the alcohol he'd consumed, Johnny's impaired vision wouldn't matter anyway. "Johnny has his guardian angel riding with him, as we do have ours."

The weekend after, we found ourselves in Boston for the Cambridge River Festival with lodgings at the Hyatt Regency on the Charles River, a beautiful hotel with an immense, glass atrium and elevator that looked out over the center of the lobby. One of the not-so-good things about playing a series of one-nighters in different cities is that you can't get too comfortable. On the other hand, one of best things about a series of one-nighters in different cities is that you can't get too comfortable.

We had a free day and night before performing, and everyone went their own way. Cody embarked upon a unique dining adventure. He checked in, alone, at the restaurant as "the Coneheads, party of four"— it would be announced over the PA this way—securing a table for four people. He sat at the table and ordered four full lobster meals, which he ate one by one, moving from chair to chair until all the meals (and two bottles of wine) had been consumed. Later that night he turned beet red and sought the services of a local doctor.

Danny Rowland received word his girlfriend in Nashville had broken up with him. He went on an immediate bender, staying holed up in his room with a neighborhood girl-for-hire.

That night, Townes and I ate dinner together. He ate very little, as usual, and then headed for the bar, while I walked around to check out the neighborhood before returning to my room, hoping for an early evening and some good rest. Two hours later, the phone rang; it was Townes, and he was talking fast and crazy.

"H, you gotta come get me! There's all these weird folks wanting to kiss and dance with me. I don't know what's happening!"

I got someone on the phone to give me directions. As I pulled up to a house in the Somerville section of the city, I saw a crowd of people in full-scale Halloween-style outfits hanging outside. It was May—a costume party in May. And why not? This was, after all, a lively metropolitan area with many fun-loving young people.

I walked inside and saw Townes in the middle of a couple dozen wildly attired people dancing in a circle around him. Turned out to be a big party of gay women and men who were so entranced by this unusual visitor that they didn't want him to leave. He had somehow become the party "mascot"; as diligently as they were trying to hug and kiss and dance with him, he was just as steadfastly refusing.

I'd seen a lot of unusual things in my twenty-eight years, but this was a first. I had to just stand back and take it in for a few minutes. Townes finally noticed me and signaled me to come into the circle. "H, you gotta get me out of here," he pleaded. "It is weirding me out!" The folks just didn't want to let him go, so I suggested we maneuver our way through the crowd over to a window and climb out, which we did.

That was the first night in Boston. Fairly harmless. Night number two, a totally different story.

At the festival during the day, Townes, Danny, and Cody performed to a very appreciative audience and did two encores. After the set, we went our separate ways through the audience, enjoying the festival vibe and doing a bit of people-watching. A few minutes later, I came across Townes squatted down next to an elderly African-American woman with long, gray, braided hair sitting on the ground. She was reading out of a small prayer manual and talking to him in a low but intense voice. I heard her say, "You have come far to get here in a red chariot of fire, and you are heading to a horrible damnation."

Townes stood up with a stricken expression; his face was sheet-white. He grasped the woman's hand, saying, "Thank you for the warning, ma'am, and may God bless you." He walked off quickly, and I followed. "What was that all about?" I asked.

"We are traveling in a red car, H. She just foretold our future, and it's scaring the hell out of me."

Back at the hotel, Townes, Cody, and I had dinner and then dispersed again. Ruester had gone from the stage back to his room without a word, still grieving the loss of his girlfriend. Townes said he was going back to his room for the night.

Around midnight, my phone rang, and a hotel security guard requested I come to the front desk, as a Mr. Townes Van Zandt was about to be arrested by local police.

I dressed quickly and rushed out to the hall. I looked down into the atrium six floors below. Townes was sitting in the lobby fountain pond, fully clothed, water jets spraying him as a crowd of onlookers began to gather. When I got to the lobby, he grinned and pointed to the security guard. "Tell this fellow I'm fishing for garth"—a fish entirely of Townes's own invention. "Grab a pole!"

Two uniformed Boston policemen arrived and conferred briefly with the guard. One of the cops turned to me. "Get him out of there, or we're going to arrest him."

I knew only one thing that would get Townes to cooperate quickly. "Townes," I said, "you're going on in five minutes!"

"Why didn't you say that in the first place?" he replied. As if he'd just come out of a trance (or maybe entered a new one), he stood up and climbed out of the water, and we started to walk off.

The hotel manager blocked our way. He was furious. "Mr. Van Zandt, you and your band need to vacate your rooms right now, or I will have the police arrest all of you." I calmed him down and said we would be gone in thirty minutes.

I went back upstairs and pounded on Danny's and Cody's doors, informing them we had to get out of the hotel immediately or be arrested. Everyone packed up and ran down the hall to the elevator to the parking garage. The police followed us out to the car. I thanked the officers for not arresting us, shook their hands, and off we sped into the night.

It was a startling farewell to a tour stop that had been fairly success-ful—musically, at least. After driving for thirty minutes on the inter-state, we decided to grab a late meal and pulled into a small restaurant a couple of miles off the highway.

I've forgotten the eatery's name, but it was definitely not part of a national chain. That was obvious when we entered and were met by a large, bright-colored painting of the Devil on the wall over the mantel. Yes, standard Devil portraiture with horns, goatee, fiery red skin, pitch-fork, and scheming, soul-stealing smile. As the waitress—a tall, thin, middle-aged woman with deep-set black eyes, jet-black hair and two-inch black-shaded fingernails—seated us, we couldn't help but notice the walls were painted dark red, a choice some folks might view as either intimate or imprisoning.

In a low voice, Townes said, "Let's get out of here right now." As we made for the door, the waitress asked if she could come with us.

"Sorry, ma'am," he replied, "but we don't have any room."

"I can sit on someone's lap."

There was dead silence. Then Townes nodded and said quietly, "Good night, ma'am," and walked out the door. We followed and piled into the car. The waitress ran out to us carrying a grocery sack filled with salad. I accepted it politely and drove out of the parking lot, all of us looking behind at this unusual woman waving goodbye, as if we'd just departed a family picnic.

When I turned the corner, Townes shouted, "Throw that bag out now!" I did, and I'm sure some nocturnal critters had a great roadside snack.

We got back on the interstate, driving eighty or ninety miles per hour. I kept looking in the rearview mirror. Townes noticed my vigilance. It was the Devil following us, he said, just as the old woman at the festival had told him earlier in the day.

We were headed south on I-95, and there wasn't much traffic at around three a.m. Danny and Cody were trying to sleep in the back seat, but were feeling the oddness as well—exacerbated, no doubt, by Townes feverishly reading the Bible out loud, random verses, mostly Old Testament prophets. I began to notice that, no matter which way the road curved, the moon remained in front of us. Some of my turns were almost ninety degrees, yet the moon was always facing us square on. There was probably a logical explanation, but none of us were in the frame of mind to entertain much logic.

Suddenly, Townes shouted, "Pull over quick! The Devil is right on our backbone!" Soon as I stopped the car on the shoulder, he leaped out and dropped onto the ground, rolling in the dirt. He picked up handfuls of dirt and gravel, splashing and rubbing it on himself, saying, "I got to wash the Devil off me!" In a few minutes, he got back in the car completely covered in dirt. "Don't stop till we run out of gas, H. We're gonna make it, we're gonna beat the Devil home!"

Whatever the potency of this purification rite, things did get mellower as we drove through the night. Three days later, we were in St. Louis at a club called Fourth & Pine for a two-day stint with John Lee Hooker. This was a gig where I think anyone suspecting the presence of a dark, occult influence in our lives might have had reason to be right.

I mentioned earlier that the tour included Townes's Bible-collecting phase. It also featured his "blood brother" phase. A number of musicians went through such a phase in the 1970s, for whatever reason. Two individuals would each make a small knife cut on their own finger, hand, or wrist, and then press the two cuts together to commingle the blood flow, the idea being that each person would be symbolically linked to the other with a lifelong pact of friendship.

I've never heard of women performing this rite with one another, but it seemed to be popular with a fair amount of male musicians back in the day.

After the second night in St. Louis, I was asleep in the hotel with my girlfriend, Michelle. Townes had relaxed the no-women-on-tour rules and allowed Michelle and his wife, Cindy, to drive in from Nashville for this one gig. In the middle of the night, my room phone rang. Cindy was on the line, screaming, "Harold, you have to come right away! There's blood everywhere!"

I dressed and rushed to Townes's room. He opened the door and stood, dazed, the front of his shirt and pants covered in fresh blood. However, I was relieved to learn the blood was not his and that *he*—for once—was not the emergency.

Instead, the person bleeding everywhere was a young guy Townes had met that night, the brother of an old friend. The guy was sitting on the bed with a serious cut to a forearm vein; his girlfriend was freaking out, and Townes and Cindy slouched off to the side, clearly stunned.

My battlefield mind-set kicked in, and I went to the bathroom, grabbed a towel, and wrapped a basic tourniquet around the guy's wound. He was conscious, so I told him to hold the towel tight, and the bleeding slowed. I called an ambulance, calmed down his girlfriend, and told Townes and Cindy we had to get out of there right away.

It was the same drill as in Boston a few days before: Get band members alerted, packed, and into the car before police arrived. We didn't need to spend conversational time with law enforcement, especially when Townes was due to perform in two days at the Kerrville Folk Festival in Texas. Luckily, I had checked us all out of the hotel before going to bed. This had become standard operating procedure.

Though nobody said anything at the time, I suspected the accident had resulted from a blood-brother ceremony gone awry, following the sharing of heroin needles. When Townes had opened the door, I could tell he'd shot up and was out of it. Two people woozing out on smack would have made precision knife-handling a challenge under the best of circumstances.

We drove off just as the ambulance and police arrived. No words were spoken by anyone until we hit the interstate with no one in pursuit.

"Do you think the guy will live?" Townes asked.

"Probably," I replied. "But you and Cindy sure as hell don't want to be there when they find the heroin."

He didn't say anything to that. The next day, he called the hospital and learned the fellow was doing better and would be okay. Which is to say, he had not died; what his status was with the police, I never learned.

Townes later told me, "This nightmare had absolutely nothing to do with me—for a change. Just people that came knockin' on my hotel door."

By this point, I had realized that danger and Townes were two natural storm forces liable to intersect any time, anywhere. And stir up the weirdest tornado you could imagine.

It was the middle of the annual Midwestern tornado season, in fact, when we returned to Madison, Wisconsin, for an encore engagement at Bunky's Nightclub, a 1930s-era urban roadhouse and Italian restaurant where Townes and the trio had done a great show a month before. This was a solo show for Townes, and when we arrived, the house was full. Just before he went onstage, he asked me to collect the money from the club owner. Seeing that the club had paid for our hotel, dinner, and drinks in addition to the performance fee, I anticipated no problems.

I entered the office, and the owner was incensed. He refused to pay, stating that Townes was drunk. Truthfully, Townes had a wee buzz on, but at this point in his career, that didn't seem to affect his performance at all. "He'll do a great show," I insisted. "Even better than last time." The owner could not be persuaded.

I found Townes just offstage waiting to go on. When he heard what was happening, he and I went to the office, and he literally kicked open the door, confronted the owner, and demanded his pay for the evening. They shouted back and forth a bit, the owner refusing to pay, claiming Townes was drunk, Townes denying it and refusing to go onstage until he was paid there and then. The owner pulled a gun from his desk drawer, pointed it at Townes, and told us to leave the office.

Round one, Bunky's.

As Townes and I walked away, he said, "Watch this, H." Striding onstage to a high-spirited audience, he proclaimed, "Thanks for coming tonight, folks. But the club owner here says he won't pay me because I'm drunk."

A spatter of laughs and murmurs from the audience . . .

"And if I'm not gonna get paid, then you shouldn't have to pay, either. Go get your money back, and I'll give you a show you won't forget!"

The room erupted in applause and cheers. The faces of owner and staff did not exhibit pleasure. I then realized this was an establishment that may have maintained an affiliation with "elements" of organized crime. I noticed that the staff—like the owner—were attired in suits with obvious bulges indicating the presence of a shoulder holster. It was going to be an interesting evening.

Townes did a dynamite set plus three encores. Before finishing, he asked the audience if they would hang around until we left. "Stick around, everybody, party's just getting started. And you press people, why don't you print what happened here tonight?" he asked. A couple of writers in the audience shouted back in the affirmative.

Townes got offstage and grabbed two bottles of vodka from the bar. "This'll be my pay for tonight," he declared; no staff member did anything. Two local policemen came in and agreed to escort us to the car. My guess is, they'd had similar experiences at Bunky's before.

As we left, the club owner said to Townes, "You come back again, I will kill you." Townes stepped outside and slammed the door in the owner's face. The cops seemed a bit rattled, as if they were half-expecting the owner and his *paesani to* burst out shooting. We were happy to see the police vehicle following behind until we hit the interstate.

As we headed south on I-90, Townes chuckled and said, "That was fun."

Fun? I was starting to understand it was normal. And that Townes always had some novel way of addressing a problem.

In early June, we found ourselves in Portland, Oregon, for two nights, and I had to check into the nearest VA hospital. One of my knees had swollen up enormously and was extremely painful, possibly as a result of driving all those weeks in the cramped Crimson Chariot and, most certainly, from the daily tour agitation.

The band dropped me off at the VA, checked into a hotel, and played both nights. My knee was drained, and I was resting in the hospital bed when Townes called me after the second night's show. "H, I know what's wrong with you. You've got too much stress dealing with me and the band, all the driving and keeping the books and whatnot."

I agreed there were a lot of moving parts to keep track of.

"Well, to fix you, I'm in the hotel room now that is several floors up from the ground. I'm opening the window"—the sound of a window sash being lifted came over the phone—"and I am throwing out all your receipts and the money made from the last couple of gigs."

I was too hoarse to scream very loudly. It wouldn't have mattered anyway.

"There goes all your stress, H. Goodnight and sleep well."

He hung up. I came close to fainting from anger. Before I could do anything or get much more upset, the painkillers kicked in, and I zonked out. I awoke to the phone ringing. It was the next morning, and Townes was asking how I was. I slowly took stock of my situation, and it seemed the swelling had gone down completely during the night.

I don't know what sort of mental jiu-jitsu had been used on me, but I figured Townes had more insights into The Unknown than I had yet to fathom.

"Good," he said. "I thought that would take care of it. We'll be by to pick you up when you're released today."

I replied that the doctors wanted me to remain for another three days of observation.

"No problem," he said. "We'll break you out." Which is, in truth, what happened. Cody came by and snuck me out of my room, down the hall, and out the back entrance to our waiting getaway vehicle. A true Jesse James moment.

Our final show for the tour was June 30 in Odessa, Texas, at the Pan American Ballroom. This was a venue shaped like an airplane hangar and possessing similar acoustic properties. Upon entering, we saw it was a rock 'n' roll show that had drawn a raucous audience with full-tilt rock 'n' roll expectations. Townes, Danny, and Cody were the opener for a popular Mexican rock band, and the crowd kept chanting "Rock 'n' roll! Rock 'n' roll! Rock 'n' roll!" over and over during the set.

Before going onstage, Townes pulled me aside. "This isn't going to go well, H. Soon as we're up there playing, collect the money from the promoter, go back to the car, and pull up by the backstage door. Lock yourself in, and keep the motor running."

I followed his instructions. Townes did a very quick set. The trio came offstage quickly, ran to the car, and jumped in. We sped off with a screech, and Townes cautioned, "H, don't stop if anyone gets in front of the car. If we are going to be robbed, it will happen in the next few minutes."

I've noted that Townes had a bent toward pranks, but this was definitely not one of those times. Townes, Danny, and Cody kept staring out the back window the next thirty minutes as we flew along the interstate. Finally, Townes announced it was safe to slow down. "I saw that coming from the moment we walked in," he said. "Have to make sure we never play that place again."

We drove straight through to Houston, where we met Townes's new manager, Lamar Fike, and his partner and cousin, Tommy McDonald. The official announcement of the change would appear in the July 1, 1978, issue of *Billboard* in the Talent Talk section: "Townes Van Zandt now represented by Lamar Fike management of Nashville."

My brother Kevin had orchestrated the switch of business manager from John Lomax to Lamar, who was a charter member of Elvis Presley's Memphis Mafia and a well-respected music-industry professional with a vast network of contacts. Lamar and Tommy had booked an upcoming national and international tour with performances by Townes and band scheduled at major music venues in Europe, Canada, and the U.S. As capable as John had been in helping Townes get a wider audience in the folk-and-college circuit, I can only assume Lamar's higher profile from his Elvis connections was the deciding factor in making the transition.

To obtain a fuller sound for the larger venues, Townes added a bassist. We went to the apartment of Jimmie Gray, just off Music Row. Back in the early 1960s out in Arizona, Jimmie had played bass in the original Waylon Jennings band, the Waylors, and was a great studio musician and live performer. Jimmie was just shy of forty years old, a laid-back, soft-spoken, long-haired American Indian hippie. Townes and Jimmie hit it off right away, and he gave Jimmie a stack of his albums to learn the songs.

With the expansion from trio to quartet, we needed a roomier vehicle. The road-weary Crimson Chariot was replaced by a brand, shiny-new Winnebago RV secured by Lamar's management company.

In late September, we drove to a Memphis car dealership, where we exchanged the Caprice for the Winnebago. Lamar had arranged for Townes and the band to do a short set at the annual Mid-South Fair in Memphis. It was the same venue Elvis Presley had frequented numerous times in the 1950s, and Lamar, with his trademark show-business flair, had a squadron of motorcycle police escort us into the fairgrounds. "We're getting the Elvis treatment!" Townes shouted as we drove through the crowd to the performers' area.

I brought the Winnebago back to Nashville and parked it at the entrance to the farm while we prepared for the tour. The night before we were set to leave, Townes and Cindy decided to sleep in the Winnebago, while I stayed alone in the cabin. The plan was that, next morning, Townes and I would drive into Nashville, pick up the band, and hit the road for the first show in Washington, D.C.

Our Crimson Chariot Tour had contained its moments of stress and crisis, but it had certainly gotten Townes into an upgraded performance circuit with enthusiastic audiences. *Flyin' Shoes* was selling well nationally, more copies so far than all of his earlier albums combined. Tomato Records had also issued a live album Townes recorded in 1973 titled *Live at the Old Quarter, Houston, Texas*, which was getting good radio airplay as well.

No doubt about it, this new tour was going to be the absolutely best he'd ever done.

Until it wasn't.

5

The Crying Tour

You've heard the old saying "Pride goeth before a fall." With this particular fall, what had goeth was one too many last rounds of drinks at a local bar.

The night before the tour was to start, Townes slipped out of the Winnebago and went into Nashville with his neighbor, Michael Ewah. I'm not sure why he did this. Townes had agreed he would make an effort to be in good physical shape for the upcoming shows; with his consent, a "curfew" had been established, as with athletes before a big sporting event.

Maybe it was a case of pre-tour nerves. Or he just felt like seeing some friends he wouldn't see in a while. But both Townes and Michael got very drunk at the Gold Rush; by some miracle, Michael managed to pilot the pickup back to the farm without incident.

But when they turned onto the property, Michael encountered the metal cattle guard at the entrance. For someone driving at a low speed, it was a minimal obstacle that would cause no damage. This early morning hour, however, the vehicle made front-on contact while careening up the road at probably forty miles per hour or more.

The truck bounced off the guard, flew into the air, and slammed smack into a large oak tree. Townes was critically injured and suffered a concussion, a broken arm, broken ribs, and a deep, three-inch cut on his cheek. Michael had minor cuts and bruises.

I was awakened by Cindy, who was in hysterics. Rushing from the cabin, we found Michael stumbling around and Townes flat on the ground. Seeing the extent of the truck damage and Townes's motionless form, my immediate impression was that he was dead. He was only unconscious, though, his face bleeding profusely. The ambulance came fairly quickly and took Townes and Michael to the hospital, Cindy and I following in my car.

Once there, I called Lamar Fike and let him know what had taken place. I went to the ER, where Townes was still unconscious. The attending doctor did not express as much optimism as I would have liked. He moved Townes to intensive care.

After several hours, Townes came to. With a lopsided grin he rasped, "Cheer up, H. It's only gonna get worse."

And it did. Lamar was enraged beyond words, saying he wanted Michael killed. Initially, I ignored these words of anger and understandable frustration; Lamar had been a part of Elvis Presley's Memphis Mafia, where over-the-top rhetorical threats were almost a performance genre in themselves.

Then again . . .

I drove to Lamar's apartment in Nashville and found him even more upset than when we'd last spoken. We stayed up all night talking and had breakfast, charting out a plan as to the next step to take concerning Townes's tour. Eventually, Lamar calmed down and said he would not have Michael killed. We rode over to the hospital, and surprisingly, Lamar was very cool, consoling Townes about his injuries and buoying him up for the tour. Clearly, it was in everyone's best interest that Townes get better physically and keep some degree of mental positivity.

I think what really bothered Lamar was that he could already see the seeds of self-destruction taking hard root in Townes. Only thirteen months before, Lamar's world had been upended by the sudden death of Elvis, his closest friend for twenty-three years. Lamar had coped with his massive grief by starting a management/booking agency and music publishing company with Tommy McDonald and redirecting his sorrow into helping Townes and other clients. Having to witness Townes's reckless behavior no doubt brought to the surface waves of frustration and déjà vu.

In a couple of days, Townes was released from the hospital, his ribs taped up and broken arm in a sling. He was given a large open prescription of codeine pills for the pain. A week later, we went on the road and did the first phase of the tour as planned.

Of course, Townes was unable to play guitar, but he held it as a prop and for balance as he sang his songs. Danny, Jimmie, and Cody provided stellar accompaniment and backing vocals, but the overall effect wasn't the same without Townes playing guitar. His playing was a vital part of his song style, but there was no other way to do the shows.

Despite the inauspicious start, I believe this quartet was—in my humble opinion—the most musically creative group I ever saw Townes perform with on a regular basis. You can hear them on the albums *Rear View Mirror, Roadsongs*, and *Rear View Mirror, Volume 2* . . . give a listen and notice the interplay between Townes's voice and the music, the diversity of instrumental textures, the subtle rhythm changes in the accompaniment, the always just-right backing vocals. If he had been able to play guitar at full strength, the performances would have garnered even more critical acclaim.

I called it "the Crying Tour," because it was a choir of tears throughout the tour, as we traveled from gig to gig. Naturally, Townes shared his codeine supply with the band, causing them to tell the saddest of personal stories; one time they were all crying at once.

I suppose it was a spontaneous, group therapy–style bonding, a sort of twelve-step program absent any intent to achieve actual recovery. I could tell Townes really enjoyed these moments of intimacy. He was by nature shy and emotionally reclusive; having everyone else share their vulnerability made for a rare moment of fellowship.

And some of the shared moments were searing. In case you're thinking I've exaggerated the dangers of the musical touring life, there's the true story of what had happened to the brother of our bassist, Jimmie Gray. In the early 1960s, Jimmie was traveling with Waylon and the Waylors. One night Jimmie's brother visited him, and after the show they were in the hotel elevator returning to their room. They were completely unaware that just a few seconds before, their floor had been the scene of a drug deal gone sour; when their elevator door opened unexpectedly, one of the paranoid dealers freaked out and fired into the elevator, hitting and mortally wounding Jimmie's brother, who died in his arms.

Jimmie quit Waylon's band and gave up touring for some time. I think the experience gave Jimmie a greater sense of calm and perspective on life. To me, Jimmie was a pillar of stability. In an emergency, I could count on him to be the most rational of any of us.

As for me, I had my own trunkload of emotional baggage. I'm sure I would have joined in the codeine and the crying, but I was too busy driving and had to stay focused on the highway ahead.

And "focus" was a constantly changing state of affairs.

We hit Chicago in mid-October and played at the Quiet Knight, a four-hundred-seat concert hall that flourished from 1969 to 1979 and featured an incredible array of American music. During the sound check, the electricity and lights and sound went out, leaving Townes standing in the dark onstage. "The room just filled up with the ghosts of all the blues greats that have played here," he said later. "By turning the room pitch-black and silent, they were letting me know this is their juke joint and I had their blessing to perform here."

The next day he bought a Chicago Blues cap, declaring, "Now I'm officially one of them blues cats." He loved the cap, wearing it tilted to the side, striding along as he walked. Townes could have been a great actor; when he was in a happy mood, he had an innate ability to create an instant "character" with words, actions, and facial expressions.

Before the sound check, however, we had an adventure involving several colorful characters. Across the street from the club was a barber shop. Townes went in for a haircut and razor shave; from the Winnebago we could see him in the barber chair. He also was getting a manicure from the barber's wife; we watched with amusement as she began expanding her service area—rubbing her hands along Townes's leg . . . thigh . . . groin . . . the barber, apparently, could not see what was going on below and kept chatting amiably with Townes, who was squirming and becoming increasingly uncomfortable as the barber shaved his long, slender neck with the long, sharp straight razor.

Soon as he was finished, Townes hopped out of the chair, paid the fee, and exited quickly to the street. Standing in front of the shop were three attractively dressed women age thirty-ish, perhaps more dressed up than that neighborhood and time of day would normally merit. Townes struck up a conversation; next thing we know, he'd brought the women into the Winnebago.

Townes, of course, had a bit of a codeine-alcohol buzz on, and his perceptive abilities were somewhat dimmed even in daylight. It was obvious to the rest of us that these women were, in fact, exquisite denizens of the local transvestite—as we said in those days—welcoming committee. One of the band guys pulled Townes aside and clued him in; Townes, ever the gentleman, announced, "Ladies, I'm sorry, but we have to go into the club for sound check." The visitors departed without incident. "Man, that was a close one!" exclaimed Townes. Definitely, close shaves were the order of the day.

Later that week, the band played a great show at Black Sheep Repertory Theatre in Manchester, Michigan, a little bit southwest of Ann Arbor. As we got in the vehicle to leave, an enthusiastic fan dashed up and gifted us with a large shopping bag of marijuana. Lovely gesture. What could go wrong?

Nothing, except that the unmarked police car secreted in the dark across the street suddenly appeared behind us after we'd driven a block from the theater. The two policemen had us file out of the Winnebago onto the street, hands up, to be frisked. They asked if we had any illegal substances. Townes replied matter-of-factly, "No, officers. Just a little weed."

In the ensuing silence, you could've heard a roach sizzle.

Amazingly, there were no arrests. The shopping bag and its contraband contents were impounded, along with most of the alcohol, except for one bottle of vodka Townes was allowed to retain. Probably because the policemen recognized him as the author of "Pancho and Lefty" and were impressed enough to grant leniency.

As we continued across the country, the Crying Tour took on the nature of any other Townes tour: moments of onstage glory, moments of offstage terror. It was a disaster for my brother's record label, for Lamar Fike's management company, and for everyone associated with advancing Townes's career.

However, it was the first time I truly began to get a deeper understanding of the forces driving his soul. And his music. Getting to know Townes and his ways was, for me, a sort of road-tour boot camp where I started to gradually comprehend, very partially understand, and—after many years—finally learn how to best cope with this extraordinary human being and help him bring his music to the public.

On the long drives during the Crying Tour, he shared with me his stories of growing up. The memories were fragmented and had been shuffled around by his shock therapy. But eventually, I could see a distinct pattern threading through his adult behavior and his songwriting.

At age fourteen Townes had been enrolled by his parents, Dorothy and Harris, at Shattuck Military Academy in Minnesota. In the late 1950s, sending a boy with behavioral issues or "nonconformist" tendencies to this type of boarding school was a common choice of last resort employed by middle and upper middle-class families. The cadet-style discipline and restricted social life, it was believed, would "straighten out" the wayward youth and get him better prepared academically for college.

Townes, of course, did not straighten out but, rather, sublimated his rebellion. He sniffed glue and orchestrated pranks, but his naturally high intelligence and curiosity for learning helped him get good grades and excel at sports. He joined the ROTC unit and sang and played guitar at campus talent shows.

During his freshman year at University of Colorado, he received much less daily supervision and, as many kids do in their late teens, engaged in daredevil activities as an attention-getting, status-claiming, persona-defining device among their peers.

It was that unique period in a young person's life when they take a more assertive (though often wildly misguided or misinformed) role to fill in the blanks and connect the dots of the adult personality they've been slowly shaping over their entire life to that point.

It was a time when Townes Van Zandt wanted to "feel" at a super-intense level. Feel what, exactly? Feel *life*. Or feel *like* he was feeling *life*. One of the popular tenets in American coming-of-age culture—as expressed in numerous works of literature, film, song—is that to feel truly and vibrantly alive, you have to have an up-close-and-personal encounter with death.

It's a glorification of bizarre risk-taking behavior and not limited to the U.S., of course. Seriously: Who thinks running down a narrow street full of rampaging bulls in Spain or climbing a nearly vertical frozen mountain face in the Himalayas is rational behavior?

But as the 1960s progressed, it seemed the attraction of challenging authority and society, of crossing norms and boundaries, had found a more receptive audience among young people than ever before.

For me, it was leaving a safe, predictable suburban milieu to join the military and spend time in a foreign country during a horrific war.

For Townes, it was letting himself lean off and fall backward from a three-story apartment balcony. But it was also secluding himself in his dorm room and immersing himself in the music of Lightnin' Hopkins, Bob Dylan, and other artists and genres that would constitute his key stylistic influences as a professional performer in the years to come.

Years later, when he and I traveled together and I saw him do the blood-brother thing and occasionally cut lines across his chest with a knife, I'd ask why. "Because I want to feel," he'd reply.

"I understand that," I'd say. "But most people just do a tiny prick; you take out a whole chunk of yourself."

"It's simple, H. I want to feel more."

I don't believe Townes's college stunts were suicidal or a desperate cry for help. I think they were just one, small point along a long, wide spectrum of a thousand crazy things kids did then, do now, and will do always to mark their unique path into adulthood.

His parents disagreed. They took him out of school, placed him in the psychiatric center at University of Texas Medical Branch in Galveston, Texas, and gave consent to the doctors' treatment plan: a four-month series of electroconvulsive therapy (ECT) treatments on his nineteen-year-old brain and body, thirty-eight treatments in all.

Shock treatment, to the layperson.

From today's vantage point of counseling and intervention protocols, the rapid and lengthy committal was an extraordinarily severe response, but clearly, his parents' deep concern for his welfare made them believe it to be the only appropriate course of action. In 1964, antidepressant drug therapy was not as widely used nor as understood as it is today. Proponents of ECT held out the promise of an *immediate* reversal of whatever mental condition was afflicting their son.

The therapy succeeded in erasing the bulk of his childhood memories, to the extent that, when his parents visited, the doctor would prep him by saying, "Townes, remember the person with the long hair is your mother. The other person is your father."

At the end of the four months, the doctors pronounced Townes substantially improved and ready to resume the "normal" life of a college student. As a way of helping him reacclimate, Townes was advised to travel and "find himself."

Looking back, that's precisely what he did. Traveling in a direction his doctors, family, and even he could never have imagined. Traveling until his very last day on earth.

Whether he succeeded in finding himself is open to question. But over the next three decades, he never stopped searching, and his music is a revealing record of that lifelong journey.

During his hospital stay, Townes received a diagnosis of bipolar disorder as the root of his adjustment difficulties. Bipolar disorder had been discussed in the medical profession since the mid-1800s as a way of characterizing behavior that was high-energy manic one moment, suddenly veered to torpid depression, and then repeated the cycle again and again and again.

An emotional roller coaster, in other words, and it describes a pattern I saw Townes go through repeatedly, up through the final hours of his life.

I think the loss of memory caused by the ECT treatments fueled the unquenchable, indefinable rage that simmered inside him. He could recall only his early years in fragments, as if he were a stranger to himself.

It was a semi-amnesiac state that I imagine was like one of those dreams where you set out after an objective, suddenly forget where you're going and why, and can never—in the dream, anyway—return to your original course.

Haven't we all had dreams like that? We wake up, rise, and go about our life. After all, it was just a dream.

But imagine if that dream pattern of constant interruption occurred continuously in our daily waking hours. The frustration of always being thrown off-course would be maddening.

While the ECT erased his memories from childhood up to the treatments, it did not necessarily erase the impact of whatever actual trauma had devastated him, the precipitating event that remained a permanent tear in Townes's spirit. Townes said he experienced this post-treatment dislocation throughout his life, and it hung over him like a dark, threatening cloud. Townes would often say, "If only I could get out from under this veil of tears." I didn't fully understand at the time what this meant; it seems clear in retrospect that the veil was a subconscious metaphor describing his unremembered trauma.

Was this veil, and his relentless struggle to escape it, the heart of what we feel in his music and lyrics?

I believe also that his time in the hospital may have opened up another area of his personality. Did it enhance his frequent ability to empathize with complete strangers? Did it cause him to subconsciously orient his songwriting toward touching people in their darkest moments? In making a connection from his ailing heart to theirs?

When John Lomax was managing Townes, he placed an advertisement in *Rolling Stone* trying to start a Townes Van Zandt fan club. The club never got off the ground, but John often said he was astonished by the number of letters from people testifying that Townes's music had saved their lives. Not making them laugh or feel lighthearted, but literally *saving* their lives. It turned out many of the correspondents were also former or current residents of mental institutions.

I can attest that up through his final tour, Townes was regularly approached by fans who would say in all seriousness, "Townes, I was

going to kill myself, but I listened to your records all night, and I didn't."
I heard variations on that statement constantly.

Townes's ECT experience was the unspoken basis of our unique, yet often tumultuous friendship. Even in the first few weeks of living with him and Cindy at the farm, I sensed his curiosity about my war experiences was more than a desire for casual chat. He saw himself as a similar type of combatant whose mind had been wounded and permanently damaged by his treatment in the mental health system.

Over two decades, Townes never stopped asking me what it was like to be in Vietnam. He sought details of the daily routine of war and death. I don't believe it was because he wanted vicarious action stories; I believe it was to see how my PTSD compared to the shock treatments he believed had taken so much away from his memory and spirit.

At the time, PTSD wasn't at all understood in the popular culture the way it is today, though it had existed as long as humans fought in battle. Yet, between Townes and me, there was a respect in the common ground of having had our emotional foundations profoundly damaged at a sensitive time in our young lives. Neither one of us ever maliciously spoke about or manipulated the other's damaged brain.

Townes intuitively understood my war years and dealing with those demons, just as I helped him grapple with the demons of his life. We discussed openly our individual fears, frustrations, and the metaphorical monkeys on our backs. We were unafraid to talk about our failures and successes in life. Sometimes he would blurt out something incredibly harsh, then turn to me and say, "It was in my head, H. I had to tell someone, and no one else but you would understand."

I think what made our bond so strong was that no matter how crazy the situation was, I was never afraid of it. Against all logic, I trusted Townes. He had brought me into his circle of trust when my heart was broken; he treated me like a brother and allowed no one to mess with me, right up to the day he died.

Which, as anyone with a sibling knows, doesn't mean everything was a day at the beach. Working and traveling with Townes was similar in many ways to life in a constant war zone. But I always felt an optimism, no matter how dark his mood or how seemingly hopeless the situation. Even though we never could control the other, we helped each other shoulder our emotional baggage—the way a soldier would aid a buddy on a long march home.

I mentioned earlier how easily freaked out Townes could get by any event that had an occult association . . . the old lady at the Boston festival, the waitress at the spooky restaurant, the washing-the-Devil-off with dirt episode, and so on.

Townes claimed to feel the presence and hear the voices of beings he described as "angels" and "demons." These were not generic demons representing negative behavior traits, or abstract guardian angels of movie lore—á la little figures sitting on opposite shoulders. He perceived them as actual entities with personalities and voices—entities that had evolved with him over the years and with whom he had an ongoing relationship.

These spiritual manifestations battled constantly in his mind, and the volume of their voices seemed to increase as the years went by. Between the angels of light and the demons of darkness, he was left with very little silence and peace throughout his life. Some say this was because of drug use and alcohol. I don't agree; having watched and heard from him how the angels and demons affected his art and life on a daily basis, I know they had a reality for him.

These entities came under the general rubric of *ghosts*. There were *gray ghosts* (demons) that were simply in the environment. *Black ghosts* heralded death; he believed they could fill a room and suffocate him with their energy. "H, I know the black ghosts are laying low, hiding in the shadows just waiting to get me," he would say. *White ghosts* (angels) gave positive guidance and succor, and could save him at the last minute from a hopeless situation.

He believed ghosts were around and talking to him all the time, especially when he went to sleep. The ghosts' words and sounds tormented him then; this was why it was unusual for him to doze for more than two or three hours. He told me his sleep was filled with nightmares and demon voices that scared him to the core. I never heard him say this to anyone else.

He would say, "When I do sleep, it's the worst time of all; the sounds and visions are beyond words." As he'd say these words, he would bend over and hold his head in anguish and torment.

Yet in a very strange way he embraced the demons as his artistic muses. Once he said to me, "Do you want me to teach you how to write songs? It isn't as hard as everyone makes it out to be."

"Sure," I would answer. "Do I have to hear the voices, like you, to do it? And can I turn the volume down when I want to?"

"Yes, you have to hear the voices, and, no, you can't turn them down when you want." He wasn't kidding. "In fact, they get louder each day."

"In that case, no thanks. I'm already unstable enough."

"Well, if you're with me all the time, the angels and demons will rub off on you eventually, whether you like it or not. I have learned to listen to their voices, and this is where I get the words and music to my songs."

On tour, when we stayed in motels or hotels, Townes and I always stayed in the same room, with two double beds; it was a necessary safety measure, so I'd know where he was and what was going on with him. He would typically wander around the room till three a.m. and get back up at five a.m., pacing around until I arose. I would go to sleep around one or two a.m. after the shows and get up around eight or nine.

Increasingly over the years, I'd wake up in the middle of the night and see him sitting up in bed, awake and watching television in a semi-trance. It was like white noise to him, something to put him in a kind of Zen zone. He had a fondness for reruns of 1960s comedies like *Green Acres*, *The Beverly Hillbillies*, and *The Andy Griffith Show*; he never watched current news or any shows with violence or dark themes.

I think those nostalgic rural shows with country folks putting it over on city slickers appealed to him; in real life, he saw himself as the hillbilly hero prevailing over the nefarious rich villain. And, truth be told, he himself had a corny sense of humor that matched the writing in these sitcoms.

Every time Townes and I left a hotel room while touring, he would leave the television on, so the room "would have company." Townes did the same when he was at his home in Mount Juliet, Tennessee, where he lived alone, or when he stayed at my condo in Austin. I really think it was to accommodate his ghosts.

No matter where we were, I would often hear Townes talking to the ghosts, saying, "Demons, leave me alone." I would come backstage and find him alone, yet he would be talking to the air. I never interrupted him—usually ignored it, or left the room for his privacy. However, if I saw it was riling him up or upsetting him, then I would say, "Who are you talking to?" That would break the conversation with the unknown, and he would come back.

"Do you really want to know?" he'd ask.

"Only if it's not going to bother me."

Then silence, as if he were transitioning from a dark, closed room into the bright, sunny outdoors.

Townes always had a Bible at hand or nearby; I think it helped him by keeping demons at bay. If not, things would have been much worse for him and anyone around him.

Another ritual involved his song "Pancho and Lefty." Each morning we were on tour, he would ask me in all seriousness, "H, who do you want to be today, Pancho or Lefty?"

Depending on my mood, I would say one and then, the next time, the other. Whatever my response, he'd smile and say, "Okay, I'll be the other."

At first it all seemed lighthearted enough . . . until one day I began to *feel* the ghosts of Pancho and Lefty. It was a peculiar sensation I can't adequately describe, but it seemed as if these characters from Townes's psyche had indeed emerged into the physical realm and were with us as we traveled.

One of Townes's habits was to finish off what was left in the vodka bottle before we checked out from a motel or hotel. I would wake up to the sounds of him cracking the bottle, gulping down a drink and orange soda chaser, and lighting a cigarette. This was the usual sunrise soundtrack, from the first day I spent on the road with him to his last. I learned to wake up when I heard he was asleep in the middle of the night, so I could take the vodka and pour it out, except for two or three drinks' worth.

Townes was at his loneliest early in the morning, for the first hour or two after waking. He didn't speak at all during this time, but often I did hear him talking to the birds and animals. His silent time in the morning seemed to be him getting a grip back on his thoughts, trying to regain an equilibrium lost while he slept.

An unanticipated effect of the 1978 tour on me was that it renewed my interest in going to church. I had been raised generic Roman Catholic and attended St. Martin's Catholic School in Bethpage, Long Island. But even during my Vietnam duty I had not made an effort to practice any regular religion, nor had my dark period of postwar adjustment and marital troubles instilled any desire to reestablish any kind of permanent spiritual practice.

Traveling with Townes changed that. I tried to go to a church in each town we passed through, often to pray for my loved ones and always for the strength to cope with Townes. And to request divine help for him. Being in a quiet, contemplative place even a short while was enormously stress-relieving. I prayed in some of the grandest churches in the world. It never mattered to me what religion the church was; just being able to enjoy spiritual time in a blessed place was crucial for my emotional sustenance.

Only once did Townes accompany me to church, and that was in Europe. It was a powerfully cathartic experience for him, and he cried profusely. But all the other times he would say, "H, pray for me when you go to church. Just maybe the good Lord will shine a light on me."

Over and over, as the years passed, I tried to get Townes to record "Amazing Grace," either singing or reciting this moving song so popular with millions of people around the world. He had written and recorded two gospel-style songs for his 1971 album *High, Low and In Between* ("Two Hands" and "When He Offers His Hand"), but "Amazing Grace" as performed by Townes would have been riveting.

He always refused, saying flatly and without a hint of humor, "I have never been saved. Me singing this song would be an untruth."

"If you did record it," I'd reply, "you might just *be* saved from your veil of tears."

"I have to live my songs before I write and record them, you know that," he'd volley back. "However, if the day ever comes that I *am* saved, I *will* perform this song on one of my future albums."

A minor concession, but it was a step forward. Every time I made the suggestion, the answer was always the same. Yet it never stopped me from asking him, right up until the end of his life. I always hoped that one day, Townes would feel as if he were saved and that all of his demons would vanish. And maybe something as simple as singing "Amazing Grace" could be the mystical catalyst.

It was another enigma wrapped in a conundrum. He read the Bible from day one that I starting working with him until his death. He could quote the Bible, and at times did as we traveled. He often said when we talked about faith, "I don't get why all these different religions are at odds with one another. It is clear there is only one God, not an individual God for each religion. We all came from Adam and Eve; that means we are all related. So what is all the arguing about?"

These few months of my initial tour had shown me that this artist capable of deep understanding and empathy preferred to live his life on the razor edge of sanity and insanity, hiding in a dark, shadowy world of addiction and violence he believed he could control. Loneliness and despair were the volatile chemicals that fueled Townes's creativity. He deliberately sought out the demons to find his next song . . . and then fervently prayed for the angels to save him at the last minute.

Did he think *I* was crazy? Probably. And I probably did become partly crazy, after being around him so much. You do become what you surround yourself with. Like my dad used to say: Show me your friends, and I'll show you who *you* are.

The more Townes and I got to know one another, the more we asked questions of each other's life. Some might characterize our relationship as *co-dependent*. I think the more apt description would be *co-independent*. By sharing our vulnerabilities over the years, we kept each other on the most even psychological keel possible. I felt like Townes was my therapist. And, I guess, to some degree, I was his.

Typically, after a gig, well-wishers and other folks would come backstage and talk to Townes. Sometimes the evening would wind down without incident; other times, something crazy happened. In either case, Townes and I would be the only ones remaining at the end.

One time he said to me, "H, don't you think it's a little odd that it always ends up with just you and me in the room? The room fills up with people, and I chase them off, and you are still sitting here. Either you are real smart, or you're as thick as a tree."

I thought about it a moment. "I'll take thick as a tree," I replied.

I'm quite certain that Townes saved my life. Dealing with his lunatic shenanigans and mercurial mental states did much to distract me from my own emotional distress. After my wife left me, I would not see her or my daughter for sixteen years. My heart was broken and kept on breaking every day for the entire time. It was not something I walked around casually discussing at the corner bar. But Townes knew the degree of pain I felt. He was a friend, the kind I had never known up to that time in my life.

And then our friendship entered a radical new phase.

After our final show of the Crying Tour, in Boston with John Lee Hooker in December 1978, Townes got word from my brother Kevin that there would be no follow-up album to *Flyin' Shoes*. In effect, this meant Townes had been dropped from Tomato Records. The planned European tour was also canceled by Lamar Fike's office.

It is my belief that Kevin and Lamar wanted to present Townes to non-U.S. audiences and critics at his very whole best. And they did not think that was possible, even after his rehab and the road gigs we'd just finished.

For Townes, losing the affiliation with Tomato was like a teenager being kicked out of the family home. He sank into a deep despair and shrank into himself, living out the lyrics of his classic, "Waiting 'Round to Die." It was the first song he'd composed when he was starting his musical journey. I'm sure I wasn't alone in wondering if he'd ever compose another.

As for me, just waiting 'round wasn't my style. I got busy taking stock of what I'd learned from my Year of Townes and began charting out a new course.

6

Interlude...Insanity Leaves, Then Sneaks in the Back Window

AFTER TOWNES was dropped from Tomato Records at the end of the Crying Tour, his career and personal life began fragmenting. He was devastated beyond words. He made no effort that I saw to gain a new label contract, and seemed to give up completely on moving forward with his career.

Wouldn't anybody?

We continued to tour sporadically; our travel vehicle was no longer the sleek, spacious Winnebago but Townes's battered pickup. He played a handful of dates in 1979 and early 1980 with the quartet; guitarist Mickey White, whom Townes had worked with in the early 1970s, came back into the musical fold that year and became a very adaptable accompanist.

In 1980, Townes and Cindy separated after a not-quite-two-year marriage; he relocated to Austin, Texas, which would be his performing and touring base until 1986. I decided to stay in Nashville and delve deeper into the music industry. During the next few years, I remained in touch with Townes by phone and occasionally went on the road with him.

Though we were geographically apart, Townes and I spent the next few years moving forward—erratically, painfully, hesitantly—along parallel life courses. I think both of us in this period came to grips with who we were going to be "when we grew up." I think we each made a commitment to pursuing this now-solidified path to our final destiny, with whatever joys and sorrows that might bring.

In Austin, Townes became a shadow of himself, touring occasionally,

writing minimally. He felt no one in the music industry wanted anything to do with him. Later, Townes would speak to me of these times as
if he had died. Darkness had consumed him to the extent it silenced his
creativity; at times, he said, he feared he had lost his source of inspiration
forever.

It was an odd paradox. As a songwriter who refused to conform to
the Nashville country-pop songwriting formula, Townes was accepted
on his own creative terms by major artists like Hoyt Axton, Emmylou
Harris, Doc Watson, Willie Nelson, Kris Kristofferson, and Bob Dylan.
Their enthusiastic acceptance, however, hadn't convinced many Music
Row label and publishing executives to back him.

Yet in 1981, just as he'd moved out of the Nashville area, his "commercial" songwriting credentials received significant validation from
the Music Row establishment. "If I Needed You" became a huge hit
for Emmylou Harris and Don Williams, peaking at No. 3 on the *Billboard* Hot Country Singles chart and reaching millions of listeners
worldwide.

And two years later, Chips Moman finally produced the Townes Van
Zandt hit single he'd been hoping for—but it wasn't by Townes. Chips's
studio version of "Pancho and Lefty" recorded by Willie Nelson and
Merle Haggard became a No. 1 country single and the title track of
a No. 1 country album, and reached No. 37 on the overall *Billboard*
charts. Townes even played a role as a *federale* in the video for the song.

Townes made guest TV spots in the early 1980s on the Nashville
Network (TNN) and Country Music Television (CMT), appearing in
interviews with hosts Ralph Emery, Bobby Bare, and other well-regarded
Music City figures. In 1984, he was a finalist in the "Songwriter of the
Year" category in the Nashville Songwriters Association International
Awards.

And in Austin, Townes was warmly welcomed by local musicians and
media as a mainstay of the city's progressive-country musical scene. He
shared stages with Gary P. Nunn, Ray Wylie Hubbard, Jerry Jeff Walker,
Rusty Wier, Steven Fromholz, Kenneth Threadgill, Butch Hancock,
Jimmie Dale Gilmore, David Halley, Calvin Russell, and Jubal Clark,

performed at the famed Armadillo World Headquarters, and made a second appearance on the prestigious *Austin City Limits* television show.

But the week Willie and Merle's "Pancho and Lefty" hit No. 1 on the *Billboard* Country chart, Townes checked in to the Austin State Hospital detox unit. Four days later, he checked out of the hospital to play his end-of-the-month rent gig at emmajoe's, Austin's premier folk club.

As for me, I had never had much of an interest in college, but residing now in a major music production capital, I wanted to learn more than what I could discover in a nightclub. I enrolled in music history courses at Tennessee State University, a historically black university on Nashville's north side, and business courses at Belmont University, a Christian school adjacent to Music Row that was one of the first four-year college institutions to offer a degree program in the nuts-and-bolts of music business.

I specifically chose Tennessee State University because I wanted to study Southern blues; doing so at a school with more than ninety percent African-American students made sense. The professors and my fellow students treated me—an obvious outsider—with respect and friendship. I learned so much about the roots of American music history and the social and political trends that shaped it.

At Belmont University, my intention was to learn all the business aspects of the music industry, from publishing to management. My goal was to have a career in music that made money, rather than just breaking even from occasional tours. When my professors found out about my background with Townes, they were impressed, surprised, and a little envious; they asked what the heck was I doing in school when the *real* education was "on the road." I was living the life they read and taught about. How, they asked, could college top that?

In time I realized they were right—making money couldn't compare to the joy I'd experienced living and touring with Townes, even though it had been (and would continue to be) quite maddening.

While I was in school, Townes's musical friends told me I was more than welcome to record their live shows. I recorded club gigs by Guy Clark, Steve Earle, David Olney, Steve Young, and others. Each time the sound demands were totally different, and the hands-on experience helped me tone up my skills in recording on the fly.

And then I got married for a second time. My new bride was a waitress at the Gold Rush bar in Nashville; two weeks into the marriage, I learned she was also an active cocaine dealer. I asked her to stop dealing, and she agreed . . . but, of course, she continued to sell drugs, and within a couple of months, we were divorced. This romantic episode convinced me that, for my own mental stability, it was time to stop dating wild and dangerous women, no matter how appealing they might be on the surface.

I still had to support myself, so I hit the bricks and walked up and down Music Row, going from office to office and applying for administrative work in publishing or management. I was invited for an interview with Patsy Bruce, the manager and wife of country singer-songwriter Ed Bruce. Patsy and Ed had co-written major chart hits such as Willie Nelson's "Mammas Don't Let Your Babies Grow Up to Be Cowboys" and Tanya Tucker's "Texas (When I Die)," and Ed was riding the crest of a series of his own Top 10 country chart hits and a co-starring television role with James Garner on NBC's *Bret Maverick*.

The interview went well, and Patsy hired me as Ed's road manager and as her assistant when we were not touring. "If you can handle working with Townes Van Zandt," she said, "then Ed will be no problem for you at all."

That was mostly accurate, and Ed certainly gave it his best shot. Though very talented as a performer and actor, he seemed to have difficulty dealing with the stress of sudden stardom.

One night, traveling on the band bus to a show, everyone was asleep except Ed, the driver, and me. We were speeding through the Arizona desert, and Ed started extolling at length his abilities as a songwriter. At *long* length.

Finally, he stopped and stared at me. "What do you think of that?" he asked.

I paused, then replied calmly, "I'm sorry, Ed. But when it comes to songwriting, you're not even close to Townes Van Zandt."

He jumped up, screaming. "Stop the bus!" The bus screeched to a halt, and he ordered me to get off in the middle of nowhere.

Not a problem.

I collected my things—including tour itinerary contacts, gig information, and the road cash of $20,000—and happily disembarked. As the bus disappeared out of sight, I wondered what nice sort of sporty road vehicle I might purchase for, say, under $20,000.

A few minutes later, here came the bus; the door opened, and Ed growled, "Get on and shut up." He didn't realize that after my exposure to Townes's extremes, he was a lightweight. No matter what he did, it wouldn't faze me a bit.

One positive aspect of the job was working with Patsy as her assistant. Her many business ventures crossed over into several music-related areas, and I learned quite a bit about the workings of the music industry in Nashville and internationally. Patsy was very influential on Music Row and had been president of the Nashville Songwriters Association International; she had served as a location and talent scout for *Urban Cowboy* and placed several songs in the film from her publishing company.

And interestingly, touring with Ed shed a bit of additional illumination on my understanding of Townes. When Ed did a show at the Double Eagle country music club in Oak Hill outside of Austin, I called Townes and invited him to stop by. He arrived while Ed and the band were inside doing sound check and asked if he could take a look inside the tour bus. I showed him around, and he walked slowly through the bus from the front to the rear, then back to the front as if lost in a private reverie.

Finally, he turned to me with a wistful gaze. "You know, H, if you had stayed working with me, this would be my bus."

It was a remark I hadn't expected, and it left me a little discomfited. We chatted some more, and Townes left before the show. Later that night, what he'd said hit me hard, and I am not ashamed to admit that I cried, thinking that if I had somehow been able to keep Townes on a regular tour schedule even after his departure from Tomato Records, it could have helped his career rise to the coveted private-bus level.

Ed's next gig was in Houston at Gilley's. My sister Nonie and her husband, Bruce Beard, brought their family to the show that night, and the first thing they asked was when I'd be going back to work with Townes. A week or so later, when Ed performed with Barbara Mandrell at the Washington State Fair in Puyallup, my sister Kathy and her husband, Mark Luckadoo, dropped by. They also asked about Townes and if I would be going back to working with him anytime soon.

It was the same whenever I spoke to my parents on the phone. "Tell Townes he is in our thoughts and prayers," they'd say. "And when are you going to be working together again?"

Clearly, the universe was sending me a message, in subtle and unsubtle ways. But for now, my responsibilities with Ed's organization were expanding. Renowned singer-songwriter Whitey Shafer was brought on to open Ed's road show. A talented pianist and guitarist, Whitey had written stellar country songs for George Jones, Merle Haggard, George Strait, Johnny Rodriguez, and Moe Bandy and co-written two monster hits—"That's the Way Love Goes" and "I Never Go Around Mirrors"— with Lefty Frizzell.

I spent a lot of miles and hours with Whitey on the tour bus, and we became friends. One day he told me that he wanted to stop opening for Ed and tour by himself. Coincidentally, at the same time he stopped working with Ed and Patsy, so did I; Whitey hired me to be his personal manager, which gave me a foothold in another part of the music business.

Whitey was a very nice person and a writer for Acuff-Rose Music in Nashville, one of the top country music publishers then and now. He arranged for me to meet with Wesley Rose, the firm's president and son of founder Fred Rose; I hoped to get some business advice on ways to boost Whitey's performing career.

Acuff-Rose had been formed in 1942 by old-time country music performer and Grand Ole Opry stalwart Roy Acuff and by Fred Rose, a 1920s and '30s pop songwriter who had played in the legendary Paul Whiteman jazz orchestra and then written several big movie songs for Gene Autry and one notable number for Acuff, "Blue Eyes Crying in the

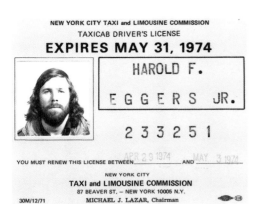

New York City, 1974, as I start my first venture into road managing my brother Kevin's artists.

Townes and I on our first tour, 1977.

From the 1978 *Flyin' Shoes* studio sessions: Townes's manager John Lomax III is center in hat and dark glasses. Above him is producer Chips Moman. Townes is just above to his left with wife Cindy Morgan. Philip Donnelly is the bearded fellow in front. I'm at top left taking it all in, with keyboardist Bobby Emmons to my left and guitarist Billy Earl McClelland opposite me at far right.

Two of my favorite Music City mentors: Whitey Shafer and Leona Williams, Nashville, 1986.

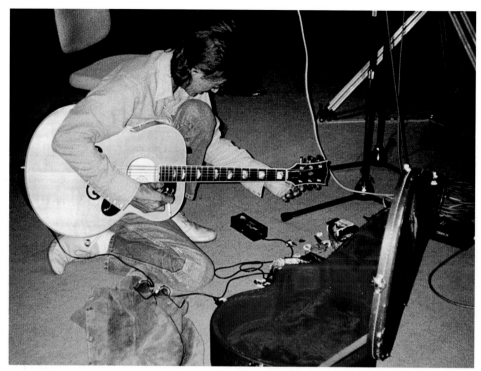

Tuning Mr. Guitar: an elaborate ritual.

Preshow: thinking positive thoughts, getting his mind right.

Postshow: after an especially emotional performance, I would often return backstage to find Townes in tears.

A soulful moment at the 1995 Mariposa Folk Festival, Toronto, Canada.

I doubt anyone enjoyed his jokes more than he did; he certainly told a lot of them.

His true home—onstage with guitar and audience.

Townes recording for his "newology" album at Pedernales Studio, Spicewood, Texas, 1990.

Townes onstage at Knust in Hamburg, where he played several times in the 1990s after Germany's reunification.

Willie Nelson's Farm Aid VI, April 24, 1993, Iowa State University, Ames, Iowa.

Townes and Larry Monroe recording interviews for audio CD *Documentary*, Austin, Texas, 1991.

Recording *No Deeper Blue* in Limerick, Ireland, 1993. *From left:* Donovan Leitch on harmonica, Townes, Sven Buick on bass, Philip Donnelly on guitar.

With the studio crew during the *No Deeper Blue* sessions, Limerick, Ireland.

Townes played a tasteful harmonica; he didn't play it often, though—it was another deep emotional well he tapped only now and then.

Performing to a standing crowd at the Borderline, London, England, December 3, 1996—his last live performance.

Townes with Alison Krauss at 1996 Cambridge Folk Festival, England.

From left: Me, Chas Cole (our U.K. booking agent), Townes, and singer-songwriter Michael Weston King, backstage at Ronnie Scott's, Birmingham, England, May 8, 1994.

Mickey Newbury was one of Townes's greatest early supporters; in February 1995, Townes and I visited Mickey's home in Springfield, Oregon.

Me, Rick Danko, and Townes relaxing before their show at Teatro Albatros di Rivarolo in Genova, Italy, December 1994.

Townes and I getting some final life lessons from blues master Brownie McGhee at his home in Oakland, California, shortly before Brownie's death in 1996.

"Grandfather Grunge" Townes with members of Mudhoney, 1994, who had recorded his "Buckskin Stallion Blues" with Jimmie Dale Gilmore on lead vocal.

A chance London, England, meeting with bluegrass great Peter Rowan in a "controlled zone." As Townes would have quipped: "Apparently not controlled enough."

From left: Me, Carla Torgeson, our European road manager Luc Wouters, Townes, and Chris Eckman. Carla and Chris were founding members of the Walkabouts, an American rock band from Seattle; they greatly admired Townes's music, and we met up with them in Germany.

Townes and Guy Clark performed many shows together. Here they are at the Texas Folklife Festival, San Antonio, Texas, August 1992.

Townes and Eric Andersen jamming, Italy, 1994.

Townes always appreciated local opening acts: this March 1995 show at the Tin Angel in Philadelphia, Pennsylvania, featured singer-songwriter Patsy Foster and her dad, Don Cogan.

Townes and I with Mary Costello, renowned BBC radio DJ, at the Borderline, London, England, his last live gig, December 3, 1996.

Townes and Irish singer-songwriter Mary Black, Belfast, 1994.

Townes and I with singer-songwriter Barb Donovan, Driskill Hotel, Austin, Texas, before Townes's performance at the 1993 Annual Jerry Jeff Walker Birthday Bash.

Courting danger wherever we could find it; on the docks in Galway, Ireland.

Townes with statue of *Den Dansk Pige* (*The Danish Girl*) by Gerhard Henning in Byparken, Bergen, Norway, November, 1994.

Visiting the National Shrine of Saint Thérèse of Lisieux, Juneau, Alaska, February 1995.

Townes enjoyed media interviews and public meet-and-greets; showing his goofy side at a record store in Edinburgh, Scotland, December 1994.

Backstage at McCabe's Guitar Shop, Santa Monica, California, with an old friend of Townes and Jack Clement. They were so happy to see each other, they danced around the room.

Before his show at Jazzhaus, Freiburg, Germany, November 25, 1994.

Townes and I with fans, Luc Wouters kneeling in front, before a concert in a castle at House of the Rising Sun, Pesina di Caprino Veronese, Verona, Italy. December 4, 1994.

On the street in Italy, we found ourselves in the company of a neon angel.

Townes and I goofing around on tour in Switzerland.

Sometimes Townes allowed his spirit to experience the awe of holy places; this is Cologne Cathedral, Germany.

Nothing like a bit of *sofortige Freundschaft* ("instant friendship"); Townes and a new fan backstage, Germany.

Three glimpses of "Bayou Self," Townes's final home in Mount Juliet, Tennessee: two outside with his dog, Feather, and an interior view that includes the fireplace that caused his broken hip in December 1996.

My Austin condo was the site for this 1995 family gathering. *Clockwise from left:* me, Townes, Kevin Eggers, dad Harold F. Eggers Sr., sister Nonie Beard, nephew Timmy Beard, mom Honora Eggers, and Cindy Soo holding our son, Harold III.

A joyous reunion Townes had predicted with my long-lost daughter, Megan East at my grandson Tristen's high school graduation, Harlingen, Texas, 2017; (from left) my granddaughter Cassidy, Megan, Tristen, me, granddaughter Ev, son-in-law Tyler East.

The High: a moment when the Angels were smiling with him.

The Low: battling the Black Ghosts.

The In Between: on the road, headed for the next town.

Rain," which later became a monster hit for Willie Nelson. Acuff-Rose became a serious player in the publishing field when they took on Hank Williams at the start of his illustrious songwriting career in the late 1940s.

Acuff-Rose had its publishing headquarters and a recording studio on Franklin Road. Wesley Rose offered me an office and use of the phones and secretaries. I immediately accepted this generous offer, along with Mr. Rose's suggestion that Whitey should record a single and an album in the Acuff-Rose studio for distribution on our own Palatial Records label.

And just like that, I was a music industry executive.

Whitey recorded two songs we put out on a burgundy-colored 45 rpm disc, Palatial P-001: side A, "Hi Yo Leon (And the Horse You Rode In On)" and side B, "Honky Tonk Amnesia."

These songs fell into the "novelty" category, but their authorial pedigree was highly distinguished—Whitey wrote "Hi Yo Leon" with Dallas Frazier and collaborated with A.L. Owens on "Honky Tonk Amnesia." Acuff-Rose song plugger Ronnie Gant served as producer with Whitey, and we hired a promotion guy to work the radio stations. The single did get a lot of airplay and sold pretty well, but never broke out big on the charts.

We then recorded the album *Whitey*, combining songs he had written with Lefty Frizzell and other songs of his that had scored previous successes for other artists. We issued it on cassette instead of vinyl, with the idea that it could be more easily circulated, and thus either picked up by a major record label or heard by other publishers and recording artists who might want to use individual songs. Acuff-Rose paid for the recordings made in their studio, along with the manufacturing costs and promotional efforts.

The Acuff-Rose affiliation gave me a serious degree of credibility in Nashville. And I was acquiring even more detailed knowledge of the music industry's actual business workings.

While working with Ronnie Gant, his girlfriend asked if I'd like to be on the VIP guest list for the Grand Ole Opry. The girlfriend was

Lorrie Morgan, a future superstar who had just become the youngest singer ever to join the Grand Ole Opry. "I'll leave your name on the regular list," she said. "That way you can come when you want and wander backstage with everyone."

My first Opry experience was pure rapture.

I sat right onstage in the old wooden church pews behind the performers. At that time I was a long-haired hippie who had never had much interest in the Porter Wagoners and Little Jimmy Dickenses of the world. But now, watching the entire Opry experience live from beginning to end, I was moved to tears. There was something so poignant, so noble, so *real* about this music. I truly felt as if I'd been in the midst of a religious service.

I attended every week for months, hearing and meeting the past, present, and future of country music. Backstage was a scene unlike any other I'd ever witnessed. Lorrie would come over and give me a hug and introduce me to the Opry family of artists and musicians she was talking with. I still recall one particular night when Lorrie and Whitey were performing together as one of the best musical memories of my life.

Whitey had suggested that whenever I was in my office at Acuff-Rose, I should drop in from time to time to the upstairs room where Wesley Rose and the song pluggers played pool each day. I did, and gradually came to know Mr. Rose to the extent that he gave me an open invitation to visit him in his office. He probably enjoyed having a new listener who hadn't heard his old stories; for me, it was a personal lesson in American music history from a wise professor.

"In this business, you can go from the bottom to the top very quickly," he told me. "You just have to keep trying." It was one of the best pieces of motivational advice I've ever received in my career.

One day while visiting in his office, he asked me if I would like to hear the recording he was most proud of working on. Sure, I said, assuming it would be a staid country-music classic. To my complete surprise, he put on a 45 record titled "Bread and Butter," the 1964 million-selling pop hit by the Newbeats, and proceeded to dance around the office singing along: "I like bread and butter, I like toast and jam." It was surreal and absolutely enjoyable to watch this buttoned-down, gray-haired music business titan grooving out in front of me.

In the 1980s, the Nashville music establishment undertook a major educational focus, using seminars and workshops to boost networking and gain new clients. It seemed like nearly every week some organization hosted an event featuring top publishers, managers, songwriters, agents, publicists, producers, studio engineers, and other industry operatives. I would attend these, and whenever Mr. Rose was on a panel, he would inevitably spot me in the audience and wave me up to sit next to him onstage.

My personal stock ascended, and I was happy to receive increased recognition in the music community. However, there was a downside. I lost count of the songwriters, musicians, agents, and managers who came by my office bearing gifts of recreational drugs, apparently with thoughts of being introduced to Mr. Rose and securing a foothold in Acuff-Rose. I was immediately up-front about telling them I had no ability to advance their interests in that matter. But, times being what they were, they kept bringing me drugs, and I kept accepting them. And ingesting them. I became very thin, and my eyes sank into their sockets with dark rings around them—the basic drug-addled raccoon look popular among music types in the 1980s.

That's a part of the business you might not hear about elsewhere. But as I write this, I hear Townes's voice in my mind: "Tell the truth, no matter what. Do not whitewash anything."

During this time I was talking regularly to my friend Susie Nelson, and I suggested she do a book about growing up with her dad, Willie Nelson. Susie did write the book, and I have no doubt that the personal mentorship and endorsement I received from Wesley Rose aided in my securing a publishing deal for her *Heart Worn Memories: A Daughter's Personal Biography of Willie Nelson*. Later I would serve as literary manager for Keri Leigh's biography *Stevie Ray: Soul to Soul* and Alan Mayor's *The Nashville Family Album: A Country Music Scrapbook*.

While I was widening my circle of contacts in the Nashville music milieu, Townes was having little commercial success in Austin. His songwriting production had waned, and his few live gigs featured erratic performances. Even so, it seemed to me that Townes was determined to get his life and music career back on track. His marriage in 1983 to his third wife, Jeanene, and the birth of their son, Will, were stabilizing forces that helped him through this fallow period.

In early 1985, I read in the newspaper that Townes was slated to perform in a few weeks at a Nashville club, 12th & Porter. I called him and asked if he wanted me to get involved in promoting his show around town. "You bet, H," was his immediate response. "Appreciate it."

I set to work creating posters, soliciting media attention, and spreading word through my Music Row network. Basically, I did what I always did: my best to make the music happen. I had no idea this chance encounter would reunite Townes and me as business partners and road companions.

Or that it would turn out to be, as the stubbornly serendipitous universe would have it, the best thirty-fifth birthday present I could ever get.

7

All Trails Lead to Townes

I GUESS you could say that, even though Nashville didn't fully accept Townes Van Zandt, they certainly did admire him there.

The Nashville music establishment saw him as an outsider, an eccentric poet-type who wrote to his own rhyme and meter and could never be properly reined in to produce consistently formulaic songs for the mainstream country market. He could always gin up interesting press and an occasional offbeat hit for a more established artist, but his own records weren't going to set country radio on fire.

So it made perfect sense that Townes's first album in seven years would be commissioned by a new bluegrass-based label, Sugar Hill Records of Durham, North Carolina. And it would be produced by Jack Clement and Jim Rooney at Jack's Cowboy Arms Studio in Nashville.

When Townes and I spoke about his upcoming 12th & Porter show, he talked at length about this new album, sounding enthusiastic and motivated—two states of mind I hadn't associated with our conversations in quite a while. The one-night performance at the small songwriter's club would serve as a tune-up for Townes and accompanists Donny Silverman and Mickey White, who would be backing him on the Cowboy Arms Studio session.

I had a sudden flash of inspiration. "Would you want me to see if I can get a live recording for you?"

He replied instantly. "Sure, H. Why not?"

I arranged for the show to be recorded by veteran Nashville engineer Jack "Stack-A-Track" Grochmal. He brought a basic sound truck with a mobile recording unit, parked it outside the club, and ran direct lines from the truck to the stage microphones; as a backup, he recorded the show inside the club on a reel-to-reel at the soundboard.

In the weeks prior to the show, I had a poster designed and printed. I spent hours hanging copies all over Nashville, especially up and down Music Row, where it would be seen not only by record-label moguls but also by any up-and-coming artist roaming the avenues (as I had done in years past) looking for some career inspiration.

I asked a leading music writer, Robert K. Oermann, if he would help spread word; he responded with a terrific advance article in the widely read "Showcase Magazine" section of *The Tennessean*. Under the headline "'Poet Laureate of Texas' Rambles into Music City," virtually every sentence of the piece hammered home the point that this show was a major musical event not to be missed.

I arranged for my friend and top-ranked Nashville music photographer Alan Mayor to document the evening. And I called my friend Susie Nelson to see if she wanted to sit in with Townes on a few songs.

When Townes arrived at the club just before the show, I was outside the front door. The window blinds were shut, and the walls and door were thick enough that you couldn't tell by sound how full the club was inside. He greeted me with a sideways glance. "You know, H, I sure hope somebody's coming to see us tonight," he said.

He opened the door, peered inside at the standing-room-only crowd, and looked at me and smiled. "Thanks, friend. You got it done."

Of all the sincere compliments Townes had paid me through our years together, I don't think I'd ever felt such pride as I did at that moment.

The room was filled with Townes's people. Nashville's top producers and engineers, songwriters, and performers were there: Rosanne Cash, Rodney Crowell, Guy and Susanna Clark, Steve Young, Neil Young, Bee Spears, John Prine, Jack Clement, and so many more.

It was a gala "Welcome Back, Townes" party, and you would have thought Hank Williams Sr. himself had risen and returned to do one last show. As Townes moved through his set with expert backing from Mickey on guitar and Donny on flute and sax, you could hear a pin drop—until each song ended, when the applause and cheers nearly blew off the roof.

As we listened to the audio Stack-A-Track had recorded, it was clear he'd caught something magical. Townes gave me the go-ahead to put together an album, and with Austin engineer Stephen Mendell co-producing and offering stellar guidance, that's what we did. The result was forty-two minutes and forty-eight seconds of vintage Townes, showcasing the most compelling live performance he'd done in years.

Live and Obscure was issued on the English label Heartland Records in 1987. Shortly after, the album Townes had been recording that summer with Jack Clement and Jim Rooney appeared as *At My Window* on Sugar Hill Records. In 1989, Sugar Hill would lease *Live and Obscure* and greatly increase the album's distribution.

Both albums received overwhelmingly positive reviews and were heralded by the music press as evidence of a bona fide "comeback" for Townes. Bringing *Live and Obscure* to full vinyl life from an offhand suggestion was a very fulfilling moment in my music career. Townes and I became full-fledged business partners; we split the ownership and profits, and that was unheard of in the music industry. Artists do not share half their recording revenue with anyone, no way, never. But we did.

Today I look back and realize how much Townes believed in me. I would go on to negotiate, with Townes's advice and approval, all the lease deals for the albums we owned together. We did six albums together when he was alive. I would compile tracks of the best of the live recordings I'd done over the years, then get him to listen and pick the keepers; he would listen to only one playing of each song, and then would approve or disapprove the final track list.

We discussed what recordings he wanted me to use in the future, in case he died. Since his death, I have succeeded in releasing another ten albums of his live material with a two-album set ready for issue.

A few months after *Live and Obscure* and *At My Window* were released, Austin documentary filmmaker Hank Sinatra and I videotaped Townes performing solo late at night in a Houston, Texas, hotel room. Issued in 2004 on Varèse Sarabande as *Houston 1988: A Private Concert,* the DVD earned rave reviews and showed Townes reflecting pensively on his life and music.

Somehow, everything I had done over the last few years had led back to working with Townes. Though we lived a thousand miles apart, I had kept in touch with him in one capacity or another and was still able to occasionally help out with advice and gig leads. Now that he was stepping back into the groove of regular public performing, the knowledge and contacts I had acquired in my Music Row phase were going to prove useful.

I do not recall asking myself at the time whether resuming the responsibilities of a road manager, coupled with the new challenges of a business partnership, was a wise decision. If I had, I might well have decided it wasn't. After all, I was working with solid, award-winning musicians and writers backed by major publishers and record labels. Why risk that kind of stability to backtrack, so to speak, to my nomadic motel-and-pickup days?

Throughout my life, I've always been a person who has sought a strong measure of closure, in my personal and business dealings. I've sought it, but admittedly, rarely found it. Yet it doesn't mean I don't keep searching. Subconsciously, I must have felt I had something to finish with Townes—a circuit that needed to be completed, a milestone that had to be reached.

That first Townes tour had not just been something for me to do while mending a broken heart. It had shown me a whole new type of music, a whole new way of creating music. The bond Townes and other singer-songwriters like him forged with their live listeners every time they performed was beyond hypnotic; their songs spoke to a precious and passionate part of the human soul.

And it showed me a whole new type of me. I wanted to be part of that mystical musical transaction, as a recipient and as a provider. Preparing for the next tour, I fervently believed the music of Townes Van Zandt was going to turn heads, bend ears, even save a few lives like never before.

For both of us, the last several years had been a tunnel of fire. We'd passed through the flames getting singed, maybe, but not scorched. The immaturity and indecision that had hindered our success in the past had been burnt away. Destiny had something big in store for us, and we needed to get back to working together again to claim it.

There was a lot to do. Who knew how much time we'd have to get it done?

8

Back on the Road, Back on the Edge

THE 1987 RELEASE of *Live and Obscure* and *At My Window* marked an upswing in Townes's musical fortunes that carried through the next decade. For an artist whose personal life was so completely intertwined with his musical fortunes, this was very good news.

Townes moved to Nashville and started to write and tour more actively. His songs were being recorded by an increasing number of artists in the country, folk, and rock fields. The mainstream music world was finally becoming more open to his style and vision, and he made numerous guest appearances on recordings by up-and-coming Texas musicians who had been inspired by his music and were now starting to get their own major-label record deals and national tours.

As I had since our first tour, I continued to record soundboard tapes of every live Townes performance at which I was present. The tapes from a series of his 1977–1981 performances would yield six albums, including the highly acclaimed *Rear View Mirror* and *Roadsongs*, nominated for Best Folk Album by the Nashville Music Awards. A track from *Roadsongs* would appear in the Coen brothers' 1998 cult hit *The Big Lebowski* (and on its soundtrack), earning him enormous posthumous visibility and credibility.

And in 1991–92, we began putting together a unique spoken-word and music CD documentary titled, appropriately, *Documentary*, which featured Townes singing ten of his favorite songs and telling stories about their connection to his life in interviews with renowned Austin radio producer Larry Monroe. *Documentary* would not be released until 1997, a few months after Townes's death, and it stands as an insightful summary of his career.

Besides the tremendous variety of material, all of these live tapes offered great insight into the evolution of Townes's performing style over the decades. And he was, indeed, charting a new course and on the move again.

In May and June of 1990, he opened for the popular Canadian band Cowboy Junkies on their North American tour of major theater and festival venues. In September, he embarked on a nine-show tour of New Zealand and Australia, followed by five weeks of shows in England, Ireland, Germany, the Netherlands, Norway, and Switzerland—his first tour in Europe, where he would find a second performing home with ever-increasing audiences over the next few years.

Townes's two months with Cowboy Junkies constituted one of the best collaborative experiences he ever had. He rode the band bus and wrote a song about the band, "Cowboy Junkies Lament." The good feelings were reciprocal, and the band returned the lyrical favor with a composition titled "Townes' Blues," released on their 1992 *Black Eyed Man* album, along with a cover of Townes's "To Live Is to Fly."

Sadly, one collaboration that did not take place was a planned European tour featuring Townes and Blaze Foley, after I secured a Heartland Records deal for Blaze. In early 1989, he was shot to death in a family dispute.

In Nashville, the country music industry had emphatically changed course during the late 1980s. The new sound was a genre variously dubbed "new country," "neo-traditional country," or "Americana"—basically, it promoted performers with a "roots" approach that incorporated stylistic elements from country music's early years. The music of Townes Van Zandt fit perfectly.

In December 1991, Townes was invited to perform at a benefit for the West Nashville Family Shelter, the annual Gift of the Heart gala concert organized by Emmylou Harris for homeless children. It featured a galaxy of country music stars. Jonell Mosser and her band went on before Townes and did a terrific set; as Townes ascended the stage, he quipped, "I don't think I can compete with a band, but I'll give it a go."

He didn't have to worry about holding the audience's attention. He launched into "Marie," his tragic narrative of a homeless man and woman, and for the next five minutes, it seemed as if nobody in that auditorium took a breath. He strummed the final chord, said thank you, and walked offstage as the audience roared.

We noticed that Bob Dylan had taken to opening his show with "Pancho and Lefty." The only lyric he changed was in the line "Living on the road, my friend." In Dylan's performance it was "Living on the edge, my friend." I can't think that edit was anything other than intentional and a tribute by a fellow master songwriter to Townes's unyielding commitment to his art.

Once again, we were living on that edge. To the max.

When it was just the two of us traveling, and Townes was sinking into a deep depression, he would attempt to exorcise the demons by repeating the chorus from the old Robert Johnson number "Stop Breakin' Down Blues," revived by the Rolling Stones on their *Exile on Main St.* album: "Stop breaking down, stop breaking down, stop breaking down . . . "—a steady, calming mantra he would intone for minutes at a time, as if trying to get himself to listen to what he was saying. He would throw off a look that said, "This is a private conversation; don't even think about saying anything." I would listen and not even glance at him while this was going on, until he went completely quiet. Then he'd look over at me with an expression that I interpreted as: "Thanks for minding your own business, friend."

It was an unspoken pact between us, a matter of respecting each other's private demons and what they caused us to do at times. As I continued to learn more about Townes, he trusted me more and more, until I learned what was really going on. Gradually, he knew all I was concealing from people and the world, and I knew the same of his demons. I covered his back door, and he covered mine. He relied on me, as I did him, for these moments of psychic sanctuary.

To redirect Townes back to present reality, I would say something funny, and usually, he would laugh and return from wherever he was mentally. But then there were times he would not come back at all, but remain silent, staring off into space.

For example, he would say ominously, "The room is filling up with ghosts."

I would reply, "Are there any pretty girl ghosts amongst them?"

"H, you better watch it. If there is any woman ghost here, she will slap your face!" Then he would laugh, and the "spell" would be broken.

If he was in a bad mood in the morning and we were packing up to leave the motel room, I would say, "What a beautiful day, eh?"

"If you like days," he'd scowl.

"You stay in a daze."

Likely as not he'd chuckle. "You're right, let's get out of this rat hole."

Speaking of rat holes . . .

Once after a tour, Townes asked me to drop him off at the Sailor Inn, an old run-down motel in downtown Nashville. He planned to isolate himself for a week or so to write new songs. In the many years I worked with Townes, he never wrote or composed a song in my presence or anyone else's, except the very few occasions he deliberately co-wrote with Susanna Clark, Mickey Newbury, or the like.

"Do you want me to call and check on you?" I asked.

"No, just drop by now and then to see if I'm alive."

When I did show up and give a knock, he wouldn't open the door. I heard a muffled, shaky voice say, "I'm alive, thanks," and nothing more. I came back three times that week, and the sequence was repeated.

On the eighth day of his sabbatical, I knocked, and the door opened. He was standing, his guitar and travel bag at the ready. "Let's get outta this rat hole," he said. We got in my car, and not another word was said between us until I dropped him off at his cabin outside Nashville. He looked at me, staring through my head, and said, "H, don't ever lose yourself."

I drove off knowing he appreciated me not asking. I learned in time that his silence and stare spoke volumes of the unknown.

When Townes felt the need for a longer period of seclusion, he would hide out in his apartment at Nashville's infamous "Rock 'n' Roll Hotel" on 20th Avenue South, just off Music Row. As the Close Quarters Hotel back in the 1970s and '80s, it had been a popular spot for major touring acts from ABBA and Kiss to Rod Stewart and the Allman Brothers and had earned a well-deserved reputation as a poster child for rock 'n' roll excess (alluded to in Bobby Bare's "Rock and Roll Hotel" on his 1980 *Drunk & Crazy* album).

It was now undergoing full renovation. Most of the first floor outside was gutted, with exposed steel beams showing. The elevator and inside stairs were shut down. Townes was living in an apartment on the third floor in the middle of the building. The only way to the second floor and above was via a rusted, dilapidated metal fire escape with narrow stairs attached tentatively to the side of the building. I would have to yell up to Townes from the ground below his apartment; he would go down the hall to open the steel fire door, as I ascended the fire escape, which rattled and swayed with each step and was extra treacherous after a rain made the metal slippery. Each time the fire door slammed shut, the whole building shook, and the ceilings in each apartment would drizzle clouds of dust and paint.

Aside from Townes and Guy Clark, who kept an apartment in the building with just a bed, chair, and desk for when he would stay over in town, the other tenants were a true motley crew of social misfits: drug dealers, folks with mental illness, and a few active criminals, one of whom would be convicted of suffocating his parents for insurance money some years later.

Townes, however, enjoyed the offbeat camaraderie and possible sources of stories for new songs; to avoid going down the dangerous fire escape, he had his hotelmates fetch vodka and food he paid for and shared with them. Sometimes he would go out for a meal and take several neighbors with him. I estimate he was spending between $1,000 to $1,500 a month on these outings, in addition to his apartment rent.

Besides the generally depressive atmosphere, the surroundings were a physical hazard to Townes's health. At one point, he suffered from a serious respiratory ailment that just wouldn't improve and was putting him into a deep psychological tailspin. Guy Clark called me in Austin and asked if I would come to Nashville to help Townes get back on some kind of normal track. I came up and stayed in Guy's apartment at the hotel for a couple of weeks, running off some of the most noxious residents and getting Townes to eat some and drink less.

Still, his breathing was getting worse, so he was taken to Vanderbilt University Medical Center and hospitalized. A week's worth of testing ran up a bill of around $30,000 and determined that the best way to avoid what he was going through was for Townes to pull up on his drinking, eat more nutritionally, live in a less toxic environment, and take better overall care of himself.

Easier said than done, as anyone who knew Townes would tell you.

Every so often I would ask Townes, "Why don't you worry more about the way you live your life?" He'd always reply with a laugh, "Why should I, when everyone else does the worrying for me?"

Guy Clark was one of Townes's oldest and closest friends, and he always made me feel welcome. Whenever he would see Townes and me, he'd say, "Here come the Bobbsey Twins!" One time Guy asked me to go to dinner, just the two of us. "Harold," he asked, "would you be up for working with me? Going on the road for my tours?"

I was flattered, of course, to be asked by an artist of Guy's stature. But I didn't respond right away, and he leaned over and said very seriously, "Harold, how can you stay in the same room with Townes Van Zandt? You have been doing this for years, man. I'm his friend, too, but it would wear me out. How do you put up with it?"

I don't remember giving a definite answer. But if Guy were to ask me this question today—and I sometimes wish he could, because that would mean he were still with us—my answer would be that you don't sweat the small stuff. Having grown up in a family of five siblings, I was no stranger to squabbling or bad moods. And military service left me with the ability to routinize almost any sort of irrational behavior. Being around Townes and his intense ways became second nature to me. Gradually, in time I acclimated to his bizarre thoughts and manner of dealing with everyday life.

I learned this in Vietnam: You can't control what you can't control.

Both Townes and I were wounded in our separate ways. For me, working with Townes was like reliving the war. A part of me thought that, if I could get things with Townes to end up right, I would atone to some degree for what had happened during my time overseas.

That might have been another thing that bonded us as friends, come to think of it. I never turned my back on him, ever. I had to see *him* through the battle, because I was convinced he would do—and was doing, in his own peculiar way—the same for *me*.

Just before our first Irish tour, I'd heard that my ex-wife Joan and my daughter Megan had moved to Ireland. At this point, I had not seen or heard from either in fifteen years, since Megan was two. The pain of separation from my daughter had not diminished, despite the passage of time.

On the flight over, the notion took root in my mind that at any given performance, a teenage Megan might possibly be in the audience—and I would have no way of identifying her. Nor would she even suspect I was connected with the performer onstage.

The notion grew into an obsession, and Townes finally said to me, "H, you have to stop tormenting yourself. Your daughter knows you love her, and one day you will see her again."

Consequently, during every show that tour, Townes would announce: "Is Megan Eggers in the audience tonight?"

No one ever stepped forward. Audience members, naturally, didn't have a clue about what was going on. And it would be years later before I did see my daughter again—not at an Irish pub, but at her high school graduation in Harlingen, Texas. But that Townes would make the effort to connect me with my child—while allaying my anxiety—was a powerful commentary on our relationship. (This year, 2017, I attended a second graduation at Harlingen High: Megan's son—my grandson—Tristen's, with my granddaughters Ev and Cassidy and Megan's husband, Tyler East, in attendance. All through the day, I felt Townes smiling down on me, feeling him at peace knowing I had finally found my own peace with my family.)

Traveling with Townes was like wandering through the thickest of fogs, not able to see ahead or behind you, always in a welter of confusion—you simply learned to enjoy the unknown. Chaos and disruption were the tactics he used to maintain a semblance of control and keep people from getting too close. His moods would change quicker than the weather in Texas, like a violent tornado that appeared out of nowhere, smashing everything apart and just as quickly departing. Even when he wasn't moving, Townes's brain never stopped.

But sometimes there seemed to be a method of sorts to his madness.

Once in front of a packed house, Townes was playing and crying while he sang. It was an incredibly emotional performance. The club owner came to me with a complaining fan in tow and said, "Man, you've got to take this guy to the hospital!"

"What for?" I asked.

"He's having a breakdown on the stage. He's crying. He's breaking down in front of the audience."

"That's Townes Van Zandt," I replied. "If you can't stand the heat, leave."

The fan protested. "How can you be so cruel? You need to take him to the hospital right now!"

I handed him the truck key. "You take him to the hospital, and I'll meet you there. I'm going to have dinner."

The show went on. I don't believe I was callous or uncaring. But by then, anyone attending a Townes show should have known that if you couldn't handle his heat, you should get out of the kitchen. I still believe that. Taking him offstage was not an option. He's up there singing a song, and he's crying. That's Townes Van Zandt to the bare-wire core. Now the audience can say they saw something even more amazing than what they came for.

In point of fact, most of Townes's performances were spot-on and mesmerizing, even when he might be under the weather or at a low physical ebb. If he had regularly put on poor shows, he could never have toured so much, especially in the later years. Many of his bookings were re-bookings with venues that were very satisfied with his work. Also, he was represented by top-echelon booking agents in the U.S. (Keith Case

& Associates) and in Europe (Berthold Seliger), who would have felt no reluctance in dropping him if he'd proved anything less than a productive asset.

On occasion, Townes would himself prove to be a veritable personal lifeline.

In 1994 in Europe, he played several shows with Rick Danko, a founding member of the famed rock group the Band. Acclaimed singer-songwriter Eric Andersen and ace Norwegian musician Jonas Fjeld were on the tour with Rick, and Lubbock, Texas, musician Joe Ely played two nights also. Rick and Townes got along very well, and Rick proposed both of them record an album together at Rick's studio in Woodstock, New York. A few minor details would have to be ironed out, of course.

I had a glimpse of those details while we were all in Italy together. Late one night in the hotel, we awoke to loud knocking and a man's frantic voice asking us to let him in. I opened the door, and Eric Andersen was there, saying that Rick had run out of heroin and was going into severe withdrawal. Townes gave Eric a full bottle of vodka and a handful of ibuprofen. "Have Rick drink the vodka and take several of the pills," advised Townes. "It will calm him down."

An hour or two later, Eric returned and reported that Townes's homemade therapy had worked. For the next few days, Townes helped Rick get through his temporary detox with vodka, ibuprofen, and good old-fashioned emotional support from a fellow habitué.

"Wouldn't you know," he said wryly, "I save Rick's life, and he drank up all my vodka."

Even so, it was another example of that special compassion I witnessed among Townes and his musical colleagues struggling to find their way through dark passages.

A recording venture with Rick Danko and his galaxy of Woodstock friends would have been a very interesting collaboration. My concern was that, as an unintended result, Townes might start to use heroin again, which he had successfully avoided for a long time. Still, the recording remained a possibility we discussed frequently, though in the ensuing

months, Rick's own health problems would limit his musical productiv-
ity.

Sometimes we caught a good break. In 1995, Townes and I were held
by custom officials at the Toronto airport en route to the Mariposa Folk
Festival, where he was headlining; it seemed that Townes had an out-
standing Canadian court fine he'd neglected to pay from some years
past. The festival liaison meeting us at the airport went to the officials
and showed them a copy of the daily newspaper, with a big festival ad
featuring a photo of Townes. They allowed us to go through.

Another time, Townes got stopped for speeding on a highway. He had
no license or identification on him, but said, "I'm a musician, and I've got
one of my albums with my picture on it. Will that work?"

The policeman took the album, went back to his car, and conferred
with his partner. A few minutes later, both officers returned and asked
Townes to get out of his car. Townes thought for sure he was going to
be arrested.

The cops laughed and said, "If you're the guy that wrote 'Pancho
and Lefty,' we want to shake your hand." Their dispatch handles and
nicknames for one another were Pancho and Lefty. Townes shook their
hands and drove away saying, "Thank you, God, for giving me this
song!" Truly, Townes had a guardian angel who traveled with him, and
had been alert and on duty that day.

There were also instances of absolutely heartfelt kindness on the road.

In December 1994, Tulane University history professor and celebrated
presidential scholar Douglas Brinkley booked a gig for Townes at the
renowned Maple Leaf Bar, a jazz and R&B hot spot in New Orleans's
Carrollton neighborhood. Dr. Brinkley's appreciation of Townes
stemmed from his own extensive scholarship on American music, which
included articles on Bob Dylan, Chuck Berry, Willie Nelson, and Levon
Helm, and his discovery of Woody Guthrie's long-lost novel *House of
Earth*, which Brinkley co-published with Johnny Depp.

The professor had his class attend the show and—as a total surprise
for Townes—flew in Ramblin' Jack Elliott, one of Townes's oldest music
friends, to perform with him. Townes was overwhelmed by the generos-

ity and consideration; he and Jack put on a terrific show the Tulane students likely never anticipated would be part of their course curriculum.

Dr. Brinkley put us up at a deluxe French Quarter hotel, and the next morning, Jack somehow got Townes to go swimming in the hotel pool. Townes was pathologically shy about being seen in shorts, but once in the water, he and Jack frolicked like little kids.

In the 1990s, my parents had retired to Blanco, Texas, about fifty miles west of Austin, to enjoy their golden years in a warmer climate and be near my sister Nonie and her family. At one point, Townes and I were passing close by, and Townes suggested we stop in and say hello. Mom cooked a great dinner, and my dad shared stories from his forty-plus years at the telephone company and union. "Mr. Eggers," Townes said to him, "you inspire me as my mother and father did."

As shy as Townes could often be, I never failed to notice that when he was with older people, he was typically attentive and sought to draw them out in conversation. I believe these moments might have triggered a flashback to his own parents, who still occupied a major part of his daily memories.

Then Townes announced, "Now that you live in Texas, folks, you need to learn how to mosey."

The lesson in Texas moseying consisted of Townes walking with my parents from the living room to the front door. Townes would take a step, then talk with my dad for five minutes, take another step, then talk to my mom for five minutes, and repeat this process two or three more times. When we finally reached the front door a half hour after starting, Townes gave my mom a hug and kiss, shook my dad's hand, and announced, "There you go, Mr. and Mrs. Eggers. I just showed you how to mosey."

In between tours, I'd met a wonderful lady, Cindy Soo, whom I would grow to love and admire. After looking for true love in many wrong places, it seemed entirely fitting I would find it at last in a South Austin recording studio.

Townes and I had dropped by Charlie Hollis's MARS Studio to deliver his *Roadsongs* album tracks for mixing. By chance, the young female manager of country fiddler Randy Crouch was in the office, and I was immediately enchanted.

Cindy was a beautiful Chinese-American woman and Houston native whose career treks through advertising, publishing, community organizing, facilities management, and accounting had brought her to Austin, where she was gaining a foothold in the local music industry. When Townes and I left the studio, he cajoled me to give her a call and ask if she would go on a date.

I did, she would, and twenty-five years later, she is very dear to me, and we are immensely proud of our talented musician/artist/innovator son, Harold III. A longtime employee at the *Austin Chronicle*, Cindy was an angel then, especially whenever my frustrations with Townes consumed me; she was a true guiding light.

Townes and I talked often about our families. When I would leave to go on tour, my baby son would wrap his arms around my leg and sit on my foot, saying, "Daddy, please don't go!" Townes would see this and say, "H, it's heartbreaking to leave our families to tour, but it is what we do; wish we could somehow bring comfort to those we leave at home."

Townes was very proud of his children: John (born 1969) with his first wife, Fran Petters, and Will (born 1983) and Katie Belle (born 1992) with Jeanene. "You know," he'd say, "I wish I could be a normal dad." Wishes don't become fishes, though, and he knew that the demands of his working life weren't going to permit normal parenting.

Even so, when he and Jeanene divorced in 1994 after eleven years of marriage, Townes signed over all of his songwriting and publishing rights to his family. He said this made him proud he was still able to be a provider, despite the ongoing vicissitudes of his professional life.

Perhaps the most unique project we undertook in the late 1980s was putting together a new anthology—a "newology," my brother Kevin would later call it—of Townes recording updated versions of his favorite songs from his earlier albums, just his voice and his guitar.

I phoned Kevin and asked if Tomato Records would be interested. Initially he declined, but I had a feeling the idea intrigued him. How could it not? Kevin had been so committed to Townes at the start of his career, I knew he'd have an interest in a new, updated project that would spotlight Townes's artistic growth over the years.

Next, I called Pete Flanagan, president of London's Heartland Records; he agreed, but it took a lengthy time to get the contract ironed out. Then my brother called me and asked if he could have another shot. I discussed it with Townes; it seemed the deal with Heartland was wavering, so Townes and I decided to sell it to Kevin's Tomato label. Heartland concurred, cutting their initial risk with the possibility of distributing the finished work later.

With Tomato's involvement, the concept grew from Townes and Mr. Guitar to a star-studded cast encompassing a three-CD set containing sixty new recordings of Townes's songs—each one intended to be a vocal duet with Townes and some of the biggest artists in the world spanning multiple musical genres. Kevin made plans to record the album at the new, state-of-the-art Fire Station Studios in San Marcos, Texas. The final cuts would be mastered at Willie Nelson's Pedernales Recording Studio in Spicewood, Texas.

Twenty of the numbers would employ the blues-based Fats Domino band, twenty would be arranged in a Tex-Mex style with Ruben Ramos & The Texas Revolution, twenty would be set in a country-folk vein with top Austin session pickers. Bob Dylan, Neil Young, Van Morrison, B.B. King, George Jones, Tammy Wynette, Johnny Cash, Tanya Tucker, Tony Bennett, Ray Charles, Beck, and Bono were among the artists invited for duet duty.

I was the project manager, with Kevin producing, Stephen Mendell engineering, and guitarist John Inmon as bandleader organizing the sidemen. Veteran record producer and former Columbia Records— Nashville head Bob Johnston was brought in as well, to contribute his sage advice and inevitable inspiration.

Besides the household names, efforts were made to include some newly emerging talent from the Central Texas scene. Jimmy LaFave was an Austin-based singer-songwriter who had a strong affinity for Townes's material and was, curiously, a native of Van Zandt County. I had gotten

his demo album, *Highway Angels . . . Full Moon Rain* to Kevin's attention, which resulted in Jimmy's first record deal with Tomato. For the
newology project, Jimmy was slated to record "Snowin' on Raton," but
then Freddy Fender dropped by the studio unexpectedly that day. Jimmy
was bumped and, unfortunately, never rescheduled.

By early 1990, all of the rhythm-track recordings were mixed, along
with a dozen or so duets by Willie Nelson, Emmylou Harris, Freddy
Fender, Doug Sahm, Jerry Jeff Walker, and others; but the project had
exceeded budget and was put on hold until more money could be raised
to finish it.

Twelve of the tracks finally made it to disc in 2001, on *Texas Rain*
(Tomato Records). Townes's singing partners on this record included
Emmylou Harris, Freddy Fender, Calvin Russell, Jerry Jeff Walker, Wil-
lie Nelson, Kimmie Rhodes, James McMurtry, Ruben Ramos, Doug
Sahm, and Kathy Mattea, with instrumental backup by Augie Meyers,
Gene Elders, Ernie Durawa, James Fenner, and Riley Osborne, and
additional accents by the Texas Revolution horns and the Chromatics
vocal backup group.

Throughout the project, Townes was as happy as I'd ever seen him.
"H, the winds of change have finally come," he said. "This could be what
will put me in the big time at last." I roomed with Townes in the motel,
as if we were on tour, and he stayed completely straight from start to
finish. Minimal drinking, no drugging, no disruptive episodes; whatever ghosts and demons might have been swirling around him remained
remarkably well behaved.

Performance-wise, I think these recordings were some of Townes's
best. Being teamed with so many excellent performers kept him engaged
and focused. Watching Townes and Kevin working in the studio day
after day until all the songs were recorded was quite the experience in
itself.

At the time, the project was probably too ambitious to attract the
investment needed to take it to conclusion. However, I believe that if
one album of the intended trilogy had been released in the early 1990s,
it would have registered such a seismic impact among music writers and

Townes's fans that the funding needed to finish the remaining forty songs would have been easily secured. Unfortunately, it seemed Townes still didn't have the kind of pulling power desired by major labels.

That changed with our next album, *Roadsongs*, a fifteen-song collection of Townes performing his favorite traditional and cover songs. Issued in 1993 on BMG Records Europe and in 1994 on Sugar Hill Records, the tracks were culled from the vast archive of tapes I'd recorded at Townes's live shows in the 1970s and '80s, and included accompaniment by Owen Cody, Jimmie Gray, Danny Rowland, and Mickey White. When the album's "Dead Flowers" cut was included in the soundtrack and final scene of *The Big Lebowski*, it represented the widest audience Townes's music had yet reached.

Roadsongs almost didn't happen. At first Townes was lukewarm to the idea of a "covers" record. To be precise, his response was: "H, you gotta be crazy!"

He elaborated. "I'm not a stylist. I'm known as a songwriter, right? These songs I'm covering—how can I cover them better than the artists who did them originally?"

I countered, "Townes, you've got your own style, and it's totally different than the original or even other covers. People will want to hear your version."

"People listen to my records because of the *songs*, not the singing. Why would they listen to an album of me *singing* other people's songs?"

"Because the way you sing *your* songs is so interesting, they want to know how you'd sing somebody else's songs."

Finally, he agreed that I would compile a demo of possibilities; he'd listen to it once and say yea or nay to each song. I made my choices, played the demo for him, and he approved them all.

Then, a week before the record came out, he started stirring up the worry pot. "You know, H, this could destroy my career. Humiliate me among my songwriting peers. This was a bad idea."

He really laid it heavy on me, to the point that I was getting big-time bummed, not only about his career, but also about *mine*. He'd bring it up each day, just drive it in a little deeper, a little deeper—and then the album came out and got rave, five-star reviews around the critical universe.

He patted me on the back, smiling, and said, "H, I knew it was going to work out."

"Then why did you put me through that?" I asked.

"Well, I was pretty worried for a while. Why should I worry about it alone?"

Typical Townes logic. That kind of thinking was why I had long wanted to get him on tape talking about his life and music. He was always very fluid and articulate in media interviews, and I believed his fans would enjoy getting to see a unique dimension to his stage persona.

He'd also once told me, "When I do a cover song, it's how I perceive myself." Of course, most singers choose to cover a song because it means something to them personally; given Townes's skill and sophistication as a songwriter, I took his comment to mean that each cover he selected showed a side of himself he could reveal only through music.

Trying to persuade Townes to reveal deeper layers of his emotional universe was the inspiration for the *Documentary* project I produced. In 1992, I arranged for Austin radio host Larry Monroe to begin a series of studio interviews with Townes. Larry was an extremely knowledgeable music historian and skilled interviewer able to draw the best from his subjects.

Townes was very absorbed in the project; he chose the songs to be used, saying, "These are the ones that tell my story the best." The resulting Normal Records CD, *Documentary*, gives some valuable insights into his personal history and approach to his music.

At one point during the interviews, Townes and I were both really sick with the flu, having just the day before straggled into Austin from an extensive tour. I suggested to Townes we should cancel the recording session, rest up, and do it another day. "No!" he said with a surprising fervor. He picked up his guitar and headed for the door, adding, "This is too important. We gotta get it done right."

And we did. When the album was finished, he said, "H, I want to sign my rights and ownership for this album over to you completely. You have believed in me all these years. This is my way of saying thank you."

It was my way of thanking him, too.

Rear View Mirror came out in 1993 on Sundown Records, a new independent label based in Austin. The tracks were from a 1978 Townes coffeehouse gig I recorded in Norman, Oklahoma, on my first tour with him, Jimmie Gray, Danny Rowland, and Owen Cody. The lease deal I secured certified that Townes and I were equal partners and co-copyright owners of the sound recordings, along with a nice advance we also split evenly. Named Best Folk Album of the Year by Tower Records' *Pulse Magazine*, *Rear View Mirror* sold so well that the next year I approached Sundown to lease a new studio album Townes would record in Ireland.

I requested a $60,000 lease payment up front, which would pay for recording expenses and travel to Ireland; Townes would retain ownership of the recording and get full ownership back when the lease period was over. The label owner agreed and invited Townes and me to come to his home and pick up the check for the full $60,000.

I was thrilled. I had just negotiated my best record deal ever and was so pleased I'd been able to do it for Townes, who—after the projected recording costs—would end up with around $14,000 cash for himself.

But the win-win didn't stop there; I was also able to strike a second deal with Sundown for an album each by Barb Donovan and Richard Dobson, two talented singer-songwriters I was representing and trying to help get a leg up in the business.

Our appointment to collect the check was at six p.m.; Townes was scheduled to perform at nine p.m. at the Cactus Café on the University of Texas campus. As we drove out way south of the city, our spirits were high, and Townes cracked a few jokes I hadn't heard before. Just before six we threaded our way through a wealthy subdivision and pulled into the driveway of a new, luxurious, suburban-style mansion. The owner and his wife both came out to greet us.

"It's so nice to meet you, Townes," said the owner, as we shook hands all around.

"Yes," said his wife, with a gracious smile. "I gave our cook the day off today, so I could personally make you a special dinner."

Replied Townes with a scowl, "I've got a gig to do. I don't have time to eat your slop."

I froze, speechless, as the owner and his wife tried to discern whether Townes's comment was a put-on. Then she took Townes by the hand. "Come with me. I'll make you a drink."

As they walked toward the kitchen, the owner turned to me. "He's a real asshole."

"Yeah," I agreed. "He can be at times. But he will make a lot of money for your company."

We went into the backyard to see the garden, and I made small talk about the lovely house, hoping to close the deal and avoid any conversation about Townes's rude behavior. We discussed a few more particulars of the contract, and my host said, "Let's go inside, and I'll write you the check."

As we walked into the front hallway, the wife and Townes were just coming out of the kitchen together. Townes was expressionless, looking at the floor, but she signaled for her husband to come over to her. They spoke briefly, she shaking her head back and forth and gesturing *no*.

Part of me knew what was going to happen next. But I didn't want to believe it.

They both walked over to us with strained smiles and put one arm behind Townes and me, escorting us toward the front door. "It's time for the two of you to leave," the label owner said. He opened the door, Townes and I stepped through, and it slammed shut behind us.

I was in total shock and turned to Townes. "What the hell is wrong with you? They were going to pay for the expense of recording, manufacturing, distribution, *everything*!"

"I don't want anyone to own me."

"It's a lease deal where you keep the ownership of the actual recording—*forever*."

"I taught you a good lesson, and my gig is more important, anyway."

"What lesson did you teach me?"

"I taught you to never bring an artist to the closing of a deal."

I lost it. "We were going to cash a $60,000 check tomorrow!" I was screaming. "$60,000! Do you hear me? $60,000!"

He shrugged, walked to the car, and got in the passenger seat.

I was able to contain myself until we got out of the driveway. Then I exploded. "It took me six months to negotiate the deal and arrange this meeting, and you blow it in fifteen minutes. This is the worst thing you have ever done to me!"

He didn't answer, and neither of us spoke on the drive back to Austin. I dropped him off at the Cactus Café. "I can't work with you anymore," I said. "I just can't work with you anymore. Goodbye."

The next week, the owner shut down the whole record label. Barb Donovan's album came out, but Richard Dobson's didn't see the light of day. Townes's inexplicable, indefensible tantrum had destroyed a lot of dreams in one fell swoop.

I had to defuse completely and didn't communicate with Cindy for days. There was no way I wanted to infect her with my fury and dismay.

It made no sense, no sense at all. Townes constantly complained about his bad breaks in the music business . . . yet, if he wanted to see the demon responsible in this case, all he had to do was look in the mirror.

I think when it finally dawned on him what he'd done, he was truly sorry and regretful. That's the way it often happens, I later learned, with victims of bipolar disorder. Their minds are so much mired "in the moment" that they easily lose all sense of a future with its consequences. But those consequences certainly do arrive, whether you see them coming or not.

It took me a couple of months to cool off. Townes was my friend, and he stuck by me; I think that meant more to me than the volatility and danger and often severe disappointment I knew our friendship would invariably bring.

Besides, he had a record to make in Ireland. If anybody could handle him, I suspected it would be the Irish.

9

"My Music Precedes Me"

TOWNES DEFINITELY flourished as an expatriate musician. During his last three years, he spent as much time abroad as he did in the U.S.—more than one hundred shows in Europe and Canada, nearly as many as he performed in America.

When Townes toured Europe, his itinerary was handled by booking agent Berthold Seliger of Berlin, who had Townes working in what seemed like every town and village in Germany, along with Italy, Netherlands, France, Belgium, Finland, Norway, Austria, and Slovenia.

Each year Townes toured in Europe, the venues got bigger and paid more. When Townes played the Cambridge Folk Festival in England for the first time in 1993 to over ten thousand people, he announced drily, "It's gonna be hard to silence a room this big."

It was an icebreaker line that always got him a laugh, but it obscured a salient fact: Townes much preferred playing to a small, intimate audience than a huge auditorium or festival crowd. The question of whether he unconsciously sabotaged several of his most prominent large shows is one we'll never answer with absolute certainty.

But there is no doubt that Townes's music found a very welcome reception among European audiences in the 1990s. I ask myself now, as I asked myself then: Why?

Several reasons. Partly, it's that Europeans still have a fascination with what they perceive as "mythic America," specifically the imagery and lore of cowboys and the Wild West. In his stage persona, Townes presented as a loner, an outsider, a throwback, all of which painted an appealing portrait of a rebel artist pursuing his own visionary path. Like so many U.S. blues and jazz artists in the 1960s, performers in the rockabilly, Western swing, Cajun, zydeco, and country-folk singer-songwriter genres found welcoming audiences in Europe during the 1990s.

Also, Townes's songs required deep listening. They were literate, not just catchphrases or simple chorus hooks. They were first and foremost poetry. I think a great many European music fans understood and appreciated that. And they showed up in large numbers to hear this American Lone Star cowboy poet perform live.

One night in late 1993, Townes had called me from Tennessee and said he'd just had a profound dream. The dream told him to make an album in Ireland with Irish musicians. As soon as possible. "The Irish have been through so much suffering, that when the wind blows, you can hear the music whispering through their bones," he said.

I'm not sure why Townes wanted to infuse his own trademark musical melancholia with an entire nation's historic suffering, as well; I think it was more him recognizing that elements of Irish traditional music had formed the basis of our American country and folk idioms, and he wanted to enrich his own music with even deeper roots.

For several years, he'd exhibited empathy for the country's contemporary political strife—the Troubles, as the civil war between Catholic and Protestant paramilitary groups in British Northern Ireland was called. Whenever we exited our motel or hotel room for Townes to play a show, he insisted on leaving a light on. "Until there's peace in Ireland," he'd say with full seriousness.

Curiously, after he fully awoke from his dream about the Irish album, he said he found a piece of paper with the phone number of Philip Donnelly. Philip was an Irishman who'd become a first-call studio guitarist in 1960s and '70s Nashville and Los Angeles, appearing on more than seventy albums by folks like Emmylou Harris, Brenda Lee, Johnny Cash, B.J. Thomas, John Prine, and Nanci Griffith. He'd played on an Everly Brothers world tour, produced music television shows for the BBC, and had served as lead guitarist on Townes's 1978 *Flyin' Shoes* album. Now he lived in an old country estate outside Limerick, Ireland.

Townes called the number on the paper. The phone rang on the other end, and, while having an early lunch five time zones in the future, Philip picked up. Townes told him about the dream and the album. Philip said, "Why not?" and this transatlantic verbal handshake got the deal in motion.

I thought it was an inspired idea and, with Townes's permission, immediately set about raising money to cover the costs and provide a small advance. I obtained a deal with Sundown Records, which, as previously described, fell through. Which meant I had to find two separate labels willing to lease the album and cover all up-front recording expenses, with Townes *maybe* getting some advance money. Ultimately, those labels would be Sugar Hill Records for U.S. rights and Veracity Records for European rights, and the album would be titled *No Deeper Blue*.

For the present, Townes was single-mindedly focused on preparing for the recording session, set for Xeric Studios in Limerick, co-owned by onetime Cranberries manager Pearse Gilmore. In the weeks leading up to the trip overseas, Townes came alive, filled with energy and the joy of a new musical challenge. "Dynamics, I want to get dynamics," he said repeatedly. "The album has to have dynamics."

As a technical term in music, *dynamics* refers to producing variation in volume between notes and/or phrases—*forte, pianissimo, crescendo,* and the like. What I think Townes meant in his use of the word wasn't so much about up-and-down volume changes but, rather, creating an album where each song had a unique feeling or identity achieved through a variety of instrumental textures, harmonic shadings, and articulation subtleties.

Philip brought in an array of instrumental textures ranging far across the tonal spectrum in the form of uilleann pipes, fiddle, accordion, bouzouki, mandolin, steel guitar, and harmonium to supplement the standard guitar, bass, piano, and drums. And there was a contribution on harmonica from none other than Donovan Leitch, who had been one of Townes's inspirations starting out in the 1960s.

However, by the time we arrived in Ireland, Townes was not in the best of physical shape. Which, to be frank, was caused by not being in the best of mental shape.

At one point, I thought he might die in the studio during the sessions, his energy was so incredibly low, his performing so erratic. If he had gone to Ireland to sample the native brand of suffering, he was fulfilling that goal in spades.

I could see that Philip was utterly drained by having to cope with Townes's behavior. But, seasoned music veteran that he was, he did not give up. He recorded Townes's vocals over and over and over and over, like a sculptor making sure to have the biggest block of stone to work with in shaping the final work of art. Putting everything together was a massive editing challenge, but Philip and his postproduction crew made it happen. The result was a magical album that scored enthusiastic reviews from around the world and revealed a different side of Townes Van Zandt at the milestone age of fifty.

When Townes's recording parts were done, we set out on a three-week tour across the whole of Ireland and even hopped across the Irish Sea for a week of gigs in England. Our driver was a man who worked for Philip—a gentle soul, but you could see he could be rough and dangerous if provoked. Before we crossed the border from the Republic of Ireland to the six counties under British control in Northern Ireland, he told us he would from this point on talk very quietly, if at all. Being overheard with his Southern Irish accent, he warned, could potentially get him killed by paramilitary vigilantes.

This was a level of paranoia I hadn't encountered since Vietnam, but in the border areas of Ireland at the time, it was warranted. A low-simmering civil war along the border was still very much in progress in the mid-1990s, and it included snipers, public bombings, kidnappings, and street riots that could ensnare anyone—even visiting Americans who blundered into the wrong place at the wrong time.

As we made our way into Belfast for Townes's gig the next night at Elmwood Hall, across from Queen's University, our driver completely ceased speaking, and we sensed his nervousness escalating. At the hotel, we were told we did not have reservations. I was certain we did and had a receipt as proof, but the clerk insisted we did not. Usually Townes did not involve himself in our lodging check-ins. This time, though, while I was on the phone to our concert promoter, Townes went into the bar and began shouting, "You bunch of stupid limeys don't have a lick of sense still fighting those religious wars! What the hell is wrong with this country?"

From the reaction of the bar denizens, it became clear that this was, in fact, a venue frequented exclusively by native-born Catholics who were highly unappreciative of being identified as "limeys," or English, and even less interested in putting up with a belligerent foreigner in their quiet pub. Over the phone, the promoter said tersely, "Shut him up and don't say another word." Meanwhile, Townes was trying to convince the bartender to gamble.

Things settled down a bit, and when the promoter arrived, he calmed everyone down and scooted us outside. "Do you have a death wish?" I asked Townes.

"No, but I don't like people treating us like that." His sticking-up-for-the-oppressed response had kicked in; the only problem was that he was haranguing the actual oppressed.

The promoter settled us in a bed-and-breakfast in a Protestant area near the venue. We saw English soldiers with guns patrolling the street, and a tank following behind. Our driver by this point was totally freaked out; once we went to our rooms, we didn't see him again until breakfast the next morning.

Townes had by now realized we were in a de facto war zone. "I saw a Chinese restaurant down the street," I said. "Do you want to get something to eat?"

"No way, H! I don't want to get killed."

"Townes, this is like when I lived in Saigon. If you show fear, the nightmare will come to your door. Let's go have a good meal."

He demurred and asked me to bring back some takeout.

On the way to the restaurant, I passed a pub and noticed Irish music coming from inside. I got a sudden burst of exhilaration and walked in. The moment I entered, the packed bar went dead quiet, with everyone looking at me. I saw no smiling, top-o'-the-mornin' faces and recalled our driver's warning about venturing alone into a strange pub where you were, literally, an unwelcome stranger. I immediately turned and left the pub, as several bar patrons rose and came toward me.

I decided to cross to the other side of the street and stepped quickly into the roadway, forgetting that in Ireland, cars drive on the opposite side of the street. I didn't even hear the screech—just felt an instant hard thump and explosion of pain in my side, as a car bumper winged me and threw me up onto the hood. My face smacked into the windshield, just as the car screeched to a halt. Stunned, I slid to the ground, bleeding from my face.

I sat up, groggy, and looked up at the guy driving the car. He was terrified, and then he saw the folks from the bar coming toward me and surmised they were going to yank *him* out of the car and administer some quick Belfast street justice. He backed up and raced off, leaving me on the ground. The group from the bar gathered around me, and I heard one say, "Ah, leave him alone; he's doing a fine job hurting himself." There was silence, then laughter as they headed back to the bar.

I was disoriented and confused, and the cuts on my face were bleeding, but not badly enough for a hospital visit. I decided I might as well pick up the food; I have no recollection of actually getting it and bringing it back to the bed-and-breakfast, but apparently I did. When I got to our room, I wasn't able to talk with my swollen lips, so I knocked and knocked until Townes opened the door; his face was a sight to behold as well as mine, no doubt.

He pulled me in the room and quickly bolted the locks. "I told you, H, if you go out there, you are going to get hurt, if not killed."

I grunted, "Yeah, the enemy got me." I could only laugh inside.

Townes wanted to know the specifics right away. I scratched on a piece of paper: "okay talk when stop bleeding."

Next morning when the driver first saw me, he asked Townes if someone had come to our room and dragged me off and beaten me up. Townes didn't answer, and neither did I, leaving it to his imagination.

That episode was a classic, if somewhat bizarre, example of the often uncertain nature of foreign travel. But there were other times when my belief in the basic goodness of human beings everywhere was reinforced.

Later that year, in November, we found ourselves in Ljubljana, Slovenia, at a venue called Klub K4. Though Slovenia had suffered only a relatively brief outbreak of war in 1991 before achieving independence, interethnic fighting among several groups would continue throughout the region up to the end of the decade. In fact, while we were in the country, vicious warfare was taking place in Croatia and Bosnia, only two hours to the east.

At the Slovenian border station, the guard asked for our passports, requested the trunk of the car be opened, and took a cursory look at our luggage and the guitar case. He came back to the car window and handed back my passport, but held on to Townes's. And kept holding. And holding, as he looked repeatedly at Townes's face and his passport photo, face to photo, face to photo.

Needless to say, a nervousness was beginning to build.

Finally, he handed Townes his passport and said, "It is nice to meet you, Townes Van Zandt. They have been playing your music on the radio nonstop, and I have been listening to it. Very enjoyable. Also they are announcing the show you will be doing. Wish I could be there—have a great visit here in Slovenia."

We drove down the road. "That was close!" I said.

Townes smiled. "It seems my music precedes me."

Ljubljana was the country's capital and very cultured, but it was clear that two world wars and almost four decades of Iron Curtain rule had not been kind to the city. Everything looked run-down, and the people we passed on the street seemed suspicious and wary.

The show promoter met us, helped us check into the hotel, and then took us to the radio station where he was a DJ. He interviewed Townes live and played several Townes songs, proudly showing us his collection of albums and 45s, telling us these were all his own records, because the radio station did not have the money to buy new releases.

He took us to dinner at a nice restaurant, and Townes ordered a steak, potato, and vegetable; I got ham and the same sides, and the DJ just drank coffee. I ate my entire meal, but Townes—as was his usual dietary m.o.—ate only two bites of the steak and had a brief nibble at the side orders.

As Townes and I got up to go to our room, I saw the promoter look down at Townes's plate of uneaten food with a disbelieving stare. Townes saw it as well; he turned to the waiter and asked, "Can I please get a to-go bag? I'll be eating this in my room." The promoter took us back to the hotel, arranging to bring us to the club later.

When the promoter left, Townes asked me, "Did you see how poor the city and people are here, H? At the restaurant, everyone was eating very modestly, and they ate everything on the plate. I could see our friend was blown away I would even think about wasting food."

We arrived at Klub K4 a little after six p.m. to do a sound check. Two grim-faced security guards were there to greet us as we were dropped off; they followed us inside and positioned themselves at attention outside our dressing room. The club was a large, concrete-walled room, and it was already packed with four hundred people. Townes did a quick sound check—a couple of guitar strums and a "Can you hear me all right?" vocal test—and then went backstage to the dressing room. Slovenia's premier folk musician, Vlado Kreslin, came by. He was a big fan of American music and well acquainted with Townes's songs; he and Townes talked for several minutes, until it was time for Vlado to go onstage and open for Townes.

Just as Townes left the dressing room to go onstage, a man approached and asked the promoter if Townes would sign an album for him. The two guards were hostile and ordered him to leave; the man hesitated, and then, without another word, the guards grabbed him, threw him on the floor, and dragged him down the hall, beating the hell out of him.

It happened in a flash, and Townes yelled for them to stop. "If they don't stop, I will not perform! Dammit, make them stop!" The promoter shouted angrily at the guards, and they stopped and backed away. Townes walked over to the man on the ground and said he was sorry. He helped him up, shook his hand, and the fan handed Townes his album to sign. Townes signed the album, put his arm round the fellow, and walked with him into the club amid a wave of perplexed murmurs from the audience. They shook hands again, and Townes said, "Good luck, my friend."

I had no idea what effect this episode was going to have on Townes's performance. Was he going to lecture the crowd on fascism? Insult the country? Burst out in a righteous rage?

What he did was deliver a pin-drop perfect concert for two solid hours. After his final encore, he invited Vlado Kreslin to perform with him, first doing a Townes song, then one of his own. The audience went nuts. Vlado and Townes came offstage arm-in-arm, hanging out with the audience, drinking and talking with everyone who got near them until it was time to go.

As we walked out of the club to the waiting car, a crowd surged behind, shaking each other's hands, shaking our hands, some crying, some laughing. An impromptu farewell reception line formed, and people came up to Townes and hugged him, talking to him in Slovene as if they'd known him for years, hugging him some more. One guy took off his hat and gave it to Townes, and then a woman gave him her scarf. Townes tried to give the hat and scarf back, but each time he did, they pushed them back into his arms until Townes hugged each of them and began crying. We finally got inside the car and started driving away slowly. The crowd surrounded the car; as we crept down the block, they moved right along with us in a festive procession.

Townes asked the driver to stop; he got out and addressed the crowd, hands clasped in front of him as if he were praying: "Thank you all so much. I will never forget you." Translations of his words echoed through the air, as he bowed his head and put a hand over his heart, crying as he got back in the car. We finally drove off, and he said, "Did you see the look of death in their eyes? They lived through a war, but the joy of music still soothes their souls."

We didn't talk again until we had crossed the border into Italy. Then Townes said, "They touched my soul. I will never forget them or this night." As we drove through the dark countryside, he drifted off into a silent reverie. Whether the silence came from torment or peace, I could not tell.

This night, it may have been a mix of both.

10

The Last Lost Highway

MY PERCEPTION of Townes, as the days and weeks on the road melded into that final year of his life, was that This Road, she was indeed a weary old train running out of track and time.

During that last year, if he had not been touring, I truly believe he would have been in a sanitarium. Full time. It was the traveling and gigging that kept him and his spirit alive, with some new adventure to look forward to. We frequently discussed our plans for the next live album. And the next. And the next. Future projects were always important to Townes.

But the fact was, as his commercial popularity began to rise again, his personal stability underwent a swift decline.

Ninety percent of Townes's performances were superb and often spellbinding—otherwise, he wouldn't have been able to tour as extensively as he did over so many years. The remaining ten percent were bad and sloppy, very intense, and the rumors of these performances generated their own urban legends, which persist today. Townes said the demons took him over during these shows, but he would gradually chase them off. My theory was the depression and alcohol converged into a perfect storm that would occasionally render a highly imperfect performance.

During this last year, he would often say to me, "I should be ashamed of myself. I am so fortunate to be able to tour and travel the world, playing my music for people that like it, but I just don't feel the joy of it anymore. I think God is going to be mad at me. He's given me a gift, and I don't appreciate it." No matter what I said, very little seemed to lift Townes out of his doldrums.

At times he would tell me, "H, there is no light. I've done all I was supposed to do in my life. I'm ready to die." These words rattled me to the bone. At times, seeing his intense sadness, I would walk off so he couldn't see or hear me crying for him.

Of more immediate concern, day to day, were the times he would turn to me and ask, "Where am I?"

Or, "What are we doing here, H? What day is it?"

I could see it was not a joke. His episodes of disjunct thoughts and disorientation were becoming more frequent and extreme. When we drove along the highway, he would gaze out the pickup window and whisper, "Sometimes I wonder what's real." He'd also begin making random rhymes—"I've had years of sorrow, fears of pain, often stayed out in the rain"—and so forth.

For someone who had for so long lived with the unknown—ghosts, demons, and so on—it seemed bizarre when seemingly trivial things got under his skin and bothered him beyond words.

The last couple of years, he started mentioning to me that his face and body were that of an old man. "The girls just don't like me anymore, H." After performing, he would come back to the dressing room, sit by himself, and cry, drained from baring his soul onstage.

To remedy this, I would go out into the audience and keep an eye out for pretty single girls rapturously consumed with his music and words. When he was doing his encores, I would go up to them individually and ask if they would like to meet Townes. They always said yes.

I would do this with about seven—for luck—girls and lead them backstage, so that when he walked in the dressing room, it was full of cute, adoring young women. I did this regularly to cheer him up.

One night he smiled at me and said, "H, you've turned into a pimp!" We laughed, but I could tell this small charade of harmless attention, no matter how fleeting or transparent, lifted his spirits.

There were times when Townes was performing, I would stand by the side of the stage watching; it seemed as if Mr. Guitar were playing by himself. I asked Townes about it, and he said that when he wasn't in shape, Mr. Guitar did indeed do the playing. As always, no Townes performance was ever the same. He sang and played guitar differently every time, his moods changing so quickly and never breaking in the same direction.

One night in Edinburgh, Scotland, at the end of a tour, Townes had just completed his show to a standing ovation and was called back for an encore. The evening had drained him physically and mentally; he shuffled back to the stage slowly, hesitantly, and I thought he might actually drop Mr. Guitar. I helped him gingerly mount the stage, then stood out in the audience to watch him do his last song, fingers crossed.

Before starting, he paused and stared at me for several seconds with a fixed, unblinking gaze—not hostile, not angry, just focused and intense. A weird sensation passed through me: a sudden light-headedness and the image of a vampire hypnotizing his victim, draining out all his strength. Townes broke eye contact, and I actually felt as if I were swaying slightly.

Townes did a terrific version of his song and strode offstage standing tall, while I felt the sort of weakness that comes after being knocked out for a few seconds, or waking abruptly from a dream.

Then I remembered that Lamar Fike, who had worked with Elvis Presley for over twenty years, once told me Elvis would affix this "vampire stare" on him every now and again when touring; Elvis said he needed to gather in Lamar's strength at that moment to make it through the show. I'd thought it was silly when Lamar said it, but now . . .

Backstage, I asked Townes to please not do that ever again; just focus on someone in the audience and take *their* strength. "I'm drained out most of the time, just being with you, especially at the end of a tour!"

Townes chuckled. "Okay. I just wanted to make sure I was taking good energy."

And he never did do that to me again. Possibly the one and only instance in which he fully complied with one of my requests.

By this point in time, Townes's daily road routine had embraced a stability of sorts. He would wake at dawn and reach immediately for the vodka bottle he had set on his nightstand the night before. After a few snorts of liquor and a chaser of orange soda to wash down a handful of ibuprofen, he would smoke a cigarette and rise and greet the day.

His food intake had devolved to a diet of popsicles and candy bars, which, coupled with travel exhaustion, had degraded his health to full-scale physical deterioration. He never had formal testing done, but the catabolysis one doctor had diagnosed him with—his body breaking down internal fat and muscle tissue in order to keep him alive—was probably in process. I had never seen him at such a low ebb of basic vitality. At the age of fifty-two, Townes possessed the ravaged appearance and infirm gait of a man twenty years older.

I had my dietary quirks as well. Eating my way through jars of Rolaids and Tums had become a staple of my food regimen for the past three or four years.

Yet despite our unhealthy behaviors, habits, and general lifestyle, we always encountered bright spots and unexpected opportunities.

As we were at the Berlin airport about to catch our plane home, Normal Records president Eduard Rühmann called with exciting news: Townes's live album *Abnormal*, which we'd released on Normal a month before, strictly as a limited-edition mail-order disc to support the European tour, had been given a five-star review by *Music Express* magazine. This was a major coup, Eduard pointed out; *Music Express* never reviewed mail-order pressings, but they'd considered *Abnormal* to be worthy of breaking precedent.

When we returned to Germany a few months later, I negotiated an agreement with Eduard to issue *Abnormal* as a regular Normal album for full distribution. Eduard also expressed interest in releasing an ongoing series of Townes albums to support our European tours. I secured a deal for three albums with possibility of more in the future.

Post-reunification Germany enjoyed a huge cultural renaissance all through the 1990s. I persuaded our friend Wolfgang Doebeling, the music writer, to press and release two Townes tracks—Ewan MacColl's "Dirty Old Town" and Michael Weston King's "Riding the Range"—on his Berlin-based Exile Records label. Townes had recorded them in

Austin with a husband-wife bluegrass duo, Jim and Royann Calvin of Nashville, backing him; the disc would be released on Exile in 1999.

The Calvins were solid, dedicated musicians in their early forties, friendly and honest, who became friends with Townes in the last year of his life. They had played a few dates with him around Nashville and in Texas a few months before, and the recording went smoothly, with the addition of Townes howling at the end of "Riding the Range."

It wasn't yodeling or old-time cowboy yippee-ki-yay vocalese; it was straight-out, wolf-in-the-wilderness howling.

Looking back, I'd have to say it was reflective of both our emotional states at the time.

One day in late 1995, Townes told me he wanted us to start work on a book about his music, life, and career. We had talked in general terms about this for the past two years or so. He knew about my securing publishing deals for the Willie Nelson, Stevie Ray Vaughan, and *Nashville Family* books, and intimated now and again that I might do something literary with him.

Yet, every time I had broached the subject, he'd laughed it off. "You can tell my life story on one page," he'd say.

"Yeah, Townes, but we can do a hell of a packaging job on that one piece of paper."

This time, though, he agreed. From that day forward, many of our daily conversations developed into him telling me details of his life. He spoke openly about everything, not holding back from any question I asked. He knew exactly what he wanted repeated about his life and in what tone it was to be told.

"Don't forget, H, in the book of my life, the most important thing is to tell the truth, no matter what," he said. "I want everyone to feel my pain, as I have shared it with you. Do not whitewash anything. Let all the ghosts and demons have their say. That's what I've done my whole life."

I was privileged to live and learn at the school of Townes Van Zandt. He was my professor in life and music, and, without me realizing it, set me up to continue promoting his music and legacy after his death. This was reflected in our business partnership, which was simple and straightforward: we were each a fifty percent owner on the sound recording rights of his live career recordings. Our division of labor was equally clear-cut: he sang and played the songs, I recorded them. We chose the album selections together, and then I would negotiate and secure contracts with the different labels.

As we traveled, we talked about new recording projects. For me, it was less about business and more about keeping him interested in life and work by focusing on future plans.

One possibility we devised was Townes recording the cover songs he'd performed live in his emerging years in Houston; obviously, these would feature some great numbers from the repertoires of Lightnin' Hopkins, Leadbelly, and other blues masters. Another was cutting an album of songs he'd written years ago but never recorded for whatever reason.

A third idea was a solo album with him playing guitar and harmonica; he would speak the words to the songs and sing the hooks, as he did in the duet "I'll Be Here in The Morning" with Barb Donovan, which appeared on *Live at McCabe's* and *Documentary*. His live performances were gradually turning into something more like poetry readings, with his guitar playing sparse and at low volume, more ghostly than ever.

The fourth potential project was a "sky songs" album, a term coined by Mississippi bluesman Bukka White to describe his technique of improvising songs on the spot—reaching up and pulling lyrics "out of the sky." Our thought was that Townes would be in the studio, just him and his guitar, making up songs as the spirits moved him. Not only would the resulting songs be absolutely unique, the album would also serve as a way for Townes to "empty his head," so to speak, and make room for new song ideas.

And then there was the serious possibility of a Townes and Bob Dylan duet album produced by Bob Johnston. The implications of such a collaboration for the singer-songwriter world were seismic.

I knew Bob Johnston from when my brother had hired him to potentially work on the Townes sixty-song anthology album. If you are not familiar with his name, I guarantee you've been hearing the amazing fruits of his studio genius every year of your music-listening life.

A Hillsboro, Texas, native, Bob is commonly referred to as the music industry's "first super-producer" and the "star behind the stars." His 1960s productions for CBS Records—Dylan's *Nashville Skyline* and *Blonde on Blonde*, Johnny Cash's *At Folsom Prison*, Simon & Garfunkel's *Sounds of Silence*, and the Byrds' *Dr. Byrds and Mr. Hyde*, to name a few of the more prominent—helped define contemporary rock-pop-country music of that era. Bob was still producing new artists up to his death in 2015 at age eighty-three.

In his prime, Bob had worked with artists as diverse as Bob Dylan, Simon & Garfunkel, Aretha Franklin, George Harrison, Leonard Cohen, Louis Armstrong, Jimmy Cliff, Marty Robbins, the Byrds, Willie Nelson, Joan Baez, Jerry Garcia, Johnny Cash, Charlie Daniels, John Mayall, Tribe After Tribe, and the Waterboys, as well as on Hollywood soundtracks and scores in films featuring Elvis Presley, Robert Redford, Warren Beatty, Gregory Peck, and Dustin Hoffman.

Naturally, he'd always really liked the music of Townes Van Zandt.

I had already spoken a couple of times to Bob about a Townes-Dylan album and finally arranged for Bob to meet with Townes at the restaurant of a downtown Nashville hotel. The meeting went very well; Townes and Bob talked for a long time and agreed to move forward with Bob producing the session at a studio in Memphis. At meeting's end, Bob invited Townes to come out to his home in the ensuing weeks to go over additional details.

The next meeting at Bob's home outside Nashville was equally congenial and productive. Bob and Townes expanded on the previous discussion, and Bob agreed to contact Dylan. As we headed out, Bob asked if he could have a word with me alone.

"This is not going to be an easy project to do," Bob warned. "Dylan will be hiding behind the couch, and Townes will be passed out on the couch. But it can be done. Heck, let's do it!"

Bob said he succeeded in contacting Dylan, who agreed to do the project when his schedule allowed. A month before Townes died, I heard him talking to Bob Johnston on the phone about the Dylan and Townes album moving forward, and Townes continued to envision the album right up to his death. The mind boggles at what might have resulted from a Townes-Dylan session . . . probably something along the lines of a poetically supercharged *Nashville Skyline* to usher in the new millennium.

It was about this time that Townes's songwriting had taken on a new urgency. His innate creativity was unquenchable. In those last two years, he wrote over twenty new songs by my count. In the hotels we stayed at on tour, I would often wake in the morning and find a crumpled sheet of paper on the floor, bed, chair, bathroom sink, wherever. It would be a new song Townes had composed the night before.

His new mission as a songsmith was to create a song that would "save the world." The world didn't need "any more sad songs," he would say.

The first time I saw a crumpled piece of paper, I unraveled it and asked if I could read the new song. Townes said yes, but to rip it up in front of him after finishing. "Until I can write the perfect song, there's no point in letting any of these out in public."

Had he lived a few more years, I think he would have fashioned exactly the song he was seeking. And maybe it wouldn't have saved the world, but it might have saved him.

I read a number of new songs Townes allowed me to see, and they were amazing. I wish he had preserved them for posterity, but, sadly, all of them were destroyed. A lot of them were incredibly painful to read, knowing as I did what mental torment Townes was going through daily.

And sometimes, what was bottled up inside would burst forth without warning.

For the first day of our fall 1996 European tour, the itinerary had been simple: I would pick up Townes at his home, drive us to Nashville airport, fly to Minneapolis for a three-hour layover, and we'd board the jet to Oslo, Norway. We would be in the Land of the Midnight Sun early the next day for a full day's rest before the first scheduled show.

Townes had been drinking vodka even before I got him that morning, but he seemed to be in good physical shape and spirits. At the Nashville airport, he drank at the bar and slept on the flight to Minneapolis. During our layover, after getting his moccasins waxed at a shoe shine stand, he insisted on going to the bar. Then he declared, "I'm going to have a smoke," and walked toward the airport entrance.

Not a minute later, I heard Townes yelling, "I need drugs! I need drugs!" I spotted him lying on the ground at the building entrance, right where the doors opened and closed automatically. The doors kept trying to close, but each time, they bonked into the supine Townes and reopened. No one could get past him, a crowd began to collect, and I saw a phalanx of police and airline security trotting toward us.

Townes continued to scream "I need drugs!" over and over. I tried to get him to stop and stand up. The first policeman asked Townes if he was okay. Townes said no and resumed shouting.

The policeman turned to me and said in a very forceful tone, "You get him up and out of here, right now, or you both are going to jail."

Police cars were now pulling up outside with sirens blaring. I told Townes to stop fooling around and get up; he ignored me. The cop took out his handcuffs, and I quickly said to Townes, "You have to get up, you're going onstage to perform."

He stopped yelling, got up, and said with a slight annoyance, "Why didn't you say that in the first place?"

The police left, but an airline representative told me Townes could not fly in that condition. We would have to come back tomorrow, and if he were not in better shape, we would not be allowed on the plane. I agreed, rescheduled the flight to Oslo, and directed Townes into a cab for a nearby hotel.

We arrived at the hotel, a posh Hilton, and I told Townes to stay in the cab while I checked in. At the desk I requested a wheelchair, figuring this was the simplest way to get him from point A to point B.

I returned to the cab, and the driver was trying to pull Townes out of the car; Townes was resisting and yelling. I realized Townes must have gotten the driver all riled up. While this fracas went on, people and staff poured out of the lobby, watching the incident escalate. I managed to get Townes out of the cab and into the wheelchair. I settled the driver down and paid the fare with a good tip; he grabbed our luggage out of the trunk and hurled it onto the ground, jumping back into the cab and driving off with a screech.

A bellhop assisted us with our luggage. We got into the elevator, and Townes began the "I need drugs!" routine, freaking out the bellhop. The elevator door opened to our floor, and the bellhop hurried out in front of us with the luggage, as I pushed Townes in the wheelchair behind. At our room, the bellhop dashed in with the bags, dropped them on the floor, and bolted out of the room, slamming the door behind him without waiting for a tip. I heard him running down the hall.

Townes smiled at me beatifically and said, "What a day! I'm getting some sleep."

Next morning, he woke me frantically: "H, what's going on?! Where are we? Are we in Oslo?"

"Don't you remember the outrageous scenes we had yesterday?"

He hesitated, clearly perplexed, and replied, "No. Anything special happen?"

We boarded the flight to Oslo that day without incident, arriving a day later than scheduled, which meant we had no time to get over our jet lag but had to go straight to the gig at the Cruise Café. The opening act was a guy who pierced fish hooks through his chest, had himself suspended from the ceiling, set himself on fire, and closed by igniting a smoke bomb that filled the club with stench and fog.

The smoke cleared, and then Townes proceeded to do a knockout performance that kept the audience silent from his first note to his last. Afterward, he said to me, "What a way to start a tour, huh, H?"

In addition to sketching out the book I was putting together with Townes and trying to nail down the Dylan details, Townes's last year was highlighted by another priority project: a new major-label record.

Though Townes and Jeanene had divorced, she had continued working to further his career. She'd contacted drummer Steve Shelley of the rock group Sonic Youth, asking if he would want to record Townes and release the album on the band's label, Ecstatic Peace! (a division of Geffen Records). It turned out to be an inspired shot in the dark.

A seminal grunge rocker since the early 1980s, Shelley had lately become highly enamored of Townes's music. Shelley agreed to produce the session with instrumental backup provided by his band, Two Dollar Guitar, a late-phase grunge outfit whose laid-back, low-key music seemed eminently suitable for the moody songs of Townes Van Zandt.

Townes's first close exposure with a contemporary rock band had been his 1990 tour with the Cowboy Junkies. Since then, the "grunge" genre of rock had risen and peaked and entered the mainstream musical pool.

Townes got a kick out of being referred to as "Grandfather Grunge" by the new generation of young music critics hearing his music for the first time. "I'm the mold the grunge was grown in," he'd say with pride. He realized this record could reach an entirely new audience of young people; certainly, the poetic alienation and despair of the grunge aesthetic was closely aligned with many of his songs.

In July 1996, Townes jammed with Two Dollar Guitar at Theatre on the Green in Cheraw, South Carolina. After the show they conferred, with Townes suggesting they write songs together and perform as a band—"just like the Rolling Stones," he kept saying. Steve Shelley eventually got everyone to agree to a workable recording format in which the band would accompany Townes with emphasis on Townes's existing but never-released songs. The scheduling process was set in motion for a studio in Memphis, with a projected recording date of late December 1996.

I've mentioned how during these last years Townes had felt the emotional weight of his advancing years. In November 1995, he had met a young German woman, Claudia Winterer, at a show in Hanau, Germany. Nothing like a little romance to regenerate a feeling of youth and vigor.

In March 1996, he invited Claudia to visit him in the U.S. and threw a welcome party at his Mount Juliet home with local friends. A couple of months later, Claudia accompanied us on our July-August tour of England and Ireland. And she was present for several gigs during the tour of Europe at the end of 1996.

I noted in Chapter 4 that wives and girlfriends were seldom permitted on our tours. And unfortunately, Claudia's presence on these last two tours became problematic. It wasn't that she herself was doing anything harmful; it was what she wasn't doing.

I typically roomed with Townes to prevent him from going overboard on the booze and freaking out about something, or sinking into the depths of depression with no one to snap him out of it. After he went to sleep, I would pour out most of what was in his nightstand vodka bottle, so that when he woke, there was only a small amount of alcohol with which he could start the day.

With Claudia along, I naturally took a separate room, so that they could be together. Townes quickly got into the habit of consuming nearly a full pint of vodka to start the day; by the time he was supposed to perform, he was walking blitzed. The result would be a poor show, but afterward, Claudia would tell him he had been great. That was kind, of course, but it wasn't how you needed to deal with a performer like Townes. If he'd done a bad show, I had no hesitation about telling him so. Now, suddenly, there was no "quality control" and his performances were getting progressively worse.

I advised Claudia on how to deal with the vodka setup. She responded, "I'm just his girlfriend, not his bottle carrier."

At that night's show in Schorndorf, Germany, Townes sang and played badly. Over the course of ninety minutes he sang only four songs, telling stories and jokes the rest of the time—despite most of the audience not speaking English. Still, he got major applause, and then did three encores of just telling stories and jokes.

"What do you think of the show?" he asked me.

"Some people applaud at funerals," I replied.

He got angry and opened the stage door so I could see the audience. "It doesn't get better than this," he snarled, slamming the door and going over to Claudia, who was waiting a few feet away. As they walked off, I heard him ask her what she thought; she said it was a great show.

I went out front to sell CDs, and virtually every person asked in broken English or with sign gestures, "Is there more music and less talking on the CDs?" A few minutes later, Townes came out to autograph the merchandise, and people asked him the same question.

"Everybody who bought a CD wants to know if there's music or just talk," I remarked.

"I get it," Townes snapped, giving me a dirty look.

There was one time, though, when Claudia may have literally saved his life. Early one morning in Germany, she called my hotel room saying Townes had fallen in the bathroom and injured himself badly. When I got to their room, I saw Townes with a bloody towel wrapped around his waist. While getting out of the bath, he had slipped and cut his buttocks on a chipped corner of the tub. At first glance, it was a very bad cut—the blood was pouring out, a chunk of skin was gone, and you could see right to the bone.

The ambulance arrived, and two of the attendants were women. Townes's shyness reared up: "No way am I showing this to those two *fräuleins!*" Meanwhile, he had gone through four towels soaking up the still-running blood. He finally agreed to let them put on temporary bandages; they suggested he don some underwear, but the only thing we could find was a pair of Claudia's panties. Now Townes was super embarrassed, but after a short stay at the hospital, he was released.

The doctor said Townes should check in at a hospital each day, no matter where he was, to have this serious cut looked at and treated with fresh bandages. We did this for the next week; each time Townes was reticent and embarrassed, but once at the hospital enjoyed flirting with the nurses.

There was always an element of weirdness he couldn't avoid even in a more tranquil European environment. One night in Dresden, while Townes, Claudia, our tour manager Luc Wouters, and I were walking to the club, I noticed a strange person following us down the street. One of his hands was inside his trench coat, as if he were holding a handgun. We reached the club, and the individual came inside, watching the whole show and staring at Townes with the most intense of expressions. After the show, I spotted him following us back to the hotel. This time, it looked as if he actually had a gun in his hand and was pointing it toward us.

I immediately went into my Saigon mind-set and told Townes and

Claudia to get close to the wall as we walked; Luc and I walked behind them, shielding them if the guy started shooting. I told them to hurry up and get back to the hotel. I walked out to the curb facing this lurking character, reached in my coat like I was taking out a gun; he stopped and ran off. When I got back to the hotel, I looked out the window, and he was back—standing on the street and looking up at Townes and Claudia's room. We thought about calling the police, but didn't. In the morning, he wasn't there.

The year's last overseas tour finished in England with a show at the Borderline in London, an upscale nightclub on Charing Cross Road. Townes started his set physically weak—voice shaky and fingers fumbly—but pulled himself together to deliver an emotionally riveting performance that stunned the audience into absolute silence. Of all Townes's shows I had witnessed over the years, this one struck me as having even more drama and intensity than usual.

Townes's longtime friend and BBC radio producer Mary Costello, the first wife of Elvis Costello, was in attendance and would happily announce to anyone who cared to listen that "Townes's worst is better than the rest's best." Townes overheard the remark and, after the show, told me how proud he was to have earned Mary's high regards. "What a great way to end this tour," he beamed.

The tour had ended not a moment too soon. When we showed up at Heathrow Airport next day to board our flight to Nashville, Townes was in such bad shape, he could hardly walk. This time he wasn't drunk or drugged, just worn out beyond belief; I got him in a wheelchair to get through customs, as we did so many times.

On the plane, we sat across the aisle from each other. I watched him awhile, then turned my face away and cried for a good few minutes, thinking how much he had physically deteriorated over the years. The last couple of years seemed to be consumed with one tragedy after another. But this had been the worst, and in my heart I knew the end was not far off. As usual, I ignored it and told myself, "He'll pull through this like always; we'll be back on the road touring again as usual."

I had seen Townes in the grip of death so many times, it had become part of the norm. What I didn't realize was how close he was getting to the shadow of heaven's door. When you live on the edge for so long, you stop seeing the boundary line and the danger waiting on the other side.

And I wasn't the only one thinking this. Throughout 1996, and especially on the last tour, Townes had frequently expressed the distinct premonition that he might not survive the year.

Of course, he had spoken of dying from the first day I was with him and never stopped talking about it to the very last night we were together—the night before he did, in fact, pass away. At the end of a typical death conversation, he would sing a line or two from "Waiting 'Round to Die."

Townes wanted to die onstage, in the recording studio, or touring on the road. That seemed natural, given that his priority was always his music, and he spent his adult life consumed by writing and performing.

On this last circuit through Europe, each show resembled a farewell performance, as if he were seeing friends one last time and offering benediction or requesting forgiveness. Most of these friends had seen him outwit death many times; if you'd have taken a poll, they would overwhelmingly expressed the belief Townes would outlive them.

Yet, his spirit was broken beyond anything I had seen in twenty years. In a sense, his spirit died long before he did. Increasingly during this trip he would tell me, "What's the use, H? I've done all I'm supposed to, drank the fullest cups of life, outran my legs till the winds of change caught my falls. Now I'm just waiting for the Reaper to come and get me."

Then he'd snarl, "Come on, Reaper, bring it on. I'm not afraid of you!"

Yet during this time he also spoke of a bright future. His plan—and remember, he *always* had a plan—was to jump-start his career in Europe. He wanted to move to Germany to take advantage of his large and growing popularity in Europe. His new plan was for the two of us to move to Europe and continue working on our intended future projects together.

Naturally, he'd continue touring extensively in North America and Europe. He had a great booking agent in Nashville and an equally talented agent in Germany. Between the two agents, Townes believed he could stay as busy as he wanted to.

I had reservations concerning my loved ones in Austin. Two decades before, I had not been able to watch my daughter grow up; I didn't want to lose the upcoming childhood years of my infant son, Harold III.

But the overall plan of moving to Europe and recording new albums was very realistic. Just talking about these possibilities cheered Townes up. The idea of a new future that would bring him before new audiences, new musicians, and even new critics to charm was a powerful motivational force in his last few months.

I still wonder if he would still be alive, if we had moved to Europe. And would he have been able to get back to being the optimistic Townes, looking toward new possibilities, and not the devastated fallen artist who spent his days and nights lamenting his lost opportunities?

Either way, first, we had to return to the States and gear up for the recording project with Steve Shelley. It was the biggest career break Townes had been waiting for, working toward—and perhaps subconsciously sabotaging—for decades.

This time, from what I could tell, it seemed as if he had the motivation and courage to make it happen.

11

No Place to Fall

TOWNES AND I returned to the U.S. the first week of December 1996 and stayed several days at my condo in Austin to get our mental land legs back before I drove him to his home in Mount Juliet for the holidays. The Geffen Records recording session was set for Memphis on December 28, and Townes said he wanted a week or so alone to prepare the material.

As a tune-up, I brought Townes over to Flashpoint Recording Studio in downtown Austin, run by my friend East Side Flash (Bennet Spielvogel), to record a few numbers. We ended the day with four songs—"German Mustard," "Where I Lead Me," and "Nothin'," written by Townes, and "Heavenly Houseboat Blues," co-written with Susanna Clark—which would be released in 2002 on the *Absolutely Nothing* CD by Normal Records.

We drove the tapes down to south Austin to Jerry and Diane Tubb's Terra Nova Digital Audio, and Jerry did the mastering then and there. Townes always referred to Jerry as "the Wizard" in deference to his extraordinary engineering skills. While we were in the studio, Jerry recorded Townes doing a few more songs for the *Documentary* CD I was producing with narration by Larry Monroe. Larry stopped by for a few minutes and was, I think, a little surprised by Townes's spacey demeanor and weakened physical condition. Still, the session finished up well, and Townes and I went back to my condo to get ready for the next day's drive to Mount Juliet.

On the trip eastward, Townes assured me that over the ensuing week he would finish recuperating from the tour and get his songs in shape for the recording. After spending Christmas in Austin, I'd fly back to Nashville the day after Christmas, stay overnight in Mount Juliet, and drive him to Memphis, where he'd make The Record he'd been striving to make for years, a record that would surely unlock the door to the commercial success his songs had provided to others.

That was the plan.

Normally, Townes did not enjoy the Christmas season at all. The shock treatments had erased his memories of childhood family holidays, and each year I noticed he got increasingly morose at this time of year. "I wish I had my memories of Christmas with my mom, dad, sister, and brother," he would say. "They must have been very happy and wonderful times." Then he'd go silent and turn away, staring into the distance, as if it might still be possible to find the wisp of a stray memory or two.

But this year was different. The new record was going to be the best Christmas present of all, ever.

Townes was very upbeat on the drive. I drank far more coffee than usual, and we cruised nine hundred miles straight across Texas, Arkansas, and Tennessee, chattering like kids waiting up for Santa. "Harold, this is it, this is the big one," he said. "I'm not going to shoot myself in the foot this time. I'm going to keep it together. Finally it's all going to come in, you know."

What came through most strongly on our drive that day was Townes's excitement about creating a new musical framework for his songs. It's easy to forget that Townes loved the guitar and had spent his early years playing it constantly, carefully crafting a unique style of his own. Having the chance to have his songs interpreted in an enhanced setting with new textures and dynamics heightened the project's appeal in his mind.

It wouldn't be the Late Great Townes Van Zandt. It would be the Latest Greatest Townes Van Zandt.

We arrived at his lake house, Bayou Self, in Mount Juliet and unloaded his gear. I was anxious to spend Christmas with my loved ones, so I immediately flew back to Austin, looking to return December 26, stay the night, and wake up fresh the next morning and drive to Memphis.

I called Townes a couple of days after getting back to Austin, and he was working on the song arrangements. He said he was writing out the chords and the lyrics for the studio musicians; when I arrived, I would rewrite it all in big letters on sheets of paper so I could hold them up while he sang, and the session would have one less hitch.

We talked again on December 20, and he repeated how much he was looking forward to the recording session, and then touring again in January. He sounded in good psychological shape and said he'd been eating and not drinking too much. The fact that he was eating at all was very encouraging.

I did note he was listening to Hank Williams every time I called. I could hear the music in the background. He was in an empty house filled with spirits, surrounding himself with the saddest of country music—which Townes claimed was happy music to him. Well, I reasoned, if it kept him psyched for the recording ahead, that couldn't be such a bad thing.

I called him on Christmas Eve, but there was no answer. I figured he might be visiting family or friends, or maybe Guy and Susanna Clark had stopped over and they'd gone out to eat or something.

But Christmas Day I couldn't get him on the phone, either. The next day, I caught the plane to Nashville, assuming that if there had been a change in recording schedule, I would have been called. If not by Townes himself, then by someone at the studio or record label.

But I felt a slow-rumbling disquiet rising in me. After twenty years, I had developed a special sense of—I don't know what to call it exactly—intuition? Premonition? Apprehension? It was that gut feeling I'd get in Vietnam as darkness fell over the air base, and you assumed the VC would attack within the next few hours. You were ready, of course, but then again . . . there was always a chance of a nasty surprise.

I tried to nap during the flight but couldn't stop thinking about what I might be walking into. Not a month before, Townes and I had gotten back from an extremely intense European tour that had drained me more than ever before. In Austin, I had stayed pretty much in bed, regrouping my physical strength and mental will for the next few days.

Whenever I flew into Nashville, Townes would meet me with his pickup truck parked right outside baggage claim. As I exited the building, I saw the truck and was instantly relieved. Until I opened the door and saw Jim Calvin in the driver's seat.

"Welcome to Nashville, Harold," said Jim with a hearty laugh. "Van Zandt Taxi Company at your service."

"How's Townes?" I asked Jim.

"Great," he replied. And then proceeded to tell me all the bad news at once.

A short while after I'd last spoken to him on the phone, Townes had embarked upon a furious bender that ended only when he tripped over the fireplace in his house and fell on his right side, incurring a massive bruise along his hip and outer thigh. The Calvins, who lived a few miles away, had come over and taken him to their house to convalesce.

Oddly, Townes had often expressed a premonition that he would die from just such a fall. He was a big fan of the great actor William Holden—also an intense alcoholic—who had died after falling and striking his head on a table in his Santa Monica apartment back in 1981. "I don't want to die alone like that," he'd tell me.

This time, it looked like he'd managed again to cheat the Reaper.

In fact, when Jim Calvin told me what had happened, I was thankful it hadn't been worse. During the last European tour, Townes's increasing fragility had caused him to fall regularly and incur cuts and bruises to his face. This tumble, I was certain, would cause some walking problems for a while, but wouldn't necessarily affect his studio performance.

The drive from the airport to Jim and Royann's home seemed to take forever. When we arrived, Townes was lying on the living room sofa, huddled in blankets and looking ragged and worn out. He poked a scrawny arm out of the blankets and motioned for me to pass him the gallon of vodka on the table stand. A pint of vodka was his normal quantity; the presence of a gallon heralded danger.

I was shocked at his appearance. He appeared even more diminished than when I'd seen him a few days before. His face was emaciated and sickly pale underneath the disheveled mop of gray-black hair and week-old growth of gray-flecked beard.

I lost it. "Why the hell have you done this to yourself?" I shouted.

His eyes fluttered open and shut as he attempted a smile. "Cheer up, H. It's only gonna get worse."

He leaned up and tried to rise from the sofa; he couldn't and fell back on his side. I tried to calm down and didn't say anything for a few moments. It was obvious he'd been drinking very hard and was even now about to pass out—but if this was the worst of it, then it wasn't *too* bad. I glanced at Jim and Royann, who were clearly embarrassed. They had tried to do their best to render aid and had gotten him to eat a bit. And at least he hadn't had to spend the holidays alone.

"Here's the plan," Townes mumbled. "Let's go to my house, I'll sober up by tomorrow. We can head for Memphis in the morning."

"What about your leg? You can't walk."

"Only a . . . only a—a . . . a basket—basketball bruise . . ." His words trailed off.

Basketball bruise. Not an exact medical term, but basically an injury you'd get from shooting hoops with friends. Would hurt like heck when it got bumped or had pressure applied, but not as serious as a broken bone or muscle tear. I figured we could rent a wheelchair and that would get him into the studio. Even in a wheelchair, he could still play guitar and sing. Suddenly, the project seemed doable.

Townes thanked the Calvins for their hospitality and concern. Jim called a medical equipment store and arranged for a wheelchair to be delivered to Townes's house the next morning. On the drive home, Townes admitted how bizarre the last week had been, apologizing somewhat for how crazy he'd made everyone around him.

The new record would perk him up, he affirmed. And when we got to his house, I suggested Townes go to bed and sleep off the booze. He said he would rather stay up and talk it off; he had a lot on his mind he wanted to get out of his head.

Over the next couple of hours, he consumed a box of ice pops. That was dinner. He spoke about the life and road he had traveled to get to where he was. Then he talked about writing his songs, a topic he seldom discussed in detail.

He believed the genuine moment of inspiration came from God—a light from the sky that might come in from the window, floor, and walls and shine directly into his head, whereupon he would immediately scribble down the words and later fashion a melody on guitar. Except for the few co-written songs he'd done, he never allowed anyone to be with him when he wrote. Over the years, when he was alone in the other room, I often heard him talking to someone. My understanding is that it was an extremely private and personal time between him and God.

As we talked, the wind outside got louder and increased the chill within the walls. The house had been owned for many years by Guy and Susanna Clark. They had sold it to Townes hoping he would find the rustic surroundings conducive to peacefulness. The wooden kitchen table Guy had made was still there. It was shaped like a big picnic table and had names of many visitors carved into the top. The Christmas Eve party scene in the *Heartworn Highways* movie was filmed with Guy, Susanna, Rodney Crowell, Steve Earle, Steve Young, Richard Dobson, and others sitting around that table singing long into the night.

There was still a little magic in that house; I sensed some of it was starting to settle in Townes.

Townes picked up Mr. Guitar and played quiet, simple chord sequences with rich, full harmonics that echoed through the house. He was winding down, and Mr. Guitar put everything at ease for Townes. He stopped abruptly and said he was feeling better. "I'm going to bed and put this veil of tears behind me, H. Let's get up early and get to Memphis and make some music."

He smiled and faded off into his bedroom.

I stayed up awhile to wind down, which didn't take long, after my early call that morning. I stepped outside to take in the wooded winter wonderland, the likes of which we rarely saw in Austin. Light snow was on the ground, the trees were bedecked in icicles. Back inside, I lay down on the couch and let my thoughts float off to my loved ones. If there were ghosts here tonight, they were acting very benevolent. Maybe they would follow us to Memphis and keep things on an even keel.

I fell asleep quickly but woke several times over the night, hearing Townes wandering about. He had never slept a full night in all the years I'd known him. Around seven a.m. I woke fully, hearing him out on the side patio feeding the birds and his dog, Feather. He was talking to the critters in the woods, and they were talking back. From what I could hear, he seemed to have sobered up.

"Good morning!" I said.

"What's good about it?"

"It's better than mourning."

He laughed. "It is a beautiful day to start this journey."

The sun was out, and we sat down at the kitchen table and drank coffee, going over the day's drive to Memphis. I saw he wasn't walking well; he leaned onto things as he made his way across the kitchen. He would grimace and emit an occasional "Ouch!" But he wasn't screaming or collapsing.

"It hurts, H," he'd comment. "But it's only a basketball bruise." Just another mishap that would heal in time.

As the morning moved on, he built a slight vodka buzz and was in very good spirits. He played Hank Williams over and over on cassette. Around eleven a.m. the wheelchair Jim Calvin had ordered arrived, and I started loading up the truck. There were two bottles of vodka in the back; this gave Townes a feeling of security.

That all changed in a microsecond.

I had finished gathering Townes's song sheets and was putting Mr. Guitar in his case, as I was talking to Townes. For no apparent reason, the guitar slipped out of my hand, and the bottom hit the floor with a thump. It bounced off the tile, and I grabbed it before it took another hit. Nothing was broken, and there wasn't even a scuff on the instrument. The slip-bounce-retrieval had happened in an instant.

I looked at Townes and saw an expression of alarm on his face. As Mr. Guitar was going down, Townes's head swirled, and he looked over just before the guitar hit the floor. I think he heard Mr. Guitar going, "Whoa!"

After a few seconds, Townes spoke in a soft voice. "H, this is not good."

I had never dropped his guitar in twenty years, though from time to time he bumped it while carrying it onstage and off. We didn't discuss it, but right then we both felt a whisper of negative energy had floated into the room. What was there to say? We finished loading up and got in the truck.

As we drove off, Townes waved goodbye to Bayou Self. "That's yesterday," he remarked. "Today and tomorrow are in front of us."

The conversation picked up as we got on the interstate headed toward Memphis. We had driven this stretch of highway many times over the years. As we headed out of Nashville, with the city skyline behind us, Townes looked back and intoned, "A city with a veil of tears over it. Broken dreams, heartache, and despair."

Yet today was a beautiful, sun-filled day warming into the fifties. Townes relaxed and talked with great anticipation about projects he wanted to do after this record. The *Sky Songs* album was one he mentioned most frequently—just him and a guitar, composing the songs on the spot. "You know what's strange," he said, "is we're going to the capital of the early blues, the city where Elvis lived and recorded, Sun Records and all the rockabillies . . . and I'm making a grunge album."

"Maybe the great blues spirits will be with you," I said. "You've earned their respect if anybody has."

Townes brought out his folder with the new songs, reading the words out loud and humming the melodies. It was great to see him focusing on the project. "Don't tell anybody this, but one of my heroes is Perry Como," he said in an almost giddy mood. "I really liked him growing up—he seemed so comfortable singing, and he made people instantly happy. But seriously, don't tell that to anybody."

About a half hour into the trip, Townes said, "Let's stop and have a good meal and get our strength up." Him suggesting we have a full meal was the most surprising occurrence yet. We pulled into a Denny's off the interstate, and to my continuing amazement, he ordered a large meal and chowed down: roast beef with gravy and mashed potatoes, and he ate it all. We got some gas, and he bought a pint vodka jug, took a couple of sips, and we were back on the road to Memphis in full high spirits.

"H, do you remember the show in New England I was doing with Guy Clark, and your sister Peggy and her husband Stephen Nolan showed up? Stephen had his mandolin with him, and I invited him to sit in on a couple songs. We rehearsed before the show—"

"And when he came onstage, you played two totally different songs."

He chortled at the memory. "But he played them perfectly and did great. Guy told Stephen afterwards, 'You know, Townes rarely lets anyone sit in with him. He tested you, and you passed.'"

The conversation kept flowing in a positive direction, touching on many points we'd talked about the last few months: moving to Germany and doing live recordings with different artists; issuing more of the live performances I'd been recording; continuing to work earnestly on our book, which he insisted cover the full spectrum of colors he lived and experienced daily.

And, finally: "H, no matter what happens, make sure I finish this album."

I assured him he would. Even at that moment, though, I sensed an element of uncertainty picking at the resolve. In all the years I knew him, Townes never showed fear for his own well-being. Heck, he spent every single day actively challenging fate. This day was no different, nor would it be any different tomorrow. It was another stroll in the danger zone, a normal day in the life of Townes Van Zandt. No different at all, outside of the immediate attention required to the details of the recording session.

As we neared the outskirts of Memphis, the weather had changed; it was now cold and rainy. During the entire drive, Townes did not speak of any pain from his injury. He had managed to get his maintenance buzz on, and the restaurant meal had been a mood elevator as well. We passed billboards advertising Elvis Presley's Graceland, and Townes launched into talking about Elvis for ten solid minutes.

For Townes, recording this new album in Memphis symbolized a kind of artistic circle of life. His first interest in performing music came from seeing Elvis on TV. Lamar Fike, one of Elvis's best friends and closest confidants, had been Townes's manager for a time. Townes's beloved Mr. Guitar was a Gibson J-200, a gift from my brother Kevin for the San Marcos newology recording sessions; Elvis had also owned this model of guitar.

And both the King of Rock 'n' Roll and Grandfather Grunge spent their adult lives fighting to overcome the dread and depression that defined so much of their offstage, personal life.

As we made our way through the city, Townes said he could feel the presence of Elvis. "He's saying, 'Welcome to my hometown! It's about time you recorded here with me and all the great music ghosts of Memphis looking over your shoulder.'"

Our hotel was the Radisson on Union Avenue in downtown. A mile or so before, we passed Methodist University Hospital. I suggested we could drop in to the hospital at some point to look at his injury. Townes became irritated. "I'm here to record this album, not go to the hospital!" He had a major fear of hospitals. He'd said more than once, "One of these days I will go into a hospital and never come out."

We pulled into the Radisson driveway. I helped Townes out of the truck into the wheelchair. "People are staring at us, H," he complained. Of course, they were; who wouldn't give a second glance to two unkempt characters hobbling out of a mud-splattered pickup? The doorman asked if we had the right hotel. Worldwide, that was the usual response at most of the hotels we checked into.

Once up in our seventh-floor room, it was the usual routine: Townes turned on the TV with no sound and propped himself up in bed equipped with the remote, a can of orange soda, and a bottle of vodka. He didn't mention his leg or any pain. I felt an infusion of excitement and went out for a walk to see if I could draw an energy uplift from nearby historic Beale Street. Maybe Townes was right . . . it was his destiny to come to Memphis and record what might be his greatest album ever.

By the time I got back, producer Steve Shelley had already come by and talked with Townes. Townes said he'd told him he was enthused and ready and that, no matter what, he wanted his parts completed before we went back to Nashville. Steve agreed and scheduled Townes for several days at the studio. It seemed like everything was on track.

Townes laid out all his songs on the bed and reviewed each one, making changes and additions. When focused, he was a professional of the highest degree. He didn't talk to anyone when he was in this mode, just spoke out loud to himself, structuring and restructuring his thoughts.

After an hour or so, he looked up and said, "I am ready for the forthcoming grunge! Let's go downstairs to the bar and check this rat hole out." Downstairs at the elegant bar, we stood out like two hobos crashing a high-society wedding. Townes immediately became friendly with the bartender, asking if it were true that Elvis used to ride his motorcycle around the city late at night, things like that. The bartender couldn't say enough about Elvis and Memphis and its great music scene past and present. We stayed for over an hour, and by now Townes had on a strong buzz. Again catching me off guard, he said he wanted to eat at the hotel restaurant. We had a good meal, Townes talking about how great life was and the wonder of it all.

He didn't speak of his physical pain until we got back to the room, mentioning it just once. In fact, in the room he was limping to get around; I thought it would be great if we could stop using the wheelchair. He called Jeanene and said how well everything was going. As they spoke, it seemed like a blanket of calmness was slowly settling on us for the night.

I walked over to the window and looked at the city below, a twinkling banner of tiny Christmas lights fused with Townes's reflection bent over the desk. I flashed back to that Christmas Eve in Saigon when my girlfriend, Lien, and I had watched the crowd in the candlelit courtyard singing "Silent Night" in Vietnamese. A sudden emotional wave swept over me—twenty-five years of constant battle had brought me here to this Memphis hotel room preparing again to deal with the unknown. Was I any safer? Any more content? Any more sure of my path in life?

The long day had done me in, and I went to bed, falling into a peaceful sleep until I woke around three a.m. Townes was wide awake and staring out the window, talking out loud; he said the ghosts had filled the room up.

"Are they white ghosts or black?"

"Both, coming and going."

"Do you want me to stay awake until they leave?"

"No. This is between me and them."

I fell back asleep with him talking to the ghosts. Around seven a.m. I woke again; he was still at the window and still talking.

"Everything all right?"

"Sure. Just another night filled with demons."

"Looks like it's going to be a nice day."

"If you like days."

"Townes, you live in a daze."

He laughed and came back to the present, fortifying himself with some vodka gulps and a cigarette. We went downstairs to breakfast— one piece of toast, coffee, and juice for him, a full breakfast for me. Heading back to the room, I wheeled him through the lobby and paused outside the hotel's front entrance for a moment. The morning sunrise was glorious. And he started a short conversation with God.

He spoke of how bad he felt about not being thankful for the life he'd been able to live, his worldly travels, his fans. Implying that the wonder of playing music and traveling didn't hold its fascination anymore. That the vivid colors of life were fading inside of him, and he couldn't control the slow dissolve.

Just as quickly as it manifested, the dark mood swung back to getting the album done. He said quietly, "I hope I can do this. Please help me, Lord."

This time it was me who cracked, "Cheer up, Townes, it's only gonna get worse." He laughed, and we rolled back through the lobby. He spent the rest of the morning going through his notes and drinking at a slow pace. His spirits were getting better, it seemed; he mentioned the room was full of ghosts, and they were friendly ones.

We reached Easley McCain Recording studio around ten a.m. As I wheeled Townes through the front door, Steve Shelley, the band, and engineers were there to greet him. They smiled and hello-ed, came up and shook his hand . . . but their faces couldn't hide hints of disbelief and sadness at Townes's weakened appearance. You could tell they were asking themselves if he'd actually be able to record.

The greetings dwindled to an awkward silence. Townes noticed and intoned, "There is a darkness on the edge of town, and it's me." Everyone laughed, and the atmosphere lightened.

Robert Gordon, the distinguished Memphis-based writer and filmmaker of American blues, rockabilly, and soul, dropped in to check out the session. A longtime admirer of Townes's music, Robert said he was looking forward to writing an article about this new album. He and Townes had a great chat; however, I couldn't help but notice the expression of surprise and dismay on his face when he entered and, like the rest, saw Townes in a wheelchair. I doubt he'd been prepared to see his friend exhibiting such an extreme degree of infirmity.

Everyone got introduced and settled in. The engineers had already set up the musicians' microphones and were now miking Townes. I had printed the lyrics in big letters on sheets of paper and would hold them up in front of him as he sang, hoping to minimize his discomfort and aid his focus.

Finally, everyone was in their places. The red recording light went on—and it was as if a noxious cloud had seeped under the doorframe, filling the room with slow-acting poison.

For no apparent reason, Townes's affability and concentration vanished, and he stumbled through several takes of the first song without ever sounding convincing. His phrasing was off, his articulation was muffled—nothing sounded like what you'd want to hear on the radio or your stereo. Something was askew. Everything was askew.

Steve told the lead engineer, Stuart Sikes, to move on to the second song. Same halting delivery from Townes, same unsatisfying result. A few minutes had turned into three hours.

Steve was getting very frustrated, but—dedicated professional that he was—was able to conceal it. He suggested a break; I rolled Townes into the control room, where he nonchalantly picked up a guitar and proceeded to sing and play perfectly the Rolling Stones' "Dead Flowers." It was like watching two different people from one room to another.

Steve and Stuart exchanged glances; perhaps they thought he'd reached the point where he was now okay—some indefinable "comfort zone" a performer needs to find before they're able to buckle down psychologically and perform in front of the microphone.

I knew better. To get Townes to do anything, you had to pass his test; you had to play his game, or he would make a mess. Of course, most things with Townes always started out with a mess and then turned out great. In fact, I had often thought that Townes should have recorded when he was signed into the mental hospitals and dry-out centers, capturing the despair firsthand. The worse the situation, the deeper the reservoir of darkness he had to work from. Steve and the crew didn't realize that riding out the storm and letting it unfold was Townes's way. And there wasn't a thing they could do to speed up the process. When Townes was ready, *then* everything would work.

I wheeled Townes back into the studio to start a third song; he reverted to the same full-tilt cantankerousness, the same screwing-up-the-recording scenario with bizarre comments and unpredictable starts and stops. He asked to take a break; soon as tape stopped rolling, he picked up a guitar and performed the song perfectly. The morale of the musicians and crew was collapsing by the minute.

In the early days working with Townes, I would just watch everything unfold, a silent bystander. As the years passed, I took a more active role in moving things along, helping things fall into place sooner. It was like a vaudeville routine, I suppose. I was the straight man feeding lines and props to the star; in this performance, getting to the punch line was taking a heckuva long time. I decided to pick up the pace.

Townes was slumped in the wheelchair. "H, I really need another drink."

"I'll give you another drink, just do the damn song." I held up the first lyric card; he stared at the floor.

"Need a drink."

"Tape's rolling. Let's go."

He stared at the far wall. "Gray ghosts are filling up the room."

I threw down the card. "Man, if you don't want to do this, what the hell are we doing here? I need to go home."

"C'mon, man, get me a drink!"

"Sure, no problem." I went to the water dispenser, drew a cup, and held it in front of him.

He glowered and turned his head away. "I'm dying!"

"You've been dead for years. Start the song."

I knew the timeline. He'd established his crazy bona fides for the folks, and they'd have exciting stories to tell their friends. Now it was time to get on track. I knew the harder I pushed now, the quicker things would click.

"Let's start the song."

"H, if I die in here, you know . . ." His voice trailed off.

"If you die, you've made your wish come true. They'll be talking about this album for years. 'The music was so powerful, it killed him.' Start the song."

"Get me a drink."

"Start the song."

It was mid-afternoon. Townes asked Steve if he could go back to the hotel to rest. I knew if we went back to the hotel, he would get completely drunk, and the day would be shot. I was more than a little surprised that Steve and the band seemed surprised by what was going on. They'd been with him before and seen him thoroughly intoxicated. Maybe they thought that in a non-casual situation—an actual meter's-running recording session—Townes would be on the mark.

They were treating him with kid gloves. You didn't treat Townes Van Zandt with kid gloves. There was that element of his mind that resembled a cat toying with a mouse. You hand him gloves, and he'll smack you. Either with words or out-there behavior. In the past, his process of keeping everyone off-balance had worked; this time, it wasn't.

It's important to realize the roots of this process. There was a deep-seated reason Townes was engaging in behavior that was, in effect, threatening to sabotage the recording session he knew could jump-start his career even at this late point in time.

It was, ultimately, about Control, with a capital C.

Over the years, Townes had repeated to me how disappointed he'd been with the final sound of his first album, *For the Sake of the Song*, in 1968. The orchestration presented Townes's vocals in a particular instrumental setting the 23-year-old songwriter felt didn't express his songs the way—even at the start of his career—he thought they should be expressed.

Without that type of setting, of course, any chance of commercial radio play would have been impossible. The great country-rock revolution of albums like *Nashville Skyline*, *Sweethearts of the Rodeo*, *Music from Big Pink*, etc., was still a year in the future.

Entering that *For the Sake of the Song* recording session, Townes had been in awe of the venerable producer Jack Clement and the superstar studio players creating the musical framework for his songs. He was happy to have the chance to learn as much as he could about professional recording. However, Townes was not asked for any input on the production; in 1968, even as enlightened a producer as Clement would have stayed with the prevailing aesthetic governing Nashville music at the time, and that aesthetic did not include artist input about orchestration.

Townes often said that, of all the albums he ever did, he liked the sound of that one the least. It was a landmark moment, early in his career; he and my brother Kevin agreed that on all future recordings Townes did for Poppy Records, Townes would have major input.

The live recordings he and I had been co-producing the last few years incorporated this principle fully. The album did not get issued unless it was according to his standards.

But here now, in Memphis, the discontent that had smoldered for thirty years was flaring up anew. Townes at this point wasn't worried about arrangements or even the sound of his radically "seasoned" voice. It was the process that mattered. He knew he was going to end up with an album he liked, even if it emerged from a crucible of chaos, pain, screaming, drunkenness, and rage. In fact, he believed, all the negativity would make the album a stronger statement in the end.

It was the same process that had taken place when Townes recorded *No Deeper Blue* in Ireland. I had seriously thought he could die in the studio during that session; he seemed barely alive. The producer, Philip Donnelly, was utterly drained by Townes but refused to yield. It had been a battle of wills, both artist and producer determined to attain their own personal goal. Philip pushed on and got from Townes what he needed to fashion a great album.

But Steve, Stuart, and the others didn't see a time-tested "process"; they saw an erratic performer incapable of completing even one song. Even though they'd witnessed some of Townes's antics at their parties a few months before, they likely had figured he'd be sober and right-minded when it came time to record for real.

They were wrong.

Despite my protests, Steve ended the session for the day; Townes and I returned to the Radisson. The evening passed quickly. I roamed around Beale Street, and Townes stayed in the room, watching TV and drinking. We discussed the day's proceedings—he complaining that the engineers couldn't get it together, me replying that he was blowing the chance he'd worked so hard for over the last year. He was starting to mention pain in his leg, but he became upset when I suggested going to the hospital to have it looked at and, possibly, treated.

The next morning at the studio was a repeat of the previous day. Townes resumed the routine of being rational when the recording button was off, then going into bizarro mode when the tape started rolling. Two more songs were partially recorded with Townes moaning more than singing; frustration and confusion were visible on the faces of Steve and the crew. Shortly after one p.m., Steve ended the session for the day and said to reconvene later that night.

That evening's session was a reprise of the first two attempts. Apparently, Steve hadn't passed Townes's test yet; at midnight, Steve said to wrap and try again the next morning.

Back at the hotel, while Townes stayed in the room reading and watching TV, I went for a walk on Beale Street, which I was getting to know quite well. A part of me hoped the ghosts of this legendary streetscape could confer enough great Memphis music vibes into my spirit that I could pass on to Townes. I wondered when the storm would break and Townes would feel the trust he needed to get serious about singing and taking true creative charge of the session. It had to happen soon.

When I came back, the storm had broken. The scene was like the aftermath of a tornado.

Townes sat on the bed, head in his hands, crying, distraught, and bewildered. Steve had just been there and said that, after talking on the phone with Jeanene, he and Jeanene had decided it would be best to cancel the session for now and reschedule at a future date. They believed Townes was in no shape to record and needed to get healthy as soon as possible, starting with a hospital visit to discern the true nature of his leg pain.

And that was that. Goodbye, Elvis. So long, ghosts of bluesmen past.

I knew deep in my gut there would be no rescheduling. Steve had been overwhelmed by the chaos. I seriously doubted he would put himself, the studio crew, and the musicians through the ordeal again.

I settled in for several hours of Townes alternating between self-abasing mea culpas and strident accusations, long-winded monologues about how disgusted he was with himself to "What's wrong with these idiots?" and rants that "My whole life has been one big misery" and "This would have been the best damn album they've ever made!"

It might seem odd to anyone who didn't know Townes that he didn't see the connection between his disruptive studio behavior and the cancellation. But the bipolar personality perceives reality from a different vantage point. I believe to this day that Townes thought everyone would hold on until it all fell in place. I do not believe the thought that the session would be terminated ever entered his conscious mind.

I saw his heart was broken. He sensed that a final line had been crossed, a last opportunity had slipped away. It was going to be a very, very long ride back home.

From our first day at the hotel, I had kept telling Townes to see a doctor. Finally, the morning we left Memphis, he agreed. I wheeled him into main admitting at the outpatient clinic across from Methodist University Hospital, and he was shown into the examination area. A few minutes later, the doctor and nurse brought him back and wheeled him outside the building entrance.

The doctor said it appeared Townes was suffering from phlebitis—inflammation of a vein (or veins) that could result in a severe blood clot (or clots) in the leg and potentially cause a pulmonary embolism—a potentially lethal stoppage of blood flow to the lungs. The doctor directed us to go to the emergency room at the hospital for a fuller examination. Immediately.

Townes said, "Well, H, you and I need to talk."

I went back in to pay the exam bill, and the desk lady said we didn't owe anything. This was a surprise. Then it dawned on me: They wanted us out of the building in case he was going to die then and there.

I went to Townes and said we needed to go to the ER. He said no. I said yes. We spent fifteen minutes in the truck arguing. I told him we weren't going anywhere except to the ER. He was adamant, even as I tried to explain the seriousness of what the doctor had said. If he were going to die, he said, it might as well be in his beloved road truck.

I realized he was not going to budge. I went back inside and called Jeanene, thinking that she and the children's pleas could help convince him to do the right thing. It worked. He agreed to go into the emergency room, but it would be in Nashville, under his conditions. As usual, Townes got his own way.

The morning we had driven to Memphis, it was beautiful and sunny; when we left that day, it was pouring rain, thunder and lightning erupting right to the hour I got him back to Mount Juliet. I drove as fast as we could. No stops. As we headed east along the interstate, the lowering clouds made the sky darker and darker. I never thought one of the most boring interstates in existence would wind up the most intense of all the roads we'd traveled together.

We talked almost continuously. He announced he would like to die like Hank Williams, in transit. "Reaper, come on and get me, I've been waiting 'round to die for a long time."

I pointed out that if he did die, I could be accused of some degree of negligent homicide, because the doctor gave me notice about going immediately to the ER. Townes said not to worry; he'd come back and straighten it all out, post-mortem. What a thought!

One of the tunes he'd wanted to record on this new album was "Dying Crapshooter's Blues," Blind Willie McTell's country-blues classic about a big-time gambler's extravagant funeral cortége. "They can play it at my funeral instead," Townes grumbled. He started singing loudly— "Little Jesse was a gambler, night and day; he used crooked cards and dice"—then abruptly stopped and lowered his head against his chest.

"What happened, H?" he whispered. "Where did it all go? Racing and stumbling through my life, chasing the next song, next gig, next album. It's like having to start all over again. It's like I never lived at all. Man, it's time to just up and die."

"Townes, you are not going to die on this highway. You're already embalmed! You've drunk so much vodka, man, you probably died years ago. Just never laid down and died!"

It was back to that old black humor, but it would keep him laughing. For a while. Maybe till we got home.

I reminded him that he could not die before tomorrow, January 1, when a new CD titled *Rare Trax* in the German edition of *Rolling Stone* would hit the newsstands. The CD featured a duet I'd produced with him and Barb Donovan—his favorite female singer-songwriter, whom he wanted to open his next round of European shows—along with cuts by major artists such as Sting, Sheryl Crow, David Bowie, and Suzanne Vega. It would greatly enhance his bookings for a new European tour.

Nor could he die until at least February 14, the fifth birthday of his daughter, Katie Belle. In fact, I calculated he would have to last for months, maybe years, certainly until Tomato Records brought out the three-CD newology collection, with its rerecordings of sixty songs, including several from *The Late Great Townes Van Zandt*. "All those people who bought *The Late Great* album back then thinking you were dead will pay to come see you now," I said. "And complain you're still alive."

Within a few minutes, I was able to steer the conversation away from the gloomy past and uncertain present to a more promising future once the holidays were over and we could get back on the road.

But it was hard to get away from the failure of the recording session. He was complaining more frequently about the leg pain and, as a result, guzzling larger than usual amounts of vodka. The man's last dream was broken. I could feel the tears of his soul even as he breathed.

At last, our conversation dwindled to silence. I was resigned to the remaining hours of the drive passing in silence. Then a very strange thing happened.

He started up talking again. Nonstop, for nearly an hour. In a soft voice and calm cadence, he embarked upon a methodical progression through his life from his earliest remaining memories to the present, a biographical highlight reel detailing his biggest hurts, his deepest loves, his most anticipated dreams.

It was the only time in all our years traveling together he'd done this.

He kept repeating two phrases: "H, listen closely to what I am saying" and "If I die . . ." It took awhile for me to grasp what was happening, but the pattern and intent became clear: he was fabricating a kind of service-man's will you find in the heat of battle.

He talked about the albums we'd already put together (*Live and Obscure, Roadsongs, Rear View Mirror, The Highway Kind, Abnormal*), the *Documentary* album we had in process, and ideas for new live albums he wanted me to produce if he "should die."

He expressed his unwavering love for his family, his parents, brother, and sister. Though he rarely mentioned his parents in public or in interviews, his most profound grief stemmed from losing them. Though they had committed him to a military academy and mental institution—two life-altering events that impacted his adult existence in major ways—he never blamed them for not fully comprehending his confusing yet always single-minded spirit. "They stuck by me no matter what," he averred.

And then he stopped, just as abruptly as he'd begun. He turned on the cassette player to what had become his favorite meditational music—a Hank Williams tape with the Leon Payne song "Lost Highway"—and sang along.

"I'm a rolling stone, all alone and lost," the distant voice quavered. "A life of sin, I've paid the cost."

It was a hillbilly homily that struck deep into every road musician's heart. I didn't know it then, but that would be the very last song I would hear him sing.

"H, you gotta make a promise to me."

"No." My standard reply anytime Townes initiated a conversation with "You gotta make a promise."

"Gram Parsons. You gotta promise."

Damn.

Before Gram Parsons died, he'd demanded his road manager cremate him and scatter the ashes in the California desert. The manager had chosen unorthodox methods to carry out the singer's wishes and gotten into serious trouble with the law.

"No, Townes, I won't. I don't want to go to jail."

"You don't know what it is I'm asking."

"No."

"You gotta promise."

"No."

"You gotta promise."

I finally gave in. He had me repeat "I promise" three times.

"So, what is it?"

"If I die in this truck, you promise to open the door and kick my body out. And look in the rear view mirror and watch my body bounce on the highway. And say, 'He's home now for good.'"

This wasn't a joke. We'd gotten past the joke point. It had crossed over to what you'd call mortuary planning.

"You're not going to die on this drive, Townes."

"You promised."

"I know."

Would I have done what he asked? If it were your closest friend, would you?

He got quieter for the rest of the drive. Townes always said the highway was his home, but that Gram Parsons request wasn't something I'd expected. Then again, I hadn't truly expected much that had taken place the last few days.

As he sat with eyes closed, I knew he was deep inside his mind, watching his life spool out like an old-time newsreel, a grainy, cacophonous montage intermeshing hopes and heartbreaks, beauty and terror, magic and fury, frame after flickering frame of disappointment, exhilaration, self-recrimination, impulse . . . yet, when the rage and tears subsided, Townes Van Zandt wasn't waiting 'round to die.

He was getting ready to write a new song. It's what he would always do, as long as he had breath left in his body and even the barest shred of a vocal cord to croak it out.

I turned slightly and thought I saw a single tear slide down Townes's cheek. Over the years I had said many prayers for Townes, but this time my heart swelled with such sadness that I cried, too—internally—and said a special prayer that he could recover from this recording debacle.

Something good would come out of the mess we'd just been through. I knew that in my heart. Something completely off the wall, something that grabbed people by their gut and made them listen.

Something.

We got to Mount Juliet late in the afternoon, and the Calvins and Jeanene, Katie Belle, and Will were there. We helped Townes into his house, and he told me to fly home that night to spend New Year's Eve with Cindy and my son, Harold III. I agreed, and we spoke briefly of rescheduling the album and getting ready for the next European tour. I said I would call tomorrow to see how things were. We shook hands, as we always did when meeting or leaving. He always had a very strong handshake, and this time the grip lasted maybe a bit longer than usual.

I got into Jim Calvin's car for the airport run. Townes called out, "H, you're deserting me!"

"No!" I yelled back. "You've already had dessert today!"

The last time I heard his voice, he was laughing.

As we pulled out of the driveway, the thought *You'll never see him again* surged across my brain, like a sudden burst from a flash grenade. I suppressed it immediately. With all the near-death situations throughout his life, I figured Townes and the Lord were on a direct line by now. As in the past, all would be well. Or at least manageably grim.

That night I was back in Austin hugging Cindy and Harold III at our impromptu New Year's Eve celebration. I didn't sleep well; too many things from the last week kept me tossing and turning. The next day, I told Cindy about the aborted session in Memphis, the initial promise and the chaotic breakdown. Still, she predicted, Townes would go on as he had before. He could tour and make records with me and with smaller independent labels. Not much would change at all.

And that, of course, was the problem. Townes had desperately wanted this Geffen album to change the story of his career. It would instead be an epitaph.

The next day Royann Calvin called me with good news. Townes had gone into the hospital the night before and gotten an x-ray revealing that his "basketball bruise" stemmed from an actual broken bone in his hip. Today, New Year's morning, Townes had undergone successful surgery to repair the fracture.

I was relieved but flabbergasted. The fact that he'd even attempted to record with that serious of an injury was nothing short of amazing; it was a powerful testament to his determination to put forth every last ounce of effort in making the album. In the end he faltered, but it was never for lack of will. He simply couldn't overcome who he was and how people were going to deal with it.

Just before Royann hung up, she said something that worried me a bit. Against the doctor's strong recommendation that Townes remain in the hospital for recovery and detoxification, he had talked his way into having Jeanene and the Calvins bring him home to Mount Juliet. He spent New Year's Day in his bed, struggling with a mild case of delirium tremens, and by evening was feeling increasing pain from the surgery. I thought about calling, but decided to leave him alone with his family. We'd talk the next day, and he'd have a funny story or two about the hospital.

I fell asleep and was drowsing away on Cindy's living room sofa, when her black lab, Jezebel, began barking furiously, scampering around the house as if pursuing an unseen visitor. I woke with a start and watched the lights flicker, then dim for several seconds before coming back up.

I tried to quiet her as two more flickering-dimming cycles occurred. Then, the lights stabilized and the dog hushed. I flopped back onto the sofa but could not fall asleep.

A half hour or so later, the phone rang. It was Jeanene, her voice a strained whisper. "Townes is gone," she said.

I paused before replying. "I know. He came to say goodbye."

12

Goodbye to All My Friends

SUNDAY, JANUARY 5, 1997. Belmont Church, Nashville, Tennessee. Less than twenty-four hours had passed since Townes Van Zandt's cremation had returned him to the literal dust from whence he had metaphorically come not quite fifty-three years before.

Yet the congregation gathered at his memorial service could not help but laugh through their tears.

"I booked this gig thirty years ago," announced a deadpan and sleep-deprived Guy Clark, as he strummed a guitar chord and prepared to play Townes's "To Live Is to Fly."

The nearly seven hundred audience members representing the cream of Nashville's songwriting community got the joke: Townes Van Zandt had spent most of his adult life seeking creative ways to hasten his death. Longtime friends like Guy and Susanna Clark, who had sold Townes the house in which he would spend his last moments, could finally finish grieving for this lost soul, a grieving that for some had begun the first instant they'd met him.

Many beneficiaries of his friendship and inspiration were sitting in the pews of the spacious Greek Revival church that afternoon—Emmylou Harris, Rodney Crowell, Steve Earle, Lyle Lovett, Nanci Griffith, Radney Foster, Larry Monroe, Lamar Fike, Kevin Eggers—several of them rising to share songs and anecdotes while agreeing that the agnostic, deliciously profane Townes would have undoubtedly preferred his final farewell take place at the Bluebird Cafe, Tootsie's Orchid Lounge, the Gold Rush, or another of Nashville's finer honky-tonks.

The end had happened so fast. Sure, everyone knew it was *possible*. But not really *now*. You just assumed that, like a pilot in a nosedive headed toward a mountain cliff, Townes would pull up the rickety old plane in time, clear the peak, and bump the wheels onto the runway. No matter what shape he'd gotten himself into, something in your heart always said, "He'll get better."

This time, the mountain had won.

Another irony, less amusing, remained unspoken in the eulogies. Townes had passed while attempting to record his first-ever album for a major label, a disc likely to bring him the commercial sales and mainstream recognition he'd diligently sought throughout his career. A lyricist hailed as "the James Joyce of Texan songwriting," "one of the greatest American poets of the 20th century," and "the greatest songwriter Texas ever produced" would attain his lifelong dream of success only after his death.

The general feeling among the mourners was that he'd at least had the good luck to die on one of the most revered dates in country music history. January 1 was the death anniversary of the legendary Hank Williams Sr., whose emotionally intense, heart-wrenching sound had transformed country music in the late 1940s and early 1950s. Both men had succumbed to a heart attack aided by a sinister confluence of alcohol and painkillers.

Before she stood and sang "Pancho and Lefty" with Rodney Crowell, Emmylou Harris recalled the first time she had seen Townes perform. "I spoke to him on the stage at Gerde's Folk City in New York. It was thirty years ago, and I remember thinking, 'My God, it's the ghost of Hank Williams.' But he was just forging his own path down the Lost Highway."

As the years passed, Harris's observation would take on a discomforting reality, as Townes slid down the same dark, dissolute path as Williams. It simply took longer for Townes to hit bottom.

Unlike Williams, who died six hundred miles from home in the freezing back seat of his Cadillac convertible, Townes departed in more comfortable circumstances: the bedroom of his house in Mount Juliet, where Jeanene had just made him a snack of cheese and crackers and put him to rest in the company of five-year-old Katie Belle and fourteen-year-old Will.

It was a surprisingly gentle, simple end to a life that had been marked by considerable harshness and difficulty. Townes's final few days were a microcosm of the existence he had created and endured over three decades—intermittent flashes of genius tempered by lengthy bouts of bipolar eruptions and alcohol-tinged psychosis, unfettered hope giving rise to impossible dreams quickly crushed, then springing anew each time he picked up his guitar or wrote out the first line to a fresh song.

As he was fond of saying to interviewers, all he had ever wanted to do was "write the perfect song that would save someone's life."

In an outpouring of email tributes and news articles over the coming weeks, fans from around the world would attest that Townes Van Zandt had indeed written songs that saved their lives, their marriages, their sanity—a feat he was never able to accomplish for himself.

Of course, Townes himself didn't want to change; he wanted only to create. No matter what his physical condition or emotional mood at any given time, he still yearned to perform for others and would do so at the drop of a hat. I believe his music was the sincerest attempt he could make to reveal who he was and ask, if not for love, at least for understanding.

Townes once told me, "H, if you want to know my life's story, listen to my records in the order they were made, and you will hear it in my songs, better than I could ever tell you in words."

Two decades after his death, Townes Van Zandt is more popular than ever. To date, his songs have been recorded by over five hundred performers worldwide, and the number continues to grow year by year.

Accolades from critics continued to multiply as well. The *Wall Street Journal* wrote, "His influence as a songwriter towers over American country and roots music . . . his entire body of work serves as a gold standard." From Amazon.com's music critic Steve Stolder came this immortalizing comparison: "The songs of Townes Van Zandt are destined to be for folk artists what the works of Gershwin are to saloon singers."

Townes had suspected this delayed recognition would be his fate. "People will only know who I am after I'm dead," he'd say. Townes knew his music had lasting value. Of course, he always hoped the appreciation would be of a more tangible nature during his lifetime.

At the memorial service, John Lomax III agreed, pointing out that "Townes may be gone, but these songs he left us will probably outlive us all. To live is to fly, and he sure did."

Kevin Eggers, Townes's longtime friend and record producer, asserted that "Townes had the extraordinary gift of looking into the darkness and bringing out the light. He saw clearer than most people."

Steve Earle observed that "Townes went into places, sometimes dark and scary places, where we were unable or unwilling to go. Sometimes I think he went so we wouldn't have to. From here on out, we're on our own."

Susanna Clark's remembrance succeeded in conveying the Whitman-esque multitudes of Townes's personality, taking on the nature of a poem itself:

> First thing each morning, at 8:30, for years, Townes called me. He'd say, "Hey, babe, this is our morning call." Guy would usually get me a cup of coffee, 'cause we'd be on the phone for at least an hour. He let me in his soul, and I let him in mine. I had the honor and privilege of having this noble, wild soul in my life. He called me his best friend and sister; I called him my best friend and brother. We always said "I love you" before we hung up. . . .
>
> This morning, 8:30 came . . . and the phone didn't ring.

When it came time for me to step forward, I kept it short and simple.

"Townes, we were on the road to the last, always with the thought in our minds we would make it home to our loved ones. Townes, you made it home the final time, blessed with the purest of love, to be in your bed, wrapped in the arms of your family. There's a big hole in the world tonight which will never be filled again. I'll miss you, old friend. When it's my time, I'll meet you on the golden highway. We'll go fishing in your heavenly houseboat. God bless you, may you rest in peace."

It was goodbye, perhaps, but not farewell.

The day before he died, Townes told me that if he died and I wanted to talk with him, I was to go out into the wind at any time and listen. "Listen, H, and you will hear me, and we can still talk like we always have over the years."

And we still do.

A good many of the voices and sounds he heard have rubbed off on me, and now I have my own crew of angels and demons with whom I converse. And can't turn off, even if I wanted to.

Describing and telling these many stories of Townes still brings tears to my eyes. Looking back, the years and miles flew by like a very turbulent thunderstorm that came out of nowhere, then suddenly disappeared and opened a sky full of sunlight.

When I drive, I believe the white lines on the highway are Townes's footprints.

Today, I listen to the live performances of Townes's words and music that I recorded years ago, and I am instantly transported back to that specific moment and place in time, my nostrils filled with the smell of thick bar smoke, my ears ringing with the din of a packed roadhouse.

A few months after Townes died, I was talking on the phone with Ramblin' Jack Elliott, the legendary folk troubadour. Booking agent Keith Case had called him, asking Jack if he would fill Townes's place on his artist roster. Jack said he felt strange taking Townes's spot; I told him that Townes would have been honored.

Jack agreed and remembered how, years back, Townes had filled in for him one night at the Exit Inn in Nashville. Jack had gotten stuck on the highway somewhere, and Townes had obligingly done the show so audiences wouldn't feel they'd come for nothing. In fact, they got more than they'd bargained for.

"He had me call in to the club phone line," said Jack. "And he had the sound man put a microphone to the phone. I was able to sing to the audience for a few songs. We even did a couple of duets."

You could always expect the unexpected when Townes Van Zandt took the stage.

Back at Belmont Church, the closing speakers were doing their best to pile on as many warm thoughts and reverential memories as they could, like a parent stuffing a son's knapsack full of extra sandwiches before sending him off to summer camp.

Steve Earle and Mickey White ended the proceedings with a rousing version of "White Freightliner Blues." When the song ended and the last echoes were fading into the cool, stone walls, there was a prolonged silence among the audience, almost a minute long, as if each person were silently determining once they left the church how to carry on the legacy of a remarkable talent they had felt privileged to experience and survive.

They all knew that Townes Van Zandt had been saying goodbye his entire life and chronicling that journey with unrivaled lyrical eloquence and passion.

I think he had a hard time being him. More than anyone I've ever known, his life was a work in progress he was constantly struggling to shape and comprehend. And he labored at that, for sure, for decades. Like the master song craftsman he was, he was never truly satisfied with the final product, but always kept giving it one more shot, one extra tweak, one last effort.

Whenever we were in Amsterdam in the 1990s, he always had us make a stop at the Van Gogh Museum; he would stand for hours looking at the paintings, sometimes an hour at one painting alone. He believed he had a powerful karmic connection with the tortured, misunderstood painter and fellow Dutchman. For Townes, these paintings came alive and consumed him; it was as if he were allowing Van Gogh's ghost to become part of his mind and spirit through the paintings.

Strange as it might seem, I always believed there was an optimism in his music, a fundamental hopefulness, no matter how harsh the tone or subject matter. An underlying belief that just by the act of crafting a story and then telling it to others, it could make a difference. If that optimism wasn't there, how else would his songs appeal to so many people?

In the end, Townes always did what he wanted. He would ask people's opinions, and he'd listen to their answers. But in the end, it was always his choice. Jeanene would give him suggestions, and he would listen, and I think she influenced him in some ways . . . but Townes always ended up doing what *he* wanted. Always. From day one I knew that. Anytime he was in bad shape and would say, "H, this is the plan," the truth of it was—it was *all* his plan.

Even his ongoing self-demolition was intentional. He set his own dynamite, laid the wire, and pushed the plunger. No matter what obstacle he faced, he found a way to live the life *he* wanted to. How many of us can say that about the lives we lead?

For whatever reason known only to himself, his decision to teach me how to be his friend was part of a plan, too. And for that, I am eternally grateful.

I'd venture to say that the chief sources of happiness in Townes's life consisted of the following: writing songs and performing to an appreciative audience; telling jokes and singing funny songs; contriving outlandish stories with dark humor; manipulating people and situations for his own personal entertainment; constantly touring and traveling to ingest as much of the world outside himself as possible; and, naturally, his mom and dad, brother, sister, wives, and children.

It was Townes's homespun wit that carried us through the rough financial patches, Townes's sly smile that defused a score of tense confrontations, Townes's deep humility that made audiences want to lean in and listen to his words and music with every fiber of their being.

And damn his legions of demons. Other people locked themselves away and hid from them. Townes flung open his door and said, "Come on in." The times he would say, "Demons are chasing me, H!" . . . I wonder if the chasing wasn't instigated by him in pursuit of another song, another truth.

Maybe success was his biggest fear. He always said he didn't want it. But I know darn well he wanted it. All performers and artists want it—singers, dancers, actors, writers, painters, clothes designers, chefs.

They want success because it means the message they're offering in whatever medium is worthwhile. It's helpful. It's useful. It may even heal. It means they've reached out and made contact. They've proven they're human, and their lives as they've chosen to live them have some immediate and possibly lasting value to others.

Townes never stopped seeking that contact, though it became an incredible burden as the years went by. They say, if you get to drink one full cup of life, you've done well. I think Townes drank a couple dozen and craved plenty more right to his very last breath.

Some might ask what value the life of an artist like Townes Van Zandt—or any artist—has in the day-to-day turmoil of our lives, the lives of billions of people walking the planet at this very moment. Songs are nice to pass the time, but what do they really do to make the world a better place?

I think of what my dad once said to me when I expressed the doubts I had about the value of my life. He said: "Son, work on your own garden and be kind to people, and this will change the world."

It took years for these words of simple wisdom to sink in to my consciousness. I think Townes felt this way, too. Though his garden was filled with rocks and weeds and may never have bloomed as full and fresh as he wanted, he never stopped trying to make his small patch of musical earth as nurturing and meaningful as he possibly could.

Townes's favorite rock band was the Rolling Stones, as they are mine. My dreams of a life in music began the day my brother Kevin took me to see them at Carnegie Hall. More than forty years later, in 2006, my son Harold III and I saw the Stones perform at Zilker Park in Austin. At one point Harold III turned to me with one of those expressions kids have that is both serious and pleased. "Dad," he said, "you know Uncle Townes is with us tonight."

Of course he was. He was in the wind, singing with the band. The Stones probably felt it, too.

I can still see the first day when I arrived in Nashville, driving up to his cabin in the hills, and he's waving a big hello as he strides toward my car.

Sometimes, it's the image of him in the wheelchair waving goodbye as I left his home in Mount Juliet for the last time.

These are among the memories that make me happy and sad at the same time.

These are the reflections of Townes Van Zandt in my life's rear view mirror.

AFTERWORD
"THE VAN GOGH OF LYRICS"
by L. E. McCullough

"I think it's a series of accidents, really, that make one persist in something."
—ALICE OSWALD

"Come, Ahab's compliments to ye; come and see if ye can swerve me . . . The path to my fixed purpose is laid with iron rails, whereon my soul is grooved to run. Over unsounded gorges, through the rifled hearts of mountains, under torrents' beds, unerringly I rush!"
—HERMAN MELVILLE, *MOBY DICK*

YOU'VE JUST FINISHED reading a memoir by Harold F. Eggers Jr. depicting the many sides of Townes Van Zandt, a talented, yet conflicted individual who could at times be stubborn, profligate, acerbic. But who was also possessed of humor, compassion, insight, and unquenchable aspiration until the very moment of his death.

A man who, like many of us, spent the majority of his waking moments as an adult seeking to live a life with as much happiness and little pain as possible, but—like many of us—not always knowing quite how to make that happen in an easy, efficient, blunder-free manner.

This account by Harold Eggers offers much more than basic biography or mere incident reporting. While it can never precisely detail the actual thought processes of Townes Van Zandt from moment to moment, Harold's personal perspective provides as much insight as we'll ever have into what it was like to share the company of an extraordinary musical artist over a twenty-year career arc. An artist who, even in his most public moments, maintained a tight cloak of emotional secrecy few were ever able to penetrate.

And you're saying, "Another Sad Artist tale . . . why should I care? What's it have to do with me?"

Let me tell you why you should care. And what it has to do with you. But first, let me tell you what it has to do with me.

I initially heard the name Townes Van Zandt in 1977 while I was finishing my PhD studies in ethnomusicology at the University of Pittsburgh and performing with various groups of Irish and Appalachian musicians. One night at a party, I met Mike Henry, a local folk guitarist. The conversation turned to new performers making their way through the area's club circuit, and Mike could not stop talking about this singer-songwriter from Texas he'd heard perform at Slippery Rock State College, a small school about an hour north of Pittsburgh.

The fellow had an unusual name for a folk singer—Townes Van Zandt—and everything about him seemed unusual, Mike recalled. Townes's "story tunes" were especially striking; the usually boisterous student audience got really quiet when the singer played. And, Mike noted, the performers he saw coming through the college's Hitchin' Post coffeehouse in the months following invariably played a Townes song or two in their sets, as if it were a special privilege and responsibility for them to impart these lines of lyrical wisdom to the world.

From Mike's reverent description, I figured this Van Zandt must be a wizened old Texan about eighty years old, rocking away his golden years on a prairie porch. Imagine my surprise after I moved to Austin in 1983 and saw Townes in the flesh—when he was, of course, not quite forty and still very much active.

A couple of years later I was hired as the country/folk music editor at the *Austin American-Statesman*, and the heart of my beat was the city's vibrant singer-songwriter community. I learned of Townes's reputation as a brilliant but unpredictable performer, yet I never spent any significant time in his presence until 1986, when I was called to perform on the *Fathers of Texas* album recounting the 1836 Texas Revolution.

I walked into Cedar Creek Recording Studio in South Austin and met project producer K.R. Wood and engineer Stephen Mendell, a well-traveled studio musician and savvy dial-spinner. The track to be recorded was an Irish folk song called "Will You Come to the Bower"; I would be contributing Irish tin whistle fills to rhythm accompaniment by acoustic guitarist Joe Forlini of the pop band the Sweaters.

The singer was Townes Van Zandt.

"Will You Come to the Bower" was written by Irish poet Thomas Moore (1779–1852) and first published in 1807 in his *Irish Melodies*, a book of 124 Irish-themed songs that was extensively republished across North America and Europe for decades after. "Will You Come to the Bower" was one of the collection's more popular songs and would certainly have been known to the fifteen or so Irish immigrants believed to be among the Alamo's last defenders.

The tune is a simple heptatonic, major-key melody in 3/4 time; like many of Moore's compositions, the lyrics are unabashedly romantic with an underlying tinge of melancholy:

Will you come to the bower I've shaded for you?
Your bed shall be flowers all spangled with dew.
Will you, will you, will you, will you come to the bower?

There under the bower on roses you lie,
With a blush in your cheek and a smile in your eye.
Will you, will you, will you, will you come to the bower?

But the roses we press shall not rival your lip,
Nor the dew be so sweet as the kisses we sip.
Will you, will you, will you, will you come to the bower?

And oh for the joys that are sweeter than dew,
From languishing roses and kisses from you.
Will you, will you, will you, will you come to the bower?

It was the type of song Townes might have written himself, had he practiced his trade in the pubs of 19th-century Dublin and not the honky-tonks of 20th-century Nashville.

In fact, there were several similarities between the two composers. Both had entered college intending to study law; both abandoned their studies, swept up in a time of extreme political and social ferment. Like Townes, the youthful Moore fell in with a bohemian crowd of artists and musicians, became intensely enamored of his nation's folk music, and spent his adult life fending off financial chaos while traveling through Europe, North America, and the Caribbean.

As we waited for the mike setup, Townes told some jokes, and the three of us did a short run-through of the arrangement. He was sober, but he quickly and seamlessly shifted the conversation to gambling: Did we want to flip pennies? Did we want to bet on what the next person coming through the door might be wearing, and so on.

We took our places inside the studio, Stephen Mendell gave the start cue, and I hit the first solo notes of the eight-bar intro. At measure five, Joe Forlini brought in his guitar, and four bars later, Townes began singing.

We nailed it on the first take. Townes's singing was assured and nuanced, the plaintive voice of a doomed soldier gazing into the dark winter sky and knowing the next sunrise will be his last, as he struggled to remember the lover he would never see again.

Even while I played, from opening breath to final hold, I could not shake the thought that this was the most achingly exquisite one minute and fifty seconds of music in which I'd ever participated.

And it was the first time that I fully grokked the *essence* of Townes Van Zandt: the disarming humor, the restless compulsion, the on-the-fly creativity, the instinctive ability to infuse even the simplest tune with unmistakable, unforgettable singularity.

I did not see the moody, soul-crushing darkness described so vividly by Harold Eggers throughout this book; on this one occasion at least, that trait was successfully transmuted into his performance channeling the long-ago spirit of a forlorn immigrant soul. Townes had not just brought an old folk tune to life; he had invited the human heart encased within that tune to speak anew to us modern listeners.

If you are an artist, storytelling is a fundamental part of a lifelong process by which you define your art and yourself. In telling *your* story, you tell the stories of others. And vice versa. In Townes Van Zandt's case, it was a particular challenge . . . he had to fill in gaps, had to replace what the shock treatments had erased from his memory bank.

While the shock treatments Townes endured at age nineteen may have broken his mind, they also may have aerated it, putting in additional space to add new components and allow his music and life to evolve in an entirely different direction.

Popular music in our time has become a way we learn about ourselves—our beliefs, our values, our hopes. Pop tunes are filled with pithy aphorisms offering concise bits of wisdom and guidance as we come of moral and psychological age: *You can't always get what you want, but if you try sometimes, you might find, you get what you need . . . you can't please everyone, so you got to please yourself . . . so often times it happens that we live our lives in chains, and we never even know we have the key . . . if you can't be with the one you love, honey, love the one you're with,* and so on.

Since the rise of rock 'n' roll in the 1950s, millions of young people around the world have cherished the dream of submitting fully to the counterculture muse, of enjoying a life of uncompromising artistry and unfettered expression, scoring salvation and bliss through the medium of meaningful music—the baby boomer equivalent of Huck Finn's lighting out "for the territory," Greeley's advice to "Go west, young man," Kerouac's on-the-road Beat mantra.

Townes Van Zandt embraced that dream each moment until the hour of his death, experiencing and reveling in the extremes of pleasure and pain, adulation and loneliness, truth and illusion that a volatile combination of music, genius, and rage can visit on a person.

Predictably, Townes received a flood of accolades after his passing. There were tribute concerts in New York City, Seattle, and Austin, dozens of memorial shows and retrospective radio broadcasts throughout North America and Europe that continue to this day, and a nationally televised *Austin City Limits* celebration featuring Willie Nelson, Emmylou Harris,

Guy Clark, Lyle Lovett, Steve Earle, Townes's son J.T. Van Zandt, and others singing Townes's songs.

The obituaries and articles praised Townes's songwriting as among the best. He had earlier been called "the van Gogh of lyrics" by *Billboard*, and the *Boston Globe* suggested he might be "the premier poet of the time."

For three decades Townes Van Zandt's fabled behavioral excesses had coexisted with a prodigious writing talent and mesmerizing performance style that rendered him, as he himself often wryly noted, "one of the most famous songwriters you never heard of."

His quirky yet literate pieces about hobos, winos, prostitutes, gamblers, and other socially marginal characters had an engaging, intimate feel marked by the directness and simplicity found in African-American country blues and Anglo-American frontier ballads. It was music that exuded a joyful melancholy, music that was by turns wistful and defiant, romantic and rakish, humorous and haunting.

And always true.

It was not the type of music one might have predicted from the scion of a prominent Texas oil family, prep school graduate, and onetime law student. Like thousands of his fellow baby boomers, Townes had tuned in to the siren call of '60s pop and dropped out of college to become an itinerant singer-songwriter on the folk circuit. Unlike most of his contemporaries, Townes stayed true to the wandering minstrel life, fully committed to the ideal that you can't really sing the blues unless you live them.

He lived them as lowdown and rough as possible, and would become his own self-fulfilling legend—the inscrutable singer-songwriter who epitomized mythic American archetypes in every aspect of his life and music: the Rambling Bluesman, the Gypsy Songster, the Brilliant Yet Destructive Artist who insisted the best and truest music came from pushing body and soul to the breaking point.

He surrendered completely, lost everything, and in so doing created a musical legacy both inimitable and timeless. The purity of his music could only be assured by the degree to which his own person evaporated from the physical world.

Question: Is an artist's obliteration of self essential to achieving creative purity?

From this account, it would seem as if Townes Van Zandt had early on decided that was the case and would require his complete, unstinting focus every day of his life.

Of course, music is a social act. Music is an art in which we listeners immerse ourselves in a community for the purpose of honing our individuality—the song or tune that speaks to "us" individually also resonates through the psyches of potentially millions of others.

Townes came of artistic maturity in an era when, for the first time in Euro-American commercial music, what truly mattered in a popular song was how a songwriter truly felt deep *inside*. A new emotional honesty had entered the idiom; a never-ending stream of singer-songwriters poured their hearts out in what became known as "soft rock." But in country music, there was a grittier side to this emotional depth—outlaw country.

In the 1960s and '70s, American country music and its folk-based derivatives came to be seen as idioms that spoke truth, or at least made an effort to locate it somewhere in the lyric of a song describing the lives of everyday people and situations.

Roots of the country-folk genre lie in ancient blues and ballad forms that speak of loneliness, sacrifice, duty, making your way, finding your destiny, submitting to fate, laughin' just to keep from cryin', feeling alienated from this world but always hoping your true home is just around the next bend in the road.

Townes Van Zandt and his country-folk songwriter peers weren't seeking world peace, divine order, or even social justice—just a modicum of basic contentment mixed with acceptance of inevitable loss. Think Jimmy Buffett's "Margaritaville," Kris Kristofferson's "Sunday Mornin' Comin' Down," Merle Haggard's "If We Make it Through December," Willie Nelson's "Funny How Time Slips Away", and hundreds of others, including "For the Sake of the Song," "At My Window," "Snowin' on Raton," "No Place to Fall," and almost every lyric Townes created.

To make their way in the world—which is to say, succeed in commu-

nicating with others—any artist of any idiom must possess three qualities: talent, discipline, and courage. You may have plenty of innate talent
and the discipline to develop your abilities, but it takes guts to draw out
the art you've painstakingly fashioned from inside yourself and present it
to the world for its acceptance, scorn, or indifference.

Townes had all three of these qualities, and his emergence as a professional songwriter coincided with the larger groundswell of a compatible
musical movement.

But at some point, he must have decided they weren't enough for
what he needed his songs to do in the world. And so he took things one
step further.

Over the last four thousand years, Hinduism has included a life stage
known as *sannyasa*, in which an individual practices a form of extreme
asceticism for the purpose of achieving *moksha*—the state of ultimate
spiritual liberation. By assuming a detachment from life and renouncing
material desires, it is believed the *sannyasin* can attain a free and blissful
existence.

When Townes Van Zandt died, all he owned was Mr. Guitar and his
pickup truck to get to the next show.

The *sannyasin* seeks to embody values and attitudes that reflect an
ever-expanding conception of himself, his aim, and his mission in life.

"If I could only write the perfect song . . ."

The *sannyasin* seeks answers to questions such as "Who am I? Of
what really do I consist? What is this cage of suffering that envelops the
human world?"

There is no doubt that Townes Van Zandt's life and music were
defined by multiple shades of love and suffering. But in sharing his lost
loves, he inspired others to think, to create, to act. The first time you saw
him perform—no matter what shape he was in—it was something you'd
likely never experienced before and would certainly never forget after.

His work embodied an immense level of respect for the process of
creation. While our modern word *respect* is usually employed to mean
"exhibiting due regard or esteem for the feelings, wishes, rights, or tra-
ditions of others," the term has a much deeper immersion in our social

consciousness, deriving from an ancient Sanskrit root denoting "one who sees" and an even older Proto-Indo European source meaning "to observe."

Townes Van Zandt spent his life observing and then attempting to transmit those observations in songs that would allow him—and us, through him—to *see* a more profound vision of the world, a vision unobscured by the haze of everyday agitation and entanglement that afflicts us all.

Respect? He was filled with enormous respect for the life-changing Art he wanted so desperately to create and disperse through the world. He had so *much* respect for this solemn calling that—like a humble *sannyasin* or other purposeful pilgrim—the need to show mundane concern for everything else, including himself, simply fell by the wayside as he woke each new day to continue his quest.

His music cast a dynamic and far-reaching spell; from his first carefree gigs in Houston beer joints to his final frustrating hours in a Memphis recording booth, he continued to use the power of song to break through the psychological barriers that constrict all of us, except for those few precious moments when a simple melody or lyric phrase can embolden us to take a daring step further along the path of personal enlightenment.

A musician creates magic. That's what we do. In a mere instant, we can change your mind with a note, a sound, a breath, a pause.

We beguile, entrance, inspire, transport, fire up, and rock your world. We mellow you out, soothe your soul, connect you with your rock-bottom emotional self, and sometimes make it possible for you to share some level of basic empathy with people you've never met.

No other human art form does this, literally, in a single moment.

And when that musical performance is live, right in front of you, it's even more powerful and potentially transformative.

Townes Van Zandt knew this. And the guitar-picking, word-rhyming, ghost-jousting *sannyasin* he had become demanded he never for a day stop living out his destiny.

And ours.

In fact, any of us *could* have been Townes Van Zandt. Thousands upon thousands of us possess wonderful artistic talents . . . but how many of us have the courage to disappear into our art the way he did?

Can we even match the courage and tenacity of Harold Eggers, resolute Ishmael to Van Zandt's implacable Ahab, who linked his fate toward furthering the singer's lifelong white-whale quest for A Perfect Song?

As they say, timing and conviction are everything in this world. Townes Van Zandt's music certainly never lacked conviction. And if the timing of his brief sojourn on this earth was too far off to yield the rewards he sought for himself, it's provided an exceptional bounty for those of us who hear him today.

A TOWNES VAN ZANDT DISCOGRAPHY
BY PATRICK HURLEY

I FIRST HEARD of Townes in 1975, at the time of the release of Guy Clark's *Old No. 1* album. In an interview discussing the album, Guy commented, "If you enjoy my album, and you have not heard him already, you really must listen to Townes Van Zandt."

I was totally mesmerized by Guy's album and, with that strong recommendation, I immediately bought *The Late Great Townes Van Zandt*, issued in the U.K. on United Artists. I was absolutely spellbound—I had never heard anything this good. I soaked up the lyrics to "Sad Cinderella," "Snow Don't Fall," "Pancho and Lefty," and "If I Needed You."

I instantly started on a mission to track down all Townes's records, which was no mean feat living in Ireland in 1975; the albums and 45s were only selectively available within the U.S., and mail order for records was in relative infancy. I telephoned a number of New York record stores and managed eventually to track them all down. Over the last forty-three years, I have bought every Townes album on the day it was released.

I have divided Townes's discography into five groups.

Releases on Poppy Records
    Established by Kevin Eggers, Poppy issued Townes's first six albums over the five-year period from his first album in 1968 to 1972, when Poppy closed.

Releases on Tomato Records

Also established by Kevin Eggers, Tomato issued Townes's albums *Live at the Old Quarter, Houston, Texas* in 1977 and *Flyin' Shoes* in 1978. It reissued five of the six Poppy albums in 1978 (excluding the first album) and in 1993 released *The Nashville Sessions* (an album recorded in 1974 but not released then). After a long spell of inactivity, Tomato issued *Texas Rain: The Texas Hill Country Recordings* in 2001, *The Best of Townes Van Zandt* in 2002, and *Be Here to Love Me* in 2005, a soundtrack album to Margaret Brown's movie about Townes's life and music.

Releases on Sugar Hill Records

Townes did not record for nine years after the 1978 *Flyin' Shoes* album. In 1987, he signed with Sugar Hill and released two albums that year: *At My Window* and *Live and Obscure* (a live recording from April 1985). Sugar Hill released four further albums between 1993 and 1997.

Releases of Live Recordings by Harold F. Eggers Jr.

Townes entered into a partnership with Harold F. Eggers Jr. (his longtime road manager, friend, and business partner) with the intention of releasing an ongoing series of live albums. The first of these albums, *Live and Obscure*, was issued in 1987. There followed a number of these live recordings; the latest—*Live at Union Chapel, London, England*—was issued in 2005.

Releases of Other Miscellaneous Recordings

To date, Townes has appeared on six albums with previously unreleased live and studio material, as well as several miscellaneous compilations, guest duets, and DVDs.

Only original LP (and later CD) issue labels and catalog numbers are listed. Reissues, of which there are many, are not noted. No compilation albums are listed, as all contain only previously released tracks. The one exception is *The Best of Townes Van Zandt* on Tomato Records, 2002, as it includes two previously unissued cuts.

ALBUMS
Releases on Poppy Records

1968   *For the Sake of the Song* [Poppy PY 40001].

1969   *Our Mother the Mountain* [Poppy PYS 40004].

1970   *Townes Van Zandt* [Poppy PYS 40007].

1971   *Delta Momma Blues* [Poppy PYS 40012].

1972   *High, Low and In Between* [Poppy PYS 5700].

1972   *The Late Great Townes Van Zandt* [Poppy PP-LA004-F].

Releases on Tomato Records

1977   *Live at the Old Quarter, Houston, Texas* [Tomato TOM 2-7001]. Recorded July 1973.

1978   *Flyin' Shoes* [Tomato TOM 7017].

1993   *The Nashville Sessions* [Tomato 598.1079.29]. Recorded 1974, not issued until 1993.

2001   *Texas Rain: The Texas Hill Country Recordings* [Tomato TOM-2001]. Recorded at the Fire Station, San Marcos, Texas, and Pedernales Studios, Pedernales, Texas, 1988–1989.

2002   *The Best of Townes Van Zandt* [Tomato TOM-2002]. Includes two tracks unavailable elsewhere.

2005   *Be Here to Love Me: A Film About Townes Van Zandt* [Tomato TMT-3005]. Soundtrack to the movie released by Palm Pictures on DVD in 2005.

Releases on Sugar Hill Records

1987   *At My Window* [Sugar Hill SH1020] [issued in the U.K. on Heartland HLD003].

1994   *No Deeper Blue* [Sugar Hill SH1046] [issued in Germany on Veracity/IRS 993.151].

Releases of Live Recordings by Harold F. Eggers Jr.

1987 *Live and Obscure* [Sugar Hill SH1026, issued in the U.K. on Heartland HLD004, reissued on Normal Records N238 with four bonus tracks]. Recorded live in Nashville, Tennessee, April 19, 1985.

1993 *Rear View Mirror* [Sundown SD2100-2, reissued on Sugar Hill SH 1054, reissued on Normal Records N203 with three bonus tracks]. Recorded live in Norman, Oklahoma, July 7, 1978.

1993 *Roadsongs* [Chlodwig 74321 13007, reissued on Sugar Hill SH1042, reissued on Normal Records N195 with three bonus tracks]. Recorded live, various venues, USA, late 1970s.

1996 *Abnormal* [Return to Sender RTS24 as limited edition of 2,000 copies, reissued on Normal Records N216 with three tracks replaced]. Recorded live throughout Europe, early 1990s.

1997 *The Highway Kind* [Sugar Hill SH1056, reissued on Normal Records N201 with two bonus tracks]. Live throughout Europe (except for three studio tracks), early 1990s.

1997 *Documentary* [Normal N211]. Interviews with Larry Monroe, 1991, plus ten songs. European version.

1997 *Last Rights* [Gregor 41290]. A re-edit primarily based on *Documentary*, but with some different interviews. American version.

1999 *In Pain* [Normal N225]. Recorded live in Germany and Austria, 1994–1996.

1999 "Riding the Range" / "Dirty Old Town" [45 vinyl, Exile Records EX7013, Germany]. Recorded at Flashpoint Studio, Austin, Texas, September, 1996.

2001 *Live at McCabe's* [Return to Sender RTS32, reissued on Varèse Sarabande 302066517, two tracks replaced and two bonus tracks]. Recorded live, February 10, 1995.

2002 *Absolutely Nothing* [Normal N235]. Recorded live in Ireland, April 1994, plus six studio tracks.

2003 *Acoustic Blue* [Tomato TOM-2087]. Recorded live in Germany and Northern Ireland, 1994 and 1996, plus one studio track.

2004   *Live at the Jester Lounge, Houston, Texas, 1966* [Normal N260].

2004   *Rear View Mirror, Volume 2* [Varèse Sarabande 302 066 608 2, reissued on Normal Records N263 with two bonus tracks]. Recorded live, various venues, USA, 1977–1981.

2004   *Houston 1988: A Private Concert* [Varèse Sarabande 302 066 698 2]. Audio recordings from a hotel room videotaping of Townes singing his songs and explaining the writing of them.

2005   *Live at Union Chapel, London, England* [Tomato TMT-3019]. Recorded live, April 24, 1994.

Miscellaneous Live Recordings

1991   *Rain on a Conga Drum: Live in Berlin* [Exile EXLP02]. Recorded live, October 25, 1990.

2001   *Steve Earle, Townes Van Zandt, Guy Clark: Together at the Bluebird Café* [American Originals AMD 4006] Recorded live, September 13, 1995.

2002   *A Gentle Evening with Townes Van Zandt* [Dualtone 80302-01119-2]. Recorded live, Carnegie Hall, New York, November 26, 1969.

2017   *Townes Van Zandt: Live at Austin City Limits* [Fat Possum Records FP11544-1]. Recorded September 30, 1975, first broadcast February 15, 1976. Released on vinyl only for Record Store Day, April 22, 2017.

Other Miscellaneous Recordings

1999   *A Far Cry from Dead* [Arista Austin 18888]. Townes's recordings 1989–1996, with overdubs added in 1998.

2003   *In the Beginning* [Compadre 6-16892-52402]. Recordings probably from 1967.

2015   *Sunshine Boy: The Unheard Studio Sessions & Demos 1971-1972* [Omnivore OVCD-15].

OTHER RECORDINGS FEATURING TOWNES
Appearances on Compilation Albums

1994   *C.J. Berkman: A Texican Tradition* [Back Porch Music BP015].
Townes recites a poem, "San Antone" by C.J. Berkman, with
musical accompaniment.

1997   *Fathers of Texas*, produced by K.R. Wood [Texanna TXA
1-001]. Townes sings two tracks, "Will You Come to the
Bower" and "Brazos River Song."

1998   *Blaze Foley: In Tribute and Loving Memory, Volume One* [Deep
South Productions, no catalog number]. Townes sings two
Blaze Foley songs, "Wouldn't That Be Nice" and "Springtime
in Uganda."

Duets

1992   *Blue Collar Blues*, Richard Dobson & State of the Heart
[Brambus 199239]. "Uncertain Texas," vocal duet with
Richard Dobson.

1993   *Endless Avenue, Direction Nashville*, various artists [Brambus
199344]. "Hobo's Lullaby," vocal duet with Dale Stumbo;
"Sage," vocal duet with Denise Benson.

1995   *Singing the Glory Down,* The Good Sons [Glitterhouse GR379].
"Riding the Range," vocal duet with Michael Weston King.

1996   *West Texas Heaven*, Kimmie Rhodes [Justice 2201-2]. "I'm
Gonna Fly," vocal duet with Kimmie Rhodes.

1997   *Angelina*, Barb Donovan [Gregor 1292/Normal N217]. "I'll
Be Here in the Morning," vocal duet with Barb Donovan. This
duet was originally issued on *Rare Trax Volume 1, Unreleased
Material & Collector's Items* by *Rolling Stone* magazine
Germany on January 1, 1997.

1998   *Kenai Dreams*, Chris Buhalis [One Man Clapping OMC-8].
"Kenai Dreams," vocal duet with Chris Buhalis.

DVDs

1975   *Heartworn Highways: Legends of Country Music's New Wave.*

Released on VHS, 1993 [Rhapsody Films, 9023]. Released on DVD, with additional footage, 2003 [Snapper Music, SMADVD 024]. A film about country music made in 1975 featuring Townes, among many others. There is some hilarious dialogue from Townes, and he sings two songs ("Waiting 'Round to Die," "Pancho and Lefty").

2004   *Houston 1988: A Private Concert* [Varèse Sarabande 302 066 610 2]. The videotape of a hotel room concert with Townes singing his songs and explaining the writing of them.

2005   *Be Here to Love Me* [Palm Pictures PALMOV 3124]. A film about Townes's life and music by Margaret Brown.

Unreleased Townes Two-Album Set

Titled *On the Road Touring: 30 Songs*, this is an unreleased collection of fifteen cover songs and fifteen original songs by Townes Van Zandt, compiled by Patrick Hurley and Harold F. Eggers Jr. Recordings were selected from 140 live performances by Townes; thirteen of the fifteen cover songs have never been released before on any Townes album. The tracks picked were unique and different from any other Townes recordings.

Disc #1: Cover Songs
    "Irene, Goodnight"
    "Molly and Tenbrooks"
    "Tying a Knot in the Devil's Tail"
    "Dirty Old Town"
    "Summer Wages"
    "Hobo Bill's Last Ride"
    "How Do You Feel"
    "Girl from the North Country"
    "The Weight"
    "Old 97"
    "Don't Be Angry"
    "Long Black Veil"
    "You Win Again"

"Jesus, Won't You Come by Here"

"North Country Fair"

Disc #2: Townes Van Zandt Songs

"Quicksilver Daydreams of Maria"

"None But the Rain"

"Waiting for the Day"

"Pancho and Lefty"

"For the Sake of the Song"

"Don't You Take It Too Bad" (duet with Barb Donovan)

"If I Needed You"

"Nothin'"

"Marie"

"Two Girls" (duet with Richard Dobson)

"Kathleen"

"White Freightliner Blues"

"Rake"

"High, Low and In Between"

"Come Tomorrow"

Patrick Hurley, a musicologist and definitive collector of Townes Van Zandt music since the 1970s, lives in Dublin, Ireland.

TOWNES VAN ZANDT DISCOGRAPHICAL DATA
BY HANS GOLVERDINGEN

HANS GOLVERDINGEN is a musicologist from the Netherlands. His discographical research as of June 2017 has documented 7,620 recordings of 133 Townes Van Zandt songs across the world.

These include: 3,601 live performances, 1,235 recordings made at Townes tributes or wakes, 1,169 original commercial recordings, and 858 video recordings, typically published on youtube.com or other websites.

Within Mr. Golverdingen's list, here are the top twenty Townes Van Zandt songs that exist in published audio form, with number of extant recordings in parentheses:

"Pancho and Lefty" (920)
"White Freightliner Blues" (824)
"If I Needed You" (518)
"Waiting 'Round to Die" (413)
"Tecumseh Valley" (304)
"Rex's Blues" (249)
"To Live's to Fly" (224)
"Snowin' on Raton" (223)
"Lungs" (222)
"Loretta" (215)
"No Place to Fall" (202)
"Rake" (164)
"Nothin'" (161)
"Colorado Girl" (154)

"I'll Be Here in the Morning" (150)
"Highway Kind" (127)
"Mr. Mudd and Mr. Gold" (116)
"Flyin' Shoes" (101)
"Marie" (98)
"Brand New Companion" (96)

As of this writing, Townes Van Zandt songs have been recorded in more than forty countries outside his native United States, including: Australia, Austria, Belgium, Bulgaria, Canada, Costa Rica, Croatia, Czech Republic, Denmark, Estonia, Finland, France, Germany, Greece, Hungary, India, Ireland, Israel, Italy, Jamaica, Japan, Latvia, Luxembourg, Mexico, Netherlands, New Zealand, Norway, Poland, Portugal, Russia, Serbia, Singapore, Slovenia, South Africa, Spain, Sweden, Switzerland, Taiwan, Thailand, and the United Kingdom (England, Northern Ireland, Scotland, Wales).

RECORDING TOWNES: PROCESS AND PHILOSOPHY
by Harold F. Eggers Jr.

I CAME UP with the idea of recording Townes's live shows shortly after I began working with him in 1977.

Townes would say, "If I could only capture Mr. Guitar and all the ghosts performing with him each night, maybe everyone could finally hear what I hear in performing these songs."

I decided to see if that were possible to achieve.

I bought a Nakamichi professional cassette tape recording machine, which I upgraded to a new model in the 1990s. For each show, I would record directly either from the venue's main mixing board (which determined what the audience would hear) or from the onstage monitors mixing board (which was what performers onstage would primarily hear).

The first live recording was the Vanderbilt University coffeehouse gig with Danny Rowland and Owen Cody I've described in Chapter 4. It went fine with no technical problems, and I figured, what the heck—I'll try this a few more times for grins.

I had no idea I'd be making hundreds of such tapes over the next two decades and that many of them would result in a series of acclaimed albums capturing Townes's kaleidoscopic moods and song interpretations.

I would listen to the first song of a set on headphones to make sure everything was coming through all right, and then monitor the sound level throughout the set, adjusting volumes if need be. I left the tape machine recording the entire time Townes was onstage; you never knew when an impromptu joke, offstage shout, or ambient house noise like a broken bottle, register ring, or door creak might add some element of embellishment or character. I mentioned this to producer Bob Johnston once, and he told me he likewise always left tape running continuously with Bob Dylan and other artists he recorded in the studio.

In the early 1980s, I took several recording classes at Belmont University, which honed my native audio instincts and gave me numerous "pro" insights into formal sound production. Guy Clark, Steve Earle, and several of Townes's singer-songwriter friends let me record their shows in Nashville; it was good practice for all of us.

Aside from making sure the technical aspects of the performance were at their best, I wanted the listener to feel the intense, all-consuming spirit of Townes's personality. Though he didn't jump around the stage or make exaggerated body motions, he was actually a very visually compelling performer; his restraint and subtlety drew the audience in even more, I believe. With the audience as the frame and canvas, I attempted to convey the sound "picture" he was painting through his music.

Recording the performance that became *Houston 1988: A Private Concert*, the DVD issued on Varèse Sarabande in 2004, was an interesting challenge. The venue was a small hotel room; the audience was myself, engineer Hank Sinatra, and three video cameras. This was Townes performing sans sound system, stage microphone, buzzing room with noisy bar. And yet, I believe the one-on-two interaction evoked music as soulful as any I've heard from any performer, ever.

Recording *Live at Union Chapel, London, England*, a two-album set released on Tomato in 2005, presented an entirely different acoustical environment. We were in a nine-hundred-seat, 1870s Gothic Revival church that had hosted performers like Tom Jones, Elton John, and Amy Winehouse and served at the time as a social and educational center for the homeless. "Great," Townes said. "The ghosts of the homeless will be onstage with me."

The show was just Townes and Mr. Guitar on the altar steps, voice and strings echoing through the building. Townes said he felt like he was flying over the audience the entire time. I think Townes left a part of himself in that chapel that night.

If you want to hear what a cross-country folk club tour sounded like in the late 1970s, listen to *Rear View Mirror, Volume 2*, released in 2004 on Varèse Sarabande. It features Townes with Danny Rowland, Owen Cody, and Jimmie Gray in a potpourri of American Heartland locales: Lawton, Oklahoma; Indianapolis, Indiana; Carrboro, North Carolina; East Lansing, Michigan; Madison, Wisconsin; Nashville, Tennessee; Athens, Georgia; Washington, D.C. Sit back, close your eyes, and you can almost smell the cigarette smoke and spilled beer.

Townes's *Documentary* album, issued in 1997 on Normal Records, stemmed from an idea I had of doing a series of documentary-style releases with renowned artists in blues, country, jazz, rock, and world music. When I told this to Townes, he said, "I'll be the first, and then you can approach others." I was honored that Townes would volunteer, and interviews by Austin DJ and radio producer Larry Monroe added a fully professional touch.

Live at McCabe's was released in 2001 on the Return to Sender label. McCabe's has been a musical instrument shop since the late 1950s, and the performing space seats about 150. The audience sits in metal folding chairs, and vintage guitars, mandolins, banjos, dulcimers, and ukuleles cover the walls. Townes took a look at the room decor and remarked, "I know all those instruments' ghosts are playing along with me. For sure, this is the first time I have ever played with a ghost guitar orchestra."

Townes said that, of his entire career's worth of recordings, most of his favorites were the live ones "with just me and Mr. Guitar." If he could have made it happen, I believe he would have performed every day of the year and spent his entire life going from town to town.

He also was pleased that he and I co-owned the albums. It was a unique business arrangement that gave us complete artistic control. To a singular artist like Townes Van Zandt, that was very important. The live albums also garnered excellent reviews, and we had a full slate of future releases in the hopper when he died.

"It's always better to be live than dead," he would joke when asked about his strategy in producing the live discs.

I believe he's right. And that these albums keep his music and memory as fresh and alive as if he were here today.

ACKNOWLEDGMENTS

HAROLD F. EGGERS JR. WOULD LIKE TO THANK:
Harold Francis Eggers Sr.; Honora Elizabeth Eggers; Cindy Soo, Harold
F. Eggers-Soo III; Megan and Tyler East; Tristen, Ev, and Cassidy
O'Rear; Gene Soo; Nonie and Bruce Beard; Kathy and Mark Luckadoo;
Pat and Dennis Eggers; Peggy and Stephen Nolan; Kevin Eggers; Joe
Oswald Jr.; Mary and Vinny Tirolo; Tommy McDonald; Lamar Fike;
Joy and Bob Johnston; Douglas Brinkley; Kathleen Hudson; Patrick
Hurley; John Wheat; Valerie, Aaron, and Edgar Campbell; Leslie,
Leslynn, Arissa, and Nate Perez; Sylvie Simmons; Susan, Chaz, and
Charlie Hollis; Jeanne Schillaci, PhD; Christine Farren; Louis Black;
Nick Barbaro; Hector Ward; Jimmy LaFave; Daniel Scardino; Buck
McKinney; Sharon Wills, PhD; Dr. Don Carleton; Margaret Moser;
George Schinler; Tony Seidl; Ben Bright; Sybil Rosen; Martin Coulter;
Kevin Triplett; Rush Evans; Valerie Fremin; Wolfgang Doebeling;
Hans Golverdingen; Jane Son; Barb Donovan; Hank Sinatra; Joe
Camacho; Don Campeau; Edith Dobson; Al Ammon; Bianca de Leon;
Jack Hyde; Kimberly Lane, LAc; Natalie Knight, LAc; Julie and Ron
McCloud; Brian Atkinson and Crystal Tabor . . . A VERY SPECIAL
THANKS TO: Bernadette Malavarca.

L. E. MCCULLOUGH WOULD LIKE TO THANK:
My wife, Lisa Bansavage; my parents, Ervin and Isabel; all the thousands
of incredible musicians of every idiom I've had the pleasure and privilege
to learn from, jam with, write about for the last fifty years. And my

first piano teachers, Mrs. Schmidt of Eagledale and Mrs. McDonald of Speedway, who could never have imagined the immeasurable tides of lifelong sonic adventure their patient instruction would release into the world.

INDEX

attitude toward music industry,
    27, 28
attitude toward paranormal,
    xix, 29, 61–64, 74, 81–83, 85,
    106, 160, 181, 205, 207
attitude toward people, xvii,
    20, 29–31, 36, 42, 46, 85, 86,
    113
attitude toward religion, 48, 49,
    83–85
Austin years-1980s, 87–89, 91
blood brother ritual, xvii, 64,
    65, 77
car accident-Nashville, 71–73
Crying Tour, 73–76, 86
death, 172, 173
diet, 34, 83, 130, 136
early emotional struggles, 76–79
early musical career (pre-1978),
    2–5, 16–18, 21, 22
early musical influences, 21, 22,
    77
effects of electroshock therapy,
    77–79
emotional volatility, 32, 33, 46,
    47, 80, 81, 109–111, 133–135,
    180–182
favorite TV shows, 82
Flyin' Shoes album recording, 37,
    38
Flyin' Shoes Tour, 39–52, 59–70
gambling habit, 31, 32, 45, 127
Geffen Records project, 142, 143,
    152–171
guitar preferences, 20–22, 42
hospitalizations, xxi–xxvi, 17,
    29, 35, 45, 72, 78–80, 89,
    108, 145, 167, 172,
law enforcement interactions,
    xxiii, 35, 50, 62, 63, 75,
    112, 141

international tours, 57–59, 104,
    123, 124, 126–132, 136,
    140–148
Newology album recording,
    114–117
No Deeper Blue album
    recording, 121–126
performing habits, xiv, 52, 53,
    57–59
philosophical moments, 51, 52
practical jokes, 48, 67, 68
residence at Harpeth River cabin,
    19
residence at Bayou Self, 31, 150,
    156, 171
residence at Rock 'n' Roll Hotel,
    106–108
residence at Sailor Inn, 106
Roadsongs album recording, 117,
    118
songwriting technique, 5, 52–56
Sundown Records episode,
    119–121
Van Zandt, Townes family
    Cindy Morgan, xv–xxii, xxv,
        xxvi, 19, 20, 36, 46, 47, 64,
        65, 70–72, 80, 87
    Jeanene Munsell, 96, 14, 142,
        159, 166, 167, 171, 172, 177,
        181
    Fran Petters, 3, 114
    Dorothy Van Zandt, 76
    Harris Van Zandt, 76
    J.T. Van Zandt, 114, 190
    Isaac Van Zandt, xii, 33
    Isaac Lycurgus Van Zandt, 33,
        35
    Katie Belle Van Zandt, 114,
        168, 171, 177
    Khleber Miller Van Zandt, 33
    Will Van Zandt, 114, 171, 177